imc investment management certificate

CFA Society United Kingdom

CW01653272

VOLUME 1
THE INVESTMENT ENVIRONMENT
OFFICIAL TRAINING MANUAL
EDITION 13

ISBN 0 950411744

First Edition March 1994; Second Edition May 1995; Third Edition August 1997; The UK Society of Investment Professionals; Fourth Edition February 2001; Fifth Edition August 2004; Sixth Edition October 2007; The CFA Society of the UK; Seventh Edition September 2008; Eight Edition July 2010; Ninth Edition December 2011; Tenth Edition October 2012; Eleventh Edition October 2013; Twelth Edition October 2014

AUTHORS

Dr Mike Buckle BA (Hons), MSc, PhD

School of Management, Liverpool University in London

Professor Stephen Thomas BSc (Econ), MSc, PhD

Professor of Finance, Cass Business School

The authors would like to thank Graham Cook, CFA and Chair of the IMC Panel, for his invaluable help in the preparation of this material. In addition, advice was greatly appreciated from IMC Panel members, and academic adviser Dr James Seaton.

INTRODUCTION

The aim of the Official Training Manual (OTM) is to provide guidance to those undertaking study for the Investment Management Certificate (IMC) examination. It provides essential reading for candidates, including worked examples, key facts, as well as self-assessment questions and a mock examination. OTM Thirteenth Edition (2016) is valid for IMC examinations taken from 1 December 2015. Candidates must check that the version of the OTM they are preparing from is valid for the period when they intend to take the examination.

IMC UPDATE

Changes will be made as necessary to keep the manual up to date. Details of the date of the latest change and of any outstanding corrections or amendments can be found on the CFA Society of the UK's website: www.cfauk.org.

Candidates should check the website on a regular basis to ensure their study material is up to date.

IMC SYLLABUS

The IMC examination is made up of two units, covering the topic areas shown below:

UNIT 1: THE INVESTMENT ENVIRONMENT

1 Financial markets and institutions
2 Ethics and investment professionalism
3 The regulation of financial markets and institutions
4 Legal concepts
5 Client advice
6 Taxation in the UK

UNIT 2: INVESTMENT PRACTICE

7 Quantitative methods
8 Micro-economics
9 Macro-economics
10 Accounting
11 Equity
12 Fixed income
13 Derivatives
14 Alternative investments
15 Portfolio management
16 Investment products
17 Investment performance measurement

WWW.CFAUK.ORG

This edition of the OTM covers the current syllabus and is published in two volumes. Volume 1 contains the materials for topic areas 1 – 6 required for the study of Unit 1: The investment environment. Volume 2 contains the materials for topic areas 7 – 17 required for the study of Unit 2: Investment practice. The IMC examination tests the IMC syllabus rather than the specific wording of the OTM. The OTM offers broad coverage of the syllabus and provides excellent preparation for the examinations. Details of the current syllabus can be downloaded from the Society website: www.cfauk.org

The IMC is developed, administered and awarded by the CFA Society of the UK. In 2003 the Society was accredited as an Examination Awarding Body by the Qualifications & Curriculum Authority and the IMC was admitted to the National Qualifications Framework as the 'UKSIP Level 3 Certification in Investment Management'. CFA UK continues to be recognised as an Awarding Organisation by the Office of Qualifications and Examinations Regulation (Ofqual), and the IMC appears on the Qualifications and Credit Framework as 'CFA UK Level 4 Certificate in Investment Management (QCF)'. CFA UK is also recognised as an Accredited Body by the Financial Conduct Authority. The IMC appears on the FCA's Appropriate Qualifications Tables as meeting the regulatory qualification requirements for undertaking Activities 14 and 10 Managing investments and/or undertaking the activity of a broker fund adviser.

LINKS TO THE CFA PROGRAM™

The IMC syllabus contains direct links to the curriculum of the Chartered Financial Analyst Program. These are listed throughout the OTM. The natural progression from the IMC is onwards to the CFA Program (administered by CFA Institute) with the IMC provided a natural stepping stone to CFA Level 1. The IMC refers directly to the CFA Code of Ethics in Topic 2. Additionally, the IMC provides UK-specific syllabus content that can augment the global curriculum of the CFA, and the two are required by many employers in combination. In 2010 the IMC + CFA Level 1 combination was formally listed as meeting the regulatory qualification requirements for those advising and/or dealing in securities and derivatives in the UK.

UNIT 1: THE INVESTMENT ENVIRONMENT

UNIT AIMS

By the end of this unit, learners should be able to demonstrate:

- An understanding of the UK financial services industry and international financial markets.
- An understanding of and ability to critically evaluate the outcomes that distinguish between ethical and compliance driven behaviour and apply the CFA Code of Ethics and Standards of Professional Conduct to business behaviours of individuals.
- An understanding of the Financial Conduct Authority's (FCA's) use of principles and outcomes based regulation to promote ethical and fair outcomes, and the ability to apply the regulatory advice framework in practice for the consumer.
- An understanding of the FCA's responsibilities and approach to regulation and the role of the Prudential Regulation Authority (PRA) for dual-regulated firms, and an understanding of and ability to apply the FCA principles and rules as set out in the regulatory framework and FCA Handbook.
- An understanding of legal concepts relevant to financial advice.
- An understanding of how the retail consumer is served by the financial services industry, the range of skills required when advising clients and an ability to apply the investment advice process.
- An understanding of the UK tax system as relevant to the needs and circumstances of individuals and trusts.
- An ability to analyse the taxation of investments as relevant to the needs and circumstances of individuals and trusts, and an ability to apply the knowledge of personal taxation to the provision of investment advice.
- An ability to analyse the role and relevance of tax in the financial affairs of individuals and trusts.

Question allocation across the syllabus is balanced on the guidance of psychometric and industry specialists. The following question allocation for Version 13 of the IMC is provided as a broad indication of the relative 'weighting' of different parts of the syllabus in IMC examinations from 1 December 2015.

CONTENT AREA	TOPIC	TOPIC NAME	QUESTION ALLOCATION
Financial markets and institutions	1	Financial Markets and Institutions	10–20
Ethics	2	Ethics and Investment Professionalism	5–15
Regulation and legal concepts	3	The Regulation of Financial Markets and Institutions	25–35
	4	Legal Concepts	
Clients	5	Client Advice	15–25
Taxation	6	Taxation in the UK	10–20

OTHER INFORMATION REGARDING THIS UNIT:

Exam format:	• 85 questions. • Online testing using standard multiple choice, item sets and gap-fill style questions.
Time allowed for exam:	1 hour and 40 minutes.
Grades:	Pass or fail.
Recommended study hours:	80 hours.
Availability of exam sessions:	Every working day through Pearson VUE testing centres.

TOPIC 1 FINANCIAL MARKETS AND INSTITUTIONS

By the end of this topic, learners should be able to:

- Demonstrate an understanding of the UK financial services industry, in its European and global context.
- Demonstrate an understanding of UK and international financial markets.

1.1 INTRODUCTION TO FINANCIAL MARKETS

1.1.1 Explain the functions of the financial services industry in allocating capital within the global economy.

1.1.2 Explain the role and impact of the main financial institutions.

1.1.3 Explain the role of government including economic and industrial policy, regulation, taxation and social welfare.

1.2 THE ROLE OF SECURITIES MARKETS IN PROVIDING LIQUIDITY AND PRICE TRANSPARENCY

1.2.1 Differentiate between a financial security and a real asset.

1.2.2 Identify the key features of: a common equity share; a bond; a derivative contract; a unit in a pooled fund; and a foreign exchange transaction.

1.2.3 Identify the functions of securities markets in providing price transparency and liquidity.

1.2.4 Identify the reasons why liquidity and price transparency are thought to be important for the efficient allocation of capital costs when trading in securities markets.

1.2.5 Calculate round trip transaction costs incorporating bid–ask spreads, dealing commission and transaction taxes, both in percentages and in absolute amounts.

1.2.6 Identify the types of securities and the market conditions where price transparency, liquidity and depth are likely to be high/low.

1.2.7 Define liquidity risk and identify why it is important.

1.3 TYPES OF FINANCIAL MARKETS

1.3.1 Identify the main dealing systems and facilities offered in the UK equities market.

1.3.2 Identify the nature of the securities that would be traded on each of the main dealing systems and facilities.

1.3.3 Explain the structure and operation of the primary and secondary UK markets for gilts and corporate bonds.

1.3.4 Explain the motivations for, and implications of, dual-listing a company.

1.3.5 Compare and contrast exchange traded and over-the-counter markets.

1.3.6 Distinguish between the following alternative trading venues: multilateral trading facilities; systematic internalisers; and dark pools.
1.3.7 Distinguish between a quote-driven and an order-driven market.
1.3.8 Explain the roles of the various participants in the UK equity market.
1.3.9 Explain high-frequency trading, its benefits and risks.

1.4 SETTLEMENT PROCEDURES IN THE UK

1.4.1 Explain the clearing and settlement procedures for UK exchange-traded securities.

1.5 THE UK LISTING AUTHORITY AND PROSPECTUS REQUIREMENTS

1.5.1 Explain the role of the FCA as the UK listing authority.
1.5.2 Identify the listing rules in Financial Services and Markets Act 2000, and relevant EU directives.
1.5.3 Explain the main conditions for listing on the Official List, AIM and ISDX.
1.5.4 Explain the purpose of the requirement for prospectus or listing particulars.
1.5.5 Identify the main exemptions from listing particulars.

1.6 INFORMATION DISCLOSURE AND CORPORATE GOVERNANCE REQUIREMENTS FOR UK EQUITY MARKETS

1.6.1 Explain the disclosures required under the disclosure and transparency rules relating to directors' interests and major shareholdings.
1.6.2 Explain the purpose of corporate governance regulation and the role of the Financial Reporting Committee in promoting good corporate governance.
1.6.3 Explain, in outline, the scope and content of corporate governance standards in the UK.
1.6.4 Explain the London Stock Exchange requirements for listed companies to disclose corporate governance compliance.
1.6.5 Explain the continuing obligations of London Stock Exchange listed companies regarding information disclosure and dissemination.
1.6.6 Explain, in outline, the UK company law requirements regarding the calling of general meetings.
1.6.7 Distinguish between annual general meetings and other types of company meetings.
1.6.8 Distinguish between the types of resolution that can be considered at company general meetings.
1.6.9 Distinguish between the voting methods used at company meetings.
1.6.10 Explain the role and powers of a proxy.

1.7 INTERNATIONAL MARKETS

1.7.1 Explain the structure, features, regulatory and trading environment of international markets, including developed markets and emerging markets.
1.7.2 Explain the structure and operation of the primary and secondary markets for eurobonds.

1.7.3 Explain the settlement and clearing procedures overseas, including the role of international central securities depositories, and the different settlement cycles and challenges in managing global assets.

1.8 THE PRINCIPAL–AGENT PROBLEM: SEPARATION OF OWNERSHIP AND CONTROL

1.8.1 Explain how capital markets allow the beneficial ownership, and the control of capital, to be separated.

1.8.2 Distinguish between beneficial owners (principals) and the various agents involved in the capital allocation process.

1.8.3 Explain how conflict between the interests of agents and principals gives rise to the 'agency' or 'principal–agent' problem.

1.8.4 Identify examples of agency costs such as: expropriation, perquisites, self-dealing and higher cost of capital, which arise when the agency problem is known to exist.

1.8.5 Identify the main reasons why it is argued that reducing the agency problem benefits the investment profession and society as a whole.

TOPIC 2 ETHICS AND INVESTMENT PROFESSIONALISM

By the end of this topic, learners should be able to:

- Demonstrate an ability to critically evaluate the outcomes that distinguish between ethical and compliance driven behaviour.

- Demonstrate an ability to apply the CFA Code of Ethics and Standards of Professional Conduct to the business behaviours of individuals.

2.1 ETHICAL AND COMPLIANCE DRIVEN BEHAVIOUR

2.1.1 Describe the need for ethics in the investment industry.

2.1.2 Identify the ethical obligations to clients, prospective clients, employers and co-workers.

2.1.3 Identify positive and negative behavioural indicators.

2.1.4 Critically evaluate the outcomes which may result from behaving ethically – for the industry, individual advisers, and consumers.

2.1.5 Critically evaluate the outcomes which may result from limiting behaviour to compliance within the rules – for the industry, individual advisers and consumers.

2.2 CFA CODE OF ETHICS AND STANDARDS OF PROFESSIONAL CONDUCT

2.2.1 Identify the elements of the CFA Code of Ethics and Standards of Professional Conduct.

2.2.2 Explain the professional principles and values on which the CFA Code of Ethics and Standards of Professional Conduct is based.

2.2.3 Apply the CFA Code of Ethics and Standards of Professional Conduct to a range of ethical dilemmas.

TOPIC 3 THE REGULATION OF FINANCIAL MARKETS AND INSTITUTIONS

By the end of this topic, learners should be able to:

- Demonstrate the ability to apply the regulatory advice framework in practice for the consumer.
- Demonstrate an understanding of the UK financial services industry, in its European and global context.
- Demonstrate an understanding of the FCA's responsibilities and approach to regulation.
- Demonstrate an understanding of UK and international financial markets.
- Demonstrate an ability to apply the FCA's principles and rules as set out in the regulatory framework and FCA Handbook.
- Demonstrate an understanding of where the PRA may also be involved for dual-regulated firms.

3.1 INTERNATIONAL AND EUROPEAN UNION DIRECTIVES, REGULATION AND GUIDANCE

3.1.1 Explain the legal status of EU directives and regulations within the UK.

3.1.2 Explain the role and powers of the European Securities and Markets Authority.

3.1.3 Explain the purpose and scope of the Markets in Financial Instruments Directive (MiFID) with respect to: passporting, roles of the home and host state, core and non-core investment services, financial instruments covered by the legislation.

3.1.4 Explain the purpose and scope of the Undertakings for Collective Investment in Transferable Securities (UCITS) Directives.

3.1.5 Explain the purpose, scope and requirements of the Alternative Investment Fund Managers Directive (AIFMD).

3.1.6 Explain the purpose and scope of the European Market Infrastructure Regulation (EMIR).

3.1.7 Explain the purpose and scope of the Foreign Account Tax Compliance Act enacted in March 2010 under US federal law.

3.2 UK REGULATION

3.2.1 Describe and distinguish between the roles of the FCA, PRA, Bank of England, Financial Policy Committee and HM Treasury.

3.2.2 Explain the different roles of the FCA and PRA for dual-regulated investment firms.

3.2.3 Explain the scope of the Financial Services and Markets Act (FSMA) 2000 (as amended by the Financial Services Act 2012).

3.2.4 Explain the scope of the Regulated Activities Order 2001 (as amended) in terms of regulated activities and specified investments.

3.2.5 Explain the purpose and scope of the FCA's rules regarding Senior Management Arrangements, Systems and Controls (SYSC).

3.2.6 Explain the function of the following bodies/persons: the Panel on Takeovers and Mergers, the Department for Business Innovation and Skills, the Competition and Markets Authority, and the Information Commissioner's Office.

3.2.7 Explain the make-up of the Panel on Takeovers and Mergers (the Takeover Panel) and how it is financed.

3.2.8 Explain the regulatory status of the City Code on Takeovers and Mergers.

3.2.9 Explain the main provisions of the City Code, including the bid timetable.

3.2.10 Explain the purpose and scope of the Trustee Act 2000: the rights and duties of the parties involved, the nature of the trust deed and the investment powers of trustees.

3.2.11 Explain the significance of the Pensions Act 2004: scheme specific funding requirement, the Pensions Regulator, the Pension Protection Fund.

3.2.12 Explain the significance of the Pensions Act 2008 and the reforms to pension rules in March 2014: automatic enrolment, National Employment Savings Trust, freedom of choice in pensions.

3.2.13 Explain the purpose of a Statement of Investment Principles.

3.3 THE FINANCIAL CONDUCT AUTHORITY: OBJECTIVES AND HIGH LEVEL STANDARDS

3.3.1 Explain the role and statutory objectives of the FCA.

3.3.2 Identify and distinguish among the blocks of the FCA handbook.

3.3.3 Identify the FCA's Principles for Businesses (PRIN 2.1.1 & 4) and explain their application and purpose (PRIN 1.1.1 & 2).

3.3.4 Explain the consequences of breaching the FCA's Principles for Businesses (PRIN 1.1.7 to 9 and DEPP 6.2.14 & 15).

3.3.5 Explain, in outline, the procedures for authorisation of firms, including knowledge of the threshold conditions, and liaison with the PRA where relevant.

3.3.6 Define an approved person, and explain the application and purpose of the Statements of Principle and Code of Practice for Approved Persons (APER).

3.3.7 Identify the main assessment criteria in the FCA's fit and proper test for approved persons (FIT).

3.3.8 Explain the application procedure for an approved person (SUP 10A) and how the PRA may also be involved.

3.3.9 Explain the procedure for an approved person moving within a group and how the PRA may also be involved (SUP 10A).

3.3.10 Define a controlled function and identify the types of controlled functions defined within the FCA handbook (SUP 10A).

3.3.11 Explain the regulatory requirements on individual accountability under Banking Reform Act 2013: Senior Managers Regime, Certification Regime, Conduct rules.

3.3.12 Explain the requirements relating to training and competence (TC 1–3).

3.3.13 Explain the professionalism requirements that have to met by retail investment advisers and investment managers (TC 1–3).

3.4 REGULATION OF INVESTMENT EXCHANGES

3.4.1 Explain the role of an investment exchange.

3.4.2 Explain the need for, and relevance of, investment exchanges needing to be recognised by the FCA.

3.4.3 Explain how the Bank of England regulates clearing houses in the UK.

3.4.4 Identify the recognised investment exchanges and clearing houses in the UK.

3.4.5 Identify and distinguish the roles of London Stock Exchange (LSE), ICE Futures Europe and ICE Clear Europe.

3.4.6 Identify the features of trading systems for derivatives.

3.4.7 Identify the main features of the regulation of derivatives.

3.4.8 Identify the main features of clearing and settlement for trading on derivatives exchanges, and when trading over-the-counter.

3.4.9 Explain the arrangements for market transparency and transaction reporting in the main derivative markets.

3.4.10 Explain the impact of MiFID and International Accounting Standards on the regulation of derivative markets.

3.5 FCA BUSINESS STANDARDS

Accepting customers for business (client categorisation)

3.5.1 Explain the purpose of client categorisation.

3.5.2 Distinguish between a retail client, a professional client and an eligible counterpart (COBS 3.4, 3.5 & 3.6).

3.5.3 Apply the rules relating to treating a client as an elective professional client (COBS 3.5.3).

3.5.4 Apply the rules relating to treating a client as an elective eligible counterparty

(COBS 3.6.4).

3.5.5 Apply the rules relating to providing clients with a higher level of protection (COBS 3.7).

3.5.6 Apply the rules relating to client agreements (COBS 8.1).

Financial promotions and other communications with customers, including information about the firm

3.5.7 Explain the purpose and scope of the financial promotions rules and the exemptions from them (COBS 4.1).

3.5.8 Explain the fair, clear and not misleading rule (COBS 4.2).

3.5.9 Explain the rules relating to communications with retail clients (COBS 4.5).

3.5.10 Explain the rules relating to past, simulated past and future performance (COBS 4.6).

3.5.11 Explain the rules relating to direct offer promotions (COBS 4.7).

3.5.12 Explain the rules relating to cold calls and other promotions that are not in writing (COBS 4.8).

3.5.13 Explain the rules relating to systems and controls in relation to approving and communicating financial promotions (COBS 4.10).

3.5.14 Explain the record keeping requirements relating to financial promotions (COBS 4.11).

3.5.15 Explain the rules relating to distance marketing communications (COBS 5.1).

3.5.16 Explain the rules relating to providing information about the firm and compensation information (COBS 6.1).

3.5.17 Explain the rules on adviser charging and remuneration (COBS 6.3 & 6.4).

3.5.18 Explain the FCA's approach to temporary product intervention.

Identifying client needs (suitability and appropriateness)

3.5.19 Explain the rules relating to assessing suitability (COBS 9.2).

3.5.20 Explain the rules relating to assessing appropriateness (COBS 10.2).

3.5.21 Explain the rules relating to warning a client (COBS 10.3).

3.5.22 Identify circumstances when assessing appropriateness is not required (COBS 10.4, 10.5 & 10.6).

3.5.23 Identify circumstances when own authority or expertise is limited and there is the need to refer to specialists.

3.5.24 Distinguish between independent advice and restricted advice (COBS 6.2A).

Dealing and managing

3.5.25 Explain the rules relating to best execution (COBS 11.2).

3.5.26 Explain the rules relating to client order handling (COBS 11.3).

3.5.27 Explain the rules relating to the use of dealing commission (COBS 11.6).

3.5.28 Explain the rules on personal account dealing (COBS 11.7).

3.5.29 Explain the purpose of the principles and rules on conflicts of interest, including: identify, recording and disclosing conflicts of interest and managing them to ensure the fair treatment of clients (PRIN 2.1.1, Principle 8, SYSC 10.1.1–1.7 & 10.1.8/1.9 & 10.2).

Investment research

3.5.30 Explain the rules relating to investment research produced by a firm and disseminated to clients (COBS 12.2).

3.5.31 Explain the rules relating to the publication and dissemination of non-independent research (COBS 12.3).

3.5.32 Explain the disclosure requirements relating to the production and dissemination of research recommendations (COBS 12.4).

Product disclosure – packaged products

3.5.33 Explain the obligations relating to preparing product information (COBS 13.1 & COLL 4.7).

3.5.34 Explain the rules relating to the form and content of a key features document and a key investor information document (COBS 13.2, 13.3, 14.2 & COLL 4.7).

3.5.35 Explain the rules relating to cancellation rights (COBS 15).

3.5.36 Distinguish between packaged products and retail investment products.

Record keeping and reporting information

3.5.37 Apply the rules relating to record keeping for client orders and transactions (COBS 11.5).

3.5.38 Apply the rules relating to occasional reporting to clients (COBS 16.2).

3.5.39 Apply the rules relating to periodic reporting to clients (COBS 16.3).

3.5.40 Explain the rules relating to reporting on the progress of an authorised fund to unitholders (COLL 4.5).

Client assets and client money rules

3.5.41 Explain the concept of fiduciary duty.

3.5.42 Explain the application and purpose of the rules relating to custody of client assets held in connection with MiFID business (CASS 6.1).

3.5.43 Explain the rules relating to the protection of clients' assets and having adequate organisational arrangements (CASS 6.2).

3.5.44 Explain the rules relating to depositing assets with third parties (CASS 6.3).

3.5.45 Explain the purpose of the rules relating to the use of clients' assets (CASS 6.4).

3.5.46 Explain the rules relating to records, accounts and reconciliations of clients' assets (CASS 6.5).

3.5.47 Explain the application and general purpose of the client money rules (CASS 7.2).

3.5.48 Explain the rules relating to the segregation of client money (CASS 7.4).

3.5.49 Explain the rules relating to records, accounts and reconciliations of clients' assets

(CASS 7.6).

3.5.50 Explain the rules relating to mandate accounts (CASS 8).

3.6 FCA SUPERVISION AND REDRESS

3.6.1 Explain the FCA's risk based approach to supervision and the enforcement and disciplinary powers of the FCA.

Complaints handling, the Financial Ombudsman Service and the Financial Services Compensation Scheme

3.6.2 Explain the FCA rules relating to handling of complaints (DISP 1.3).

3.6.3 Explain the role of the Financial Ombudsman Service (DISP Introduction and DISP 2).

3.6.4 Apply the rules relating to determination by the Financial Ombudsman Service (DISP 3).

3.6.5 Distinguish between compulsory and voluntary jurisdiction (DISP Introduction).

3.6.6 Explain the procedure and time limits for the resolution of complaints (DISP 1.4, 1.5 & 1.6).

3.6.7 Apply the rules relating to record keeping and reporting concerning complaints (DISP 1.9 & 1.10).

3.6.8 Explain the purpose of the Financial Services Compensation Scheme (FSCS) (COMP 1.1.7).

3.6.9 Identify the circumstances under which the FSCS will pay compensation (COMP 1.3.3, 3.2.1, 4.2.1 & 4.2.2).

3.6.10 Identify the limits on the compensation payable by the FSCS (COMP 10.2.1, 10.2.2 & 10.2.3).

3.7 FINANCIAL CRIME

3.7.1 Explain the various sources of money laundering and counter-terrorism regulation and legislation (FCA rules, Money Laundering Regulations, Proceeds of Crime Act 2002).

3.7.2 Explain the role of the Joint Money Laundering Steering Group (JMLSG).

3.7.3 Explain the main features of the guidance provided by the JMLSG.

3.7.4 Explain the three stages involved in the money laundering process.

3.7.5 Explain the four offence categories under UK money laundering legislation.

3.7.6 Explain the meaning of 'inside information' covered by the Criminal Justice Act (CJA) 1993.

3.7.7 Explain the offence of insider dealing covered by the CJA 1993.

3.7.8 Identify the penalties for being found guilty of insider dealing.

3.7.9 Explain the FCA's powers to prosecute insider dealing.

3.7.10 Describe the behaviours defined as market abuse (MAR 1.3–1.9).

3.7.11 Explain the enforcement powers of the FCA relating to market abuse (MAR 1.1.4, 1.1.5 & 1.1.6).

3.7.12 Explain the main features of the Bribery Act 2010.

TOPIC 4 LEGAL CONCEPTS

By the end of this topic, learners should be able to:

- Demonstrate an understanding of legal concepts relevant to financial advice.

4.1.1 Explain legal persons and power of attorney.
4.1.2 Explain basic law of contract and agency.
4.1.3 Explain the types of ownership of property.
4.1.4 Explain insolvency and bankruptcy.
4.1.5 Explain wills and intestacy.
4.1.6 Describe the main types of trusts and their uses.

TOPIC 5 CLIENT ADVICE

By the end of this topic, learners should be able to:

- Demonstrate an understanding of how the retail consumer is served by the financial services industry.
- Demonstrate an ability to apply the investment advice process.
- Demonstrate an understanding of the range of skills required when advising clients.

5.1 TYPES AND CHARACTERISTICS OF INVESTORS

5.1.1 Describe and compare different types of investors.
5.1.2 Explain the obligations of a firm towards retail clients.
5.1.3 Explain the main needs of retail clients and how they are prioritised.

5.2 THE CLIENT'S FINANCIAL OBJECTIVES

5.2.1 Explain the importance of establishing and quantifying a client's objectives.
5.2.2 Explain the need to prioritise objectives to accommodate a client's affordability.

5.3 THE CLIENT'S CURRENT CIRCUMSTANCES

5.3.1 Explain the importance of the fact-find process in establishing a client's current financial circumstances and requirements.
5.3.2 Identify the factors shaping a client's circumstances.

5.4 THE CLIENT'S ATTITUDE TO RISK

5.4.1 Analyse the main types of investment risk as they affect investors.

5.4.2 Explain the role of diversification in mitigating risk.

5.4.3 Analyse the impact of timescale on a client's attitude to risk.

5.4.4 Explain the key methods of determining a client's attitude to risk.

5.5 ADVICE AND RECOMMENDATIONS

5.5.1 Explain why asset allocation always comes before investment or product selection.

5.5.2 Explain the key roles of charges and the financial stability of the provider as criteria within the fund selection process, and the use of past performance.

5.5.3 Explain the importance of stability, independence and standing of trustees, fund custodians and auditors in the fund selection process.

5.5.4 Identify benchmarks and other performance measures.

5.5.5 Explain the importance of reviews within the financial planning process.

5.6 SKILLS REQUIRED WHEN ADVISING CLIENTS

5.6.1 Describe the need for advisers to communicate clearly, assessing and adapting to the differing levels of knowledge and understanding of their clients.

5.6.2 Identify and apply suitable investment solutions to suit different needs of retail clients.

5.7 THE OBJECTIVES OF PENSION FUNDS, LIFE ASSURANCE AND GENERAL INSURANCE COMPANIES AND THE FACTORS THAT IMPACT UPON THEIR INVESTMENT DECISIONS

5.7.1 Explain the features and objectives of the following funds in the UK: pension funds (defined benefit and defined contribution), life assurance, general insurance.

5.7.2 Distinguish among the typical asset allocations for DB and DC pension funds, life assurance and general insurance funds.

5.7.3 Explain the return objectives of the major fund types.

5.7.4 Classify funds by their income/capital growth requirements.

5.7.5 Explain the effect of each of the following on a fund's asset allocation: time horizons, liability structure, liquidity requirements.

5.7.6 Explain the taxation of the various types of funds in the UK.

5.7.7 Explain the effect that taxation legislation may have on the stock selection and asset allocation of a fund.

5.7.8 Identify other types of legal requirements that affect pension funds, insurance funds and retail clients.

TOPIC 6 TAXATION IN THE UK

By the end of this topic, learners should be able to:

- Demonstrate an understanding of the UK tax system as relevant to the needs and circumstances of individuals and trusts.
- Demonstrate an ability to analyse the taxation of investments as relevant to the needs and circumstances of individuals and trusts.
- Demonstrate an ability to analyse the role and relevance of tax in the financial affairs of individuals and trusts.
- Demonstrate an ability to apply the knowledge of personal taxation to the provision of investment advice.

6.1 THE UK TAX SYSTEM AND THE TAXATION OF INVESTMENTS

6.1.1 Describe the principles of income tax applicable to earnings, savings and investment income in the UK.

6.1.2 Describe, in relation to income tax, the system of allowances, reliefs and priorities for taxing income.

6.1.3 Explain the taxation of the income of trusts and beneficiaries.

6.1.4 Describe the system of National Insurance contributions (NICs).

6.1.5 Describe the principles of capital gains tax (CGT) in the UK.

6.1.6 Describe the principles of inheritance tax (IHT).

6.1.7 Explain the limitations of lifetime gifts and transfers at death in mitigating IHT.

6.1.8 Explain the implications of residence and domicile in relation to liability to income tax, CGT and IHT.

6.1.9 Describe the system of UK tax compliance including self-assessment, pay as you earn (PAYE), tax returns, tax payments, tax evasion and avoidance issues.

6.1.10 Describe the principles of stamp duty land tax (SDLT) as applied to property transactions (buying/selling and leasing).

6.1.11 Describe the principles of stamp duty reserve tax (SDRT).

6.1.12 Explain how companies are taxed in the UK.

6.1.13 Describe, in outline, the principles of value added tax (VAT).

6.1.14 Analyse the taxation of direct investments including cash and cash equivalents, fixed interest securities, equities and property.

6.1.15 Analyse the key features and taxation of indirect investments including pension arrangements, different types of individual savings accounts (ISAs), and child trust funds, onshore and offshore life assurance policies, real estate investment trusts, venture capital trusts and enterprise investment schemes.

6.2 INVESTMENT ADVICE AND TAX PLANNING

6.2.1 Evaluate the tax considerations shaping clients' needs and circumstances.

6.2.2 Analyse the key principles of income tax planning.

6.2.3 Analyse how the use of annual CGT exemptions, the realisation of losses, the timing of disposals, and sale and repurchase of similar assets can mitigate CGT.

6.2.4 Calculate the most common elements of income tax, NICs, CGT and IHT, including the impact of lifetime transfers and transfers at death.

6.2.5 Select elementary tax planning recommendations in the context of investments and pensions advice.

CONTENTS

CHAPTER 1

FINANCIAL MARKETS AND INSTITUTIONS

Banks, insurance companies, pension funds, savers and other participants in the UK financial services industry all play their own part in allocating capital within the UK and the global economy. This chapter describes how financial markets and the key participants operating within them function, and the benefits they can offer.

Bank deposits made by individuals, loans made by banks, portfolios held by insurance companies and companies raising capital by issuing equities and bonds all play some role within a functioning financial market. By understanding the main types of financial securities traded between participants and how they are issued to raise capital, we can build a picture of how an efficient market serves both capital raising bodies and investors by offering trading venues with liquidity and price transparency.

The parties all exist in a market governed by regulations such as the UK listing rules, legal considerations such as the principal–agent relationship (together with shareholder protection offered by the Companies Act 2006 and effective corporate governance) and administrative processes such as clearing and settlement.

Financial markets are constantly evolving and it is not only necessary to understand how established trading venues such as the London Stock Exchange operate, but also to examine the role of alternative trading venues such as dark pools.

This chapter gives a broad introduction to the functions served by financial markets and a detailed discussion of key market rules, processes and trading venues.

CHAPTER 1 SECTION 1

INTRODUCTION TO FINANCIAL MARKETS

SECTION AIMS

By the end of this section, learners should be able to:

- Explain the functions of the financial services industry in allocating capital within the global economy.
- Explain the role and impact of the main financial institutions.
- Explain the function of government, including economic and industrial policy, regulation, taxation and social welfare.

The financial services industry provides four main functions in an economy:

1. **Financial intermediation.** A financial system provides the mechanisms to channel funds from savers to those who need to borrow funds. Financial intermediaries significantly reduce information and transaction costs in the economy. They provide suitable services and products for savers to become investors, ensure the adequate provision of information, and minimise the costs for borrowers in relation to the number of savers that would otherwise have to be approached and to the variety of terms that they would demand. Figure 1.1 illustrates some of the main flows that take place in a financial system. Savers can supply funds directly by holding the debt and equity securities issued by borrowers (the dotted lines in Figure 1.1) or they can supply funds via an intermediary, such as a bank or investment institution (the unbroken lines). While there can be circumstances in which direct financing through capital markets is appropriate, most forms of capital raising and capital saving involve financial intermediaries.

FIGURE 1.1: CAPITAL FLOWS

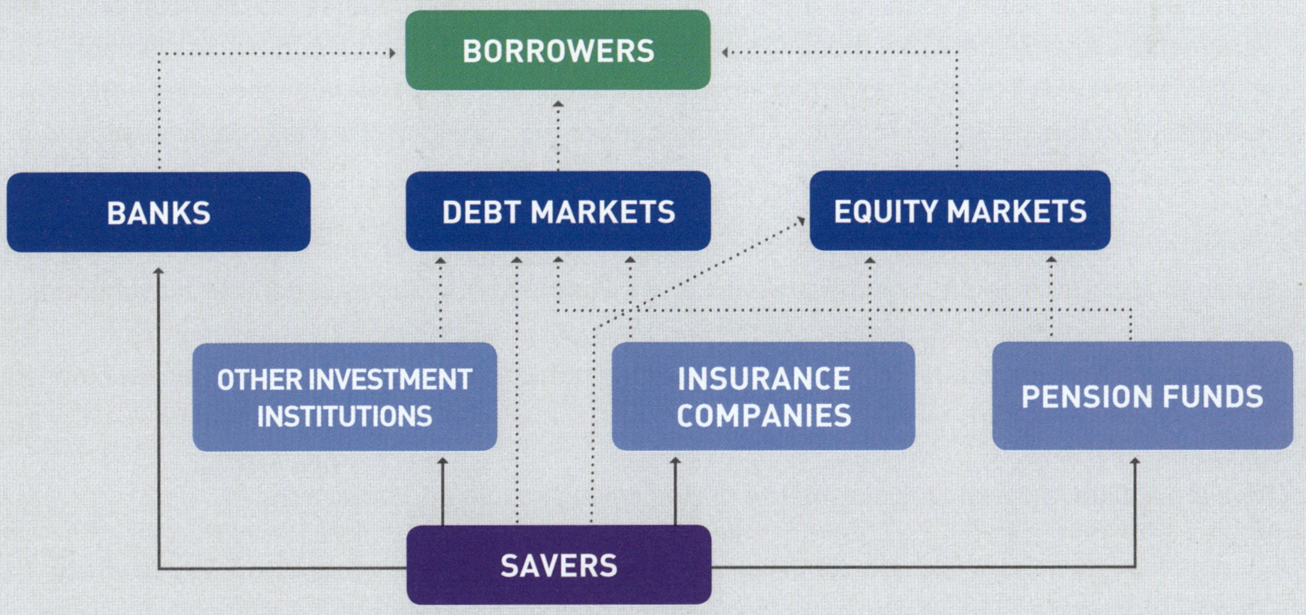

Banks and other credit institutions, such as building societies, have traditionally been a key source of finance for individuals, companies and other borrowers, and a vehicle through which individuals can save. They perform an intermediation function themselves. Increasingly, the banking sector interacts with the securities markets to raise capital (rather than relying on retail deposits) or to invest in those markets. Securities have grown much faster than bank deposits as a share of total financial assets in recent years. Insurance companies, pension funds and other investment institutions or vehicles (such as open-ended investment companies (OEICs), unit trusts and investment trusts) also perform an intermediation function by collecting funds from savers and investing those funds in securities issued by borrowers. Investment companies, such as insurance companies, also purchase the securitised assets of banks.

2. Pooling and managing risk. The financial services industry provides mechanisms that efficiently manage risk. This could be achieved through pooled investment funds, insurance or derivative products. Pooled investment products such as unit trusts, OEICs and investment trusts allow multiple savers to pool their funds and invest in a wider variety of investments, therefore reducing each individual's overall risk exposure. Insurance allows individuals and companies with a risk exposure to transfer this to the insurance company in return for payment of a fee. This transfer of responsibility for selecting borrowers to an institution allows pooling and more efficient management to take place. Derivatives, such as options and futures, also allow investors and borrowers to manage their risk exposures.

3. Payments and settlement services. The financial system provides the mechanisms for money and other financial assets to be managed, transmitted and received. Banks are the main providers of payments systems that allow money to be exchanged and debts to be settled. Settlement services are provided by clearing houses to ensure that buyers and sellers of securities complete the transaction they have entered into. Clearing houses are considered in more detail in section 4 of this chapter.

4. Portfolio management. The financial system allows investors to manage their wealth through access to financial markets, specialist advice and investment management services. Investment advice and investment management are the two main services provided by the investment industry, and are the focus of most of the discussion in this volume of the Official Training Manual.

1. INSTITUTIONS

There are a wide range of financial intermediaries linking savers and borrowers.

A central bank is a financial institution involved in setting the monetary framework within which both the economy and other financial organisations operate (see chapter 9, section 3). Financial intermediation involves the transfer of funds between surplus and deficit agents. Surplus agents are deposit-accepting institutions, such as banks and savings institutions, and deficit agents are investment institutions, such as insurance companies, mutual funds and pension funds.

Deposit institutions accept deposits from economic agents. The deposits become liabilities of these institutions, which lend funds as direct loans or investments. These institutions include commercial banks and building societies. However, the banking sector contains a wide range of different types of banks, including universal banks, which offer financial services as well as traditional deposit and lending facilities, and investment banks, which act as brokers, underwriters and mergers' advisers. Like banks, savings institutions accept deposits and make loans, although they usually operate under different rules to banks.

Investment institutions are also intermediaries, but unlike banks they invest the funds they raise in tradable securities such as bonds and equities. Investment institutions include insurance companies that offer protection against unfortunate events in exchange for a premium. Life insurance deals with death, illness and retirement policies, whereas general insurance involves loss or damage to property, homes, vehicles and so on. The different nature of life and general insurance is reflected in their different investment strategies. Life insurance policies tend to cover longer periods and so insurers tend to hold longer term assets. However, general insurance companies tend to hold shorter term assets, reflecting their greater need for immediate cash. Mutual funds, or unit trusts and investment trusts, are also important collective savings vehicles. Pension funds are now significant institutional investors in many countries, especially with falling state pension payments and aging populations.

Many of these institutions operate in the global financial system. Over the last 30 years or so, capital flows across national borders have increased dramatically. The large US current account deficit for most of this period has seen a flow of dollars into the world economy and a large part of these funds have been recycled, with central banks in many Asian and Middle-Eastern exporting economies purchasing US Treasuries in large quantities. Companies in one country may choose to list on the stock market in another country in order to raise capital in a more liquid market. Companies may also raise capital across borders by issuing bonds in another country (see section 7 of this chapter). Investment companies, such as pension funds and mutual funds, have increased their holdings of foreign assets over time. Individual investors in the UK increasingly look to invest internationally in Europe, the US and emerging markets through investment vehicles such as mutual funds and exchange-traded funds (ETFs). All of these developments mean that investment by savers and capital-raising by firms has a global dimension. The gradual removal of capital controls by individual nation states and the globalisation of the world economy have contributed to this phenomena of global capital flows.

2. THE ROLE OF GOVERNMENT

Broadly speaking, governments perform four functions.

1. The provision of services which private firms are either unwilling to provide or are not allowed to provide (or at least not exclusively). This is often referred to as 'market failure' and examples include defence, law and order and maintenance of roads. Industrial policy may involve grants and subsidies to promote certain sectors considered worthy of support, and for which the market may not provide a satisfactory solution (e.g. 'green' activities), or for which the market does not punish externalities (e.g. carbon taxes, tobacco taxes).

2. The regulation of firms, principally to protect the consumer. This includes regulation to promote competition, prevent fraud and so on. Governments also regulate markets through restrictions on entry into the market and rules governing behaviour in markets. In the UK, the Financial Conduct Authority (FCA) plays the main role in regulating conduct in financial markets. The Prudential Regulation Authority (PRA) regulates the capital and liquidity of banks, insurance companies and large investment intermediaries. Finally, the Financial Policy Committee (FPC) is responsible for managing systemic risk within the financial system. These regulatory bodies are covered in more detail in chapter 3. Government regulation may also include banning dangerous chemicals, promoting food and hygiene standards, ensuring drug safety standards, maintaining road and air safety, and so on.

3. To intervene in the distribution of income generated by private market transactions in order to conform to some criterion of equity, for example, a minimum wage guarantee. Redistribution of income and wealth is also a policy of most governments, and this is often achieved through transfer payments to households – for example, state pension payments and other welfare payments. Taxation is also used to achieve a better distribution of income among the population.

4. The stabilisation of the economy by attempting to reduce fluctuations in income and employment, and to control movements in the general price level. In many economies today, emphasis is placed on controlling inflation by using interest rates. In the UK, this is carried out by the Bank of England – covered in more detail in chapter 9, section 3. In 2008/09, many governments intervened to stabilise the financial system through capital support for distressed financial institutions.

CHAPTER 1 SECTION 2

THE ROLE OF SECURITIES MARKETS IN PROVIDING LIQUIDITY AND PRICE TRANSPARENCY

SECTION AIMS

By the end of this section, learners should be able to:

- Differentiate between a financial security and a real asset.
- Identify the key features of: a common equity share; a bond; a derivative contract; a unit in a pooled fund; and a foreign exchange transaction.
- Identify the functions of securities markets in providing price transparency and liquidity.
- Identify the reasons why liquidity and price transparency are thought to be important for the efficient allocation of capital costs when trading in securities markets.
- Calculate round trip transaction costs incorporating bid–ask spreads, dealing commission and transaction taxes, both in percentages and in absolute amounts.
- Identify the types of securities and the market conditions where price transparency, liquidity and depth are likely to be high/low.
- Define liquidity risk and identify why it is important.

1. TYPES OF INVESTMENTS

One of the main reasons for the existence of the financial services industry is to provide a link between savers that have funds to invest (also referred to as lenders or investors) and spenders that need funds (also called borrowers).

The main lenders in an economy are households – generally, households will have a surplus of income after spending. Not all households will be saving in a particular period; some will, some will be borrowing and some will be both saving and borrowing. Taken together, though, households are normally the main lenders in an economy. Lenders could lend their surplus directly to borrowers in the form of a loan, for example to help fund a business. The borrower typically pays interest to the lender until the loan is repaid. The main borrowers in an economy are typically companies and governments. Some companies will want to invest in physical capital (e.g. new plant or machinery) but will have insufficient funds and therefore need to borrow. Governments need to borrow when spending is greater than taxation income. Direct lending from lenders to borrowers is uncommon, although the growth of peer-to-peer lenders has provided some impetus to this type of lending. More commonly, households will lend/invest their savings indirectly through intermediaries in a range of assets.

Assets are items that have value and include real assets and financial assets. Real assets are physical assets, such as land, buildings and gold. Financial assets are claims representing the right to some return (such as a bank deposit or a bond) or could represent ownership of physical assets. For example, a share represents ownership in a company. This share gives its owner, the shareholder, rights to some of the company's assets and earnings. We can categorise these two different types of financial assets as debt and equity.

- Debt claims are loans that lenders make to borrowers. Lenders expect borrowers to repay these loans and to make interest payments until the loans are repaid. A simple example of a debt security is a bank savings deposit. This may pay a fixed rate of interest over some term or the rate of interest may vary. A bank deposit represents a claim the lender has on the bank and is not tradable. Most debt claims are tradable and one example of a tradable debt is a bond. A tradable claim is also referred to as a security. Bonds are issued by governments and companies and generally pay a fixed rate of interest, as such they are often referred to as fixed-income securities.

- Equity securities are also called shares. Like bonds these are tradable securities. Shareholders have an ownership stake in the company they have invested in. The company has no obligation either to repay the money invested by the shareholders (i.e. shares are not repaid by the company) or to make regular payments, called dividends. However, investors who buy shares expect to earn a return by being able to sell their shares at a higher price than they bought them and, possibly, by receiving dividends (a share of the earnings made by the company).

Places where buyers and sellers can trade securities are known as securities markets or financial markets. A distinction is generally made between money markets, for securities that have maturity shorter than a year, and capital markets, for securities that have maturity longer than a year. An example of a money market security is a Treasury Bill – a short term debt security issued by a government with a typical maturity of one or three months. Examples of capital market securities include bonds and shares.

Savers often rely on individuals or firms in the investment industry to help them navigate financial markets. The investment industry is a subset of the financial services industry comprising a range of entities that facilitate savers investing their money and borrowers obtaining the funds they need. The major investment industry participants include exchanges, investment brokers, investment dealers, financial advisers and investment analysts.

So far, we have described two of the main financial assets that savers can invest in – shares and bonds. Households and individuals generally invest in these assets indirectly through an intermediary, such as insurance companies, pension schemes and pooled investment vehicles. Savers will therefore invest in the products created by the intermediary, such as an investment share or unit created by a unit trust. The intermediary will then invest in a range of assets including shares, bonds, property, commodities and derivatives. The advantage to the saver of indirect investment is a reduction in risk due to:

- More extensive diversification.
- A reduction in transaction costs (as the intermediary will be able to trade financial assets at lower cost than the individual saver, although the intermediary will charge a fee for its services).
- Access to specialist expertise in the financial assets being invested in.
- The ability to invest in assets that would not be available to a small investor, such as large properties.

Let us take a unit trust that specialises in UK equities as an example of a pooled investment vehicle. These vehicles are known as 'open ended'; when investors want to invest, the fund issues new units in exchange for cash that the investor pays for the units. When existing investors want to withdraw money, the fund redeems (repurchases) their units and pays the investors cash. The fund can therefore increase or shrink in size according to demand for its units – hence the term 'open-ended'. The fund manager will then invest the cash received from its many investors in UK shares. If the fund is well managed and the value of UK equities increase, then the value of the units in the fund will increase. The investor can realise this gain by selling the units. Unit trusts and other investment vehicles are covered in chapter 16.

An investment intermediary, such as a pension fund or unit trust, may use a derivative contract to achieve its objectives. A derivative contract is a financial contract 'derived' from some other asset (normally called the underlying asset) in such a way that the price movements of the derivative and the underlying asset will be highly correlated over time. An example of a derivative is a FTSE 100 index futures contract. This can be used to hedge against falls in the value of the FTSE 100 over some future time period. The value of the index and the price of the derivative are positively correlated with each other. A fund manager holding a portfolio of large UK stocks will see the value of that portfolio fall if the value of the FTSE 100 falls, and so can sell FTSE index futures contracts to hedge (protect) against such a fall. If the FTSE 100 falls, the value of the index futures contract will fall. As the fund manager has sold the index futures contract initially, reversing this position (i.e. buying the index futures contract) will yield a gain. This gain compensates for the fall in value of the UK shares in the portfolio.

Derivative contracts can also be used to speculate (i.e. make gains from anticipated movements in the price of an asset). A derivative contract is often used if the underlying asset is difficult to buy or has high costs associated with investing in it. One example is speculating on anticipated movements in the price of oil. Buying the oil directly is expensive but buying a derivative contract is less costly. Derivatives are covered in chapter 13.

Finally, an investor may use a foreign exchange market transaction. For example, a UK-based fund manager may want to purchase US securities. To achieve this, the manager will need to convert pounds sterling into US dollars. This transaction will be carried out in the foreign exchange markets (also referred to as the currency markets). For large value transactions, the purchase of dollars for pounds may take place directly with a dealer (typically a bank). The dealer will quote bid and offer prices representing the prices they buy and sell dollars in relation to pounds. For smaller value transactions, the purchase of dollars will take place with a broker who will arrange for the dollars to be purchased. More detailed examination of the workings of the foreign exchange market is covered in chapter 9, section 4.

2. THE FUNCTIONS OF SECURITIES MARKETS

Securities such as equities and bonds are traded in securities markets. Securities markets bring buyers and sellers of financial securities together. Such markets provide a number of important functions.

The raising of capital (in the capital markets). Capital is long-term funds raised for the purpose of investment in physical productive assets. A firm can raise capital by issuing equities (ordinary shares) or bonds (corporate bonds). The funds raised can then be used to purchase new machinery, and other resources that enable the firm to grow. Growing firms contribute to a nation's economic growth. The other essential part of this process, facilitated by financial markets, is the mobilisation of savings. The liquidity provided by markets encourages savers to purchase the claims issued by borrowers. This leads to a greater flow of savings into productive investment.

The transfer of risk (in the derivatives markets). We have seen that risk can be hedged using derivative contracts. A fund manager can hedge the risk that the value of an equity portfolio may fall by using equity index futures contracts. A company can protect itself from a rise in interest rates (which would increase its borrowing costs) by using interest rate futures contracts. The fund manager and the company have obtained protection against the risk by using a derivative contract but this risk has not disappeared. It has been transferred to the counterparty of the derivative contract. In the case of the fund manager seeking protection against a fall in the value of the FTSE 100, we saw the fund manager achieve this by selling FTSE 100 futures contracts. In the event the FTSE 100 fell, the fund manager would then buy FTSE 100 futures at a lower price than they were sold and make a gain from the futures position that would compensate for the loss of value of the FTSE 100. The counterparty to the fund manager would be a trader who expected the FTSE 100 to rise in the future and would buy futures contracts initially to take advantage of that expectation.

Price discovery. This refers to the revealing of the equilibrium price through trading. The orders placed by buyers and sellers into a market leads to the emergence of a price that both buyers and sellers can agree to trade at. In dynamic markets, such as the equity markets, this process takes place continuously while the market is open. If a market is efficient (discussed in chapter 15, section 4) then the equilibrium price will change only when new information arrives in the market.

Creation of liquidity. Securities markets enable investors who hold investments to sell (liquidate) them. This ability to sell investments makes them more attractive to hold and encourages investors to buy securities in the first place. Liquidity in a financial market is typically defined as the ability to sell a security without causing a significant movement in its price and with minimum loss of value. A liquid market is therefore one in which there are many buyers and sellers. A seller is more likely to sell at a price they wish to sell at if there are many buyers willing to trade at the same time.

One important distinction is the difference between primary and secondary markets. Primary markets are those where initial sales of securities are made to investors. For example, a company may issue new ordinary shares in order to raise capital. Where the issue is the first issue into the markets, the company is said to be making an initial public offering (IPO). Where the company has already issued shares and makes a subsequent issue this is said to be a secondary or seasoned offering.

After the shares (whether from an IPO or secondary offering) have been sold to investors, any subsequent trading of those shares is said to take place in the secondary market. Clearly the primary market trades are important because this is where issuers raise new capital. However, the secondary market also plays an important role in providing liquidity to investors in securities – i.e. the ability to turn those securities into cash with little loss of value. This liquidity provision makes it more likely that issuers of securities can make that first issue to raise capital and may even increase the price that the securities are first sold at. Buyers will be willing to pay more for securities that are easy to sell later. This in turn will reduce the cost of issuing for issuers.

For secondary market trading there are essentially two types of trading arrangements: order-driven and quote-driven. Order-driven markets use rules to match trades between buyer and sellers. Most shares, futures contracts and standard option contracts are traded on exchanges that primarily use an order-driven system. Most of these systems are electronic order matching, though some commodity futures are still traded using a floor-based order matching system. In section 3 of this chapter we will examine the nature of trading on SETS, the electronic order-matching system used for trading most shares listed on the London Stock Exchange.

On such markets, there are essentially two types of orders submitted to the market. First, a market order can be submitted which specifies the quantity that the trader wishes to buy or sell and is then matched with the best order available. So an order to buy 1,000 Vodafone shares will be matched with the lowest priced order to sell 1,000 Vodafone shares. Second, a limit order can be submitted which specifies both the quantity to be traded and the price the trader wants to buy/sell at. This order will not be matched straight away if there are no other trades offering to take the counterparty position for the price specified. Limit orders sit in the order book waiting to be matched. Such limit orders provide liquidity in order-driven markets as their existence provides an opportunity for a trader who needs to sell quickly to submit a market order and be matched immediately with the best price in the order book.

Most of the trading of bonds, currencies and commodities for immediate delivery (spot commodities) trade in quote-driven markets. In addition, many non-standard derivatives such as swaps trade over-the-counter (i.e. not on an organised exchange) using a quote-driven system. These markets are termed quote-driven (or price-driven) markets because investors trade with dealers at the prices quoted by the dealers. Depending on the instrument traded, the dealers work for commercial banks, investment banks, brokers/dealers, or proprietary trading houses. The dealers will quote two prices: a bid price, which is the price they are willing to buy at, and an offer (ask) price that they are willing to sell at. The difference between the bid and ask price, known as the bid–ask spread, represents the profit (or compensation for risk) made by the dealer. The dealer will hold an inventory of securities thus guaranteeing to always be in a position to fulfill a buy or sell trade. By guaranteeing to be always able to trade at the prices quoted, the dealer is supplying liquidity to the market.

Another important distinction in financial markets is whether a trader is on the sell-side or the buy-side. Sell-side firms – such as investment banks, brokers and dealers – primarily provide transaction services and investment products. Buy-side firms – investment managers – purchase these services and products. This classification scheme is somewhat arbitrary and not easily applied to many large integrated firms. Many investment banks have divisions or wholly owned subsidiaries that provide asset management services. These functions are on the buy-side, even though investment banks are sell-side firms. 'Buy-side' is also used to refer to the investors who purchase investment services and products from the sell-side. For example, mutual funds, pension funds, hedge funds and insurance companies are all considered buy-side.

3. PRICE TRANSPARENCY AND LIQUIDITY

As well as determining the equilibrium price, markets also disseminate that price to the public. There are two types of price dissemination:

- A market is pre-trade transparent if it publishes real-time data about quotes and orders.
- A market is post-trade transparent if it publishes trade prices and sizes soon after trades occur.

Buy-side traders value transparency because it allows them to better manage their trading, understand market values and estimate their potential transaction costs. Sell-side traders, however, prefer to trade in opaque markets because, as frequent traders, they have an informational advantage over counterparties (particularly buy-side traders). Organised markets, such as the London Stock Exchange, tend to be more transparent than an over-the-counter market, such as the market for credit default swaps. In Europe, pre- and post-trade transparency for many securities (especially equities) is required under the Market in Financial Instruments Directive (MiFiD).

Many investors assess a market's liquidity by looking at bid–ask spreads. Bid–ask spreads tend to be wider in opaque markets because finding the best available price is harder for traders. Transparency reduces bid–ask spreads, which benefits investors. In order-driven markets, liquidity can be judged by the difference between the best buy and sell prices in the order book.

A market may also be considered deeply liquid if there are a lot of ready and willing buyers and sellers. This is related to market depth that is a measure of the size of order that is needed to move the market (have an impact on price) by a certain amount. Therefore, a deep stock market would have a sufficient volume of pending orders on both the bid and ask side, preventing a large order from significantly moving the price.

An asset is illiquid if it is difficult to sell because of uncertainty about its future market value or if there is a lack of market depth. During the 2008 financial crisis, mortgage-backed securities became illiquid because of uncertainty about their future market value. Infrequently traded shares, such as some of the shares traded on AIM (see section 3 of this chapter) are relatively illiquid. During times of market uncertainty, when most securities are falling in value, those securities may become difficult to sell, as most traders will have similar pessimistic expectations about the future value of those securities. An example of a deeply liquid market is the US Treasuries market; the large volume of transactions, low bid–ask spreads and high depth (low market impact of a trade) make transaction costs very low.

Investors tend to demand a higher return on securities with low liquidity to compensate for the risk that it may be difficult to sell the security quickly. The price may move against them (fall) while they are waiting to sell. Liquidity risk – the risk of not being able to sell quickly with the potential for loss of value – is generally priced in the security.

4. TRANSACTION COSTS

Trading securities incurs significant transaction costs. These include brokerage commissions, bid–ask spreads and market impact. Most traders employ brokers to trade on their behalf and pay their brokers commission for arranging their trades. Commissions are usually a fixed percentage of the principal value of the transaction or a fixed price per share, bond or contract. Commissions compensate brokers for the resources that they must use to fill orders, such as costs for order routing systems, market data systems, accounting systems, exchange memberships, office space and personnel to manage the trading process. Brokers also pay exchange, regulatory and clearing fees on behalf of their clients via their commission and fixed transaction charges.

EXAMPLE

Broker commission

Broker commission varies according to the type of trader and frequency of trading. Retail customers typically pay around £5.00 to £12.50 per trade (the more frequent the trading, the lower the commission). Institutional investors pay significantly less with typical costs being 10 to 20 basis points for large trades.

Generally, traders who want to trade quickly buy at higher prices than the prices at which they sell. The difference comes from the price concessions that they give to encourage other traders to trade. For small orders, the trader will have to buy at the ask or sell at the bid, thus incurring the bid–ask spread. For large trades, buyers who want to trade quickly must raise prices to encourage other traders to sell to them. Similarly, impatient sellers of large trades must lower prices to encourage other traders to purchase from them. These price concessions, called market impact or price impact, often occur over time as large-trade buyers push prices up and large-trade sellers push them down in multiple transactions. For large institutions, the price impact of trading large orders generally is the biggest component of their transaction costs.

EXAMPLE

Bid–ask spread

Consider a stock that is trading with a bid price of £9.95 and an offer price of £10.00. The bid–ask spread in this case is £0.05. The spread as a percentage is ((£0.05/£10.00) × 100), or 0.50%.

A buyer who acquires the stock at £10.00 and immediately sells it at the bid price of £9.95 would incur a loss of 0.50% of the transaction value due to this spread. The purchase and immediate sale of 100 shares would entail a £5.00 loss, while if 10,000 shares were sold, the loss would be £500.00. The percentage loss resulting from the spread is the same in both cases.

Traders who are willing to wait until other traders want to trade with them generally incur lower transaction costs on their trades. In particular, by using limit orders instead of market orders, they can buy at the bid price or sell at the ask price. However, these traders incur the risk that they will not trade when the market is moving away from their orders. The cost of not executing a trade is called an opportunity cost.

Traders choose their order submission strategies to minimise their transaction costs and their opportunity costs of not trading. Market participants can use various techniques to reduce their transaction costs. They employ skillful brokers, use electronic algorithms to manage their trading and use hidden orders or dark pool trading systems to hide their size.

EXAMPLE

Tax and other charges

UK traders purchasing shares pay stamp duty reserve tax of 0.50% of the transaction value. A further levy of £1 on all purchases and sales of shares in excess of £10,000 is levied to finance the Panel on Takeovers and Mergers (the PTM levy).

EXAMPLE

Total round-trip transaction costs

Round-trip transaction costs are the total costs of completing a transaction, including bid–ask spread, commissions and taxes. The assumption made in this example is that the purchase and sale occur simultaneously so the quoted bid and ask prices are used as buying and selling prices.

For a retail investor that wants to purchase 5,000 shares in Barclays, assume the current bid–ask quotes for this order quantity are 213.75p–213.85p and commission per trade is £5. The total round-trip transaction costs will be:

	COST
Buy 5,000 shares at 213.85p	£10,692.50
Sell 5,000 shares at 213.75p	(£10,687.50)
Commission (for two trades)	£10.00
Stamp duty reserve tax	£53.46
PTM levy	£2.00
Net cost (absolute terms)	£70.46
Net cost (percentage terms)	0.659%

5. THE IMPACT OF WELL-FUNCTIONING MARKETS

Well-functioning financial markets provide significant benefits to traders, borrowers and society as a whole. Markets in which trades are easy to arrange with low transaction costs are operationally efficient. Such markets have small bid–ask spreads and can absorb large orders without substantial impact on prices. This will encourage traders to trade and in turn encourage savers to invest their funds in claims issued by borrowers, therefore increasing the flow of capital to productive uses in the economy.

An important by-product of operational efficiency is informational efficiency where trading leads to asset prices reflecting all relevant information about the value of the asset. Informational efficiency is enhanced by price transparency. Where all investors have access to good quality, timely information about securities, then the prices of those securities are more likely to reflect fundamental information about value. If prices reflect the fundamental value of those securities, then investors will direct funds to those securities yielding the highest returns. In well-functioning markets, the highest returns are likely to be earned on securities issued by firms investing in the most productive assets. Thus funds will be allocated to the most productive uses in society (i.e. there is greater allocative efficiency).

CHAPTER 1 SECTION 3

TYPES OF FINANCIAL MARKETS

SECTION AIMS

By the end of this section, learners should be able to:

- Identify the main dealing systems and facilities offered in the UK equities market.
- Identify the nature of the securities that would be traded on each of the main dealing systems and facilities.
- Explain the structure and operation of the primary and secondary UK markets for gilts and corporate bonds.
- Explain the motivations for, and implications of, dual-listing a company.
- Compare and contrast exchange trading and over-the-counter markets.
- Distinguish between the following alternative trading venues: multilateral trading facilities; systematic internalisers; and dark pools.
- Distinguish between a quote-driven and an order-driven market.
- Explain the roles of the various participants in the UK equity market.
- Explain high-frequency trading, its benefits and risks.

1. UK EQUITY MARKET

The London Stock Exchange offers two market models for trading UK shares: SETS and SETSqx. Domestic stocks are assigned to market models according to their liquidity and index to ensure that buyers and sellers are brought together efficiently. SETS is an electronic limit order book used to trade stocks including all FTSE All-Share constituents, as well as many of the most traded AIM and Irish securities. SETSqx is a trading platform for stocks that are less liquid than those covered by SETS. It combines a periodic electronic auction book along with standalone non-electronic quote-driven market making, with four uncrossings taking place each day. The uncrossings allow order book execution through auctions taking place at 9am, 11am, 2pm and at closing. Investors therefore have a choice of trading in either the quote-driven or order book auction service. SEAQ is a quote-display system used as the price reference point for telephone execution between market participants and registered market makers. This is used for fixed interest securities and AIM securities that are not traded on either SETS or SETSqx.

International securities are traded on the London Stock Exchange through the International Order Book, an electronic order book for trading international securities in the form of a depository receipt on the London Stock Exchange. Other trading services provided by the London Stock Exchange include, firstly, the European Quoting Service (EQS) – a quote-driven market-making and trade-reporting platform that supports all European Union (EU) liquid securities (excluding those traded on SETS and SETSqx). With this platform, market-makers enter non-electronically executable quotes during the Mandatory Quote Period (MQP).

The European Trade Reporting service enables clients to meet their post-trade reporting obligations whether trading on- or off-exchange. This is achieved either by:

- on-exchange off-book trade publication – for all trades regulated under the exchange's rules; or
- OTC trade publication – for any unregulated trades executed away from the exchange's markets, whether acting as a systematic internaliser or not.

Finally, the London Stock Exchange provides an electronic Order Book for Retail Bonds (OBR). Launched in 2010, this order-driven trading service offers retail investors access to a select number of gilts, supranational and UK corporate bonds.

LCH.Clearnet is the central counterparty to all SETS trades at the point of execution. This ensures that clearing members acting on behalf of firms trading on SETS are not exposed to any risk in the event that a clearing member defaults. LCH.Clearnet assumes the risk itself, but manages it by collecting margin from members.

A dual-listed company (DLC) is a corporate structure in which two corporations function as a single operating business through a legal equalisation agreement, but retain separate legal identities and stock exchange listings. Virtually all DLCs are cross-border and have tax advantages for the corporations and their shareholders. The equalisation agreements are legal contracts that specify how ownership of the corporation is shared, and are set up to ensure equal treatment of both companies' shareholders in voting and cash flow rights. The contracts cover issues related to dividends, liquidation and corporate governance. Usually, the two companies will share a single board of directors and have an integrated management structure. Some examples of DLCs (together with the countries where the two corporations making up the DLC are listed) are:

- BHP Billiton (Australia and UK).
- Carnival Corporation & plc (US and UK).
- Investec Bank (South Africa and UK).
- Royal Dutch Shell (UK and Netherlands).
- Reed Elsevier (UK and Netherlands).

One important advantage of a dual-listed structure is tax. Capital gains tax could be owed if an outright merger took place, but no such tax consequence would arise with a DLC deal.

The shares of the DLC parents represent claims on exactly the same underlying cash flows. This implies that in efficient financial markets, stock prices of the DLC parents should be the same. In practice, however, large differences between the prices of the two parents can arise. For example, in the early 1980s Royal Dutch NV was trading at a discount of approximately 30% relative to Shell Transport and Trading plc. This, of course, creates arbitrage opportunities for investors, assuming the two prices eventually converge. The evidence on DLC mispricing is that convergence can take many years and therefore an arbitrage strategy of this kind would require a very long investment horizon. Such arbitrage is therefore very risky.

Dual-listing is not to be confused with cross-listing. Cross-listing is when a firm lists its shares on one or more foreign stock exchange(s) in addition to its domestic exchange. There are a number of possible reasons for firms to cross-list. These include the traditional argument, which is that the firm expects to benefit from a lower cost of capital that arises because their shares become more accessible to global investors whose access would otherwise be restricted because of international investment barriers. Another possible motivation is that cross-listings on deeper and more liquid equity markets could lead to an increase in the liquidity of the stock and a decrease in the cost of capital.

2. GILTS

The UK government bond market is commonly referred to as the 'gilt-edged' or 'gilts' market. Although the issued bonds carry a variety of names (e.g. Treasury, Exchequer, Consols), all bonds are the direct obligation of the UK government. The government's agent issues gilts, which usually pay coupons semi-annually, to finance the public sector net cash requirement, which is the shortfall between government expenditure and government revenue. This used to be known as the public sector borrowing requirement. In April 1998, the management of the UK government's debt was passed to the Debt Management Office (DMO), which is an agency of the Treasury.

Although now quite rare, the government has in the past issued gilts via the 'tap' method, where the issue is announced and investors are invited to tender for the issue. If bidders do not offer the price required by the DMO, that part of the issue not taken up originally can be temporarily withdrawn and released slowly into the market as market conditions become more favourable. In recent years, however, the DMO has begun issuing gilts via an auction, and this is now the favoured method. Issuing gilts by auction is also the method preferred in a number of other countries, most notably the US.

All gilt holders are able to receive coupon payments in gross form. New holdings automatically receive gross tax treatment (unless the holder indicates otherwise). The main holders of government gilts are UK pension funds, UK insurance companies, overseas investors, UK banks and building societies and private individuals. The accrual convention for interest is based on an actual/actual basis. This means that when calculating accrued interest over a period, it is based on the actual number of days since the last coupon and the actual number of days in the coupon period. Although this sounds quite normal, it is not the case in many other overseas government bond markets.

Gilts normally go ex-dividend seven business days before the coupon date. UK gilts are now quoted on a decimal basis, where previously they had been quoted in 32nds of £1. Gilt settlement is made via CREST.

The key participants in the market for UK gilts are the gilt-edged market makers (GEMMs) who are required by the DMO 'to make on demand and in any trading condition, continuous and effective two-way prices in gilts at which they stand committed to deal'. This means that they must continually quote two-way (bid and ask) prices for gilt issues and must trade at these prices so that investors always have a source of liquidity. In addition, the GEMMs are expected to participate in primary gilt issuance, provide the DMO with relevant data about the gilts market and accept the DMO's monitoring arrangements.

For example, the Gilt-Edged Market Makers' Association (GEMMA) provides data at the end of each day to the DMO relating to gilt prices. This is where the gilt prices quoted in the financial press come from. In return for providing these services, the DMO makes certain facilities available to the GEMMs. These include a special dealing arrangement with the DMO, access to the competing inter-dealer brokers (IDBs) and the exclusive right to strip and reconstitute gilts with the introduction of the market for gilt strips on 8 December 1997.

Inter-dealer brokers (IDBs) are intermediaries that market makers use when dealing on their own account. By trading through an IDB, the market makers can be assured of anonymity so that a fair market is maintained.

When corporate bonds are issued, they may be sold as an open offer for sale or directly to a small number of professional investors, a so-called private placing; the former involves a syndicate of banks with one as lead manager buying the bonds and then reselling them to investors. Hence the sale of the bonds is underwritten by the banks (who charge for this service). If the lead bank buys all the bonds and sells them to the syndicate this is called a 'bought deal'. The syndicate members could then sell the bonds on at varying prices. More usually, the lead manager and the syndicate buy the bonds together and offer them at a fixed price for a certain period – a so-called fixed price re-offering.

Corporate bonds mainly trade in decentralised, dealer-based over-the-counter markets, with market liquidity provided by dealers and other market participants committing risk capital. When an investor buys or sells a bond, the counterparty to the trade is almost always a bank or securities firm acting as a dealer. In some cases, when a dealer buys a bond from an investor, the dealer carries the bond 'in inventory'.

On 1 February 2010, the London Stock Exchange launched an electronic ORB. This order-driven trading service offers access to a number of gilts and UK corporate bonds and has been developed in response to strong demand from retail investors for access to an onscreen secondary market in fixed income securities.

In June 2015, more than 60 gilts and over 100 corporate bonds (tradable in denominations of £1,000 or similar) were available for trading on the ORB. The ORB offers an electronic order-driven model similar to SETS with continuous two-way pricing provided by market makers (submitted as named executable quotes). Other market participants are able to enter market orders and limit orders. Standard settlement cycles are followed with T+1 for gilts and T+2 for corporate bonds.

3. EXCHANGE TRADING, OVER-THE-COUNTER AND ALTERNATIVE TRADING VENUES

An over-the-counter (OTC) market involves the trading of securities in a decentralised way, usually via telephone, fax or electronic network rather than on a physical trading floor or other centralised meeting place (an 'exchange'). These securities may not be listed on an exchange, and trading takes place via dealers who carry inventories of the securities to satisfy buy and sell orders. OTC refers to a bilateral contract in which two parties agree on how a trade or agreement is to be settled in the future. Often, it is between an investment bank and its clients directly. Forwards and swaps are examples of such contracts, and they are mostly done via computer or telephone.

Dark pools are electronic crossing networks that provide liquidity that is not displayed on a conventional order book of an organised exchange. Dark pools are useful for traders wishing to buy/sell large numbers of shares without revealing themselves on the open market as neither the price nor identity of the trading firm is displayed.

Multilateral trading facilities (MTFs) are trading platforms organised by investment firms or market operators which bring together third-party buyers and sellers, often banks and large institutional investors. This may involve OTC instruments or exchange-traded securities, thereby providing additional liquidity to participants (e.g. BATS Chi-X Europe, Turquoise). They can be owned by conventional exchanges. In addition, a systematic internaliser is an investment firm which deals on its own account by executing customer order flows in liquid shares outside either a regulated market or a multilateral trading facility. MiFID requires such a financial firm to publish and honour buy and sell prices up to standard market size; they have to honour their prices and are not able to improve their price when dealing in retail size or with retail clients.

4. QUOTE-DRIVEN AND ORDER-DRIVEN MARKETS

SEAQ is a 'quote-display' system, while SETS is an 'order book', i.e. an order-driven system. Here, we explain in simple terms the differences between the two and when each type is used.

Some securities are highly liquid – i.e. are traded in large volumes, so that when an investor wants to buy a stock there is a counterparty who can be readily found. More than this, the price the buyer is willing to pay is acceptable to the seller. When securities have these characteristics, it is sufficient for markets to be run under an order-driven system. Under these systems, orders from all customers are input to an electronic order book. Buyers state the security, volume and price they are willing to pay. Similarly, sellers state the prices they are willing to accept.

Orders are automatically 'matched' and then proceed to the settlement system. Remainders of orders, where not fully matched, may be then left on the system until completed. The priority for matching is first by price, and then by the time the order was input – i.e. on a first-in-first-out basis.

A simplified example of an order book for XYZ PLC's shares is as follows:

BUY		SELL	
Volume	Price	Volume	Price
5,000	303	12,100	304
10,880	303	650	305
4,666	303	18,221	305
10,000	302	4,326	306
860	301	14,100	307
5,000	301	1,500	307

The table shows the volume of shares for each order, together with the prices buyers are willing to pay and that sellers are willing to accept. As well as the volumes and prices, the times that the orders are entered would also be recorded. The orders shown in the table are those that have not been matched – the highest price buyers are willing to pay (303p) is below the price that sellers are willing to accept (304p). If an order is entered to buy 10,000 XYZ PLC shares 'at best', then this will be matched against the selling order at the top of the right-hand column with a price of 304p.

An electronic order-driven system automatically gives customers the best price available. This is not the case with quote-driven systems.

SEAQ is an example of a quote-driven (or 'price-driven') market. When securities are too illiquid to be traded on an order-driven system, market makers are required to maintain liquidity and efficiency in trading. Market makers are financial institutions that have an obligation to continually quote firm bid and ask prices for a given security and be ready and able to buy or sell at those publicly quoted prices. Of course, if the market maker does not want to trade in a particular stock, they will not quote a good price. Market makers in equities in the UK may elect which securities they wish to trade in. GEMMs must deal in all gilt issues, or none at all.

Market makers must indicate firm prices up to a required volume (set by exchanges). For example, the London Stock Exchange sets that minimum volume in the UK (known as the normal market size). For volumes greater than this, they may give indicative prices.

Market makers input their prices to a central market system (e.g. SEAQ) which market participants have access to view. Broker-dealers can then identify the market maker that gives their client the most favourable price, and can call that market maker to strike a deal. The market maker will then update the system as required.

5. HIGH-FREQUENCY TRADING

Algorithmic trading, also known as automated trading, is the use of electronic platforms for entering trading orders with an algorithm deciding on aspects of the order, such as the timing, price or volume of the order, or in many cases initiating the order without human intervention. Algorithmic trading is widely used by institutional traders (buy-side traders), such as pension funds and mutual funds, to divide large trades into several smaller trades to manage market impact and risk. Sell-side traders, such as market-makers and some hedge funds, also generate and execute orders automatically and in doing so provide liquidity to the market.

High-frequency trading (HFT) is a kind of algorithmic trading in which computers make decisions to initiate orders based on information that is received electronically before human traders are capable of processing the information they observe. This has resulted in a dramatic change in the market microstructure, particularly in the way liquidity is provided. HFT essentially looks to identify predictable patterns in financial data. The trading is characterised by short portfolio holding periods (often just a few seconds or even milliseconds) and very large volumes. There are four key HFT strategies: market-making based on order flow, market-making based on tick data information, event arbitrage and statistical arbitrage.

It is estimated by Tabb Group LLC that HFT accounted for 77% of transactions in UK markets in 2010. The Tabb Group estimates there are between 35 and 40 independent HFT firms operating in the UK.

HFT has been the subject of intense public focus since the US Securities and Exchange Commission (SEC) and the Commodity Futures Trading Commission (CFTC) stated that both algorithmic trading and HFT contributed to volatility in the 6 May 2010 Flash Crash. On 6 May 2010, US stock markets opened down and trended down most of the day on worries about the debt crisis in Greece. At 2:42pm, the equity market rapidly began to fall, and dropped 600 points in five minutes. By 2:47, the market had an almost 1,000 point loss on the day. Twenty minutes later, the market had regained most of the 600 point drop. According to the joint SEC/CFTC investigation report, at 2:32pm, against a 'backdrop of unusually high volatility and thinning liquidity' that day, 'a large fundamental trader (a mutual fund complex) initiated a sell program to sell a total of 75,000 E-Mini S&P 500 contracts (valued at approximately US$4.1bn) as a hedge to an existing equity position'. The report states that this was an unusually large position and that the computer algorithm used to trade the position was set to 'target an execution rate set to 9% of the trading volume calculated over the previous minute, but without regard to price or time.'

As the seller's trades were executed in the futures market, buyers included HFT traders, and these HFT firms also started aggressively selling the long futures positions they first accumulated mainly from the mutual fund. HFT traders then began to quickly buy and resell contracts to each other, generating a 'hot potato' effect as the same positions were rapidly passed back and forth. The combined sales by the large seller and HTF traders quickly drove the market down. However, this version of events has been challenged by the exchange the contracts were traded on and by a number of academic papers. Despite this, HFT is likely to have played a prominent role in driving the market down rapidly.

Another example of the risks created by HFT occurred on 1 August 2012, when Knight Capital Group experienced a technology issue in their automated trading system causing a significant loss of money for the trading firm. The problem was related to Knight's installation of trading software and resulted in Knight sending numerous erroneous orders in NYSE-listed securities into the market. This software has since been removed from the company's systems. Clients were not negatively affected by the erroneous orders, and the software issue was limited to the routing of certain listed stocks to NYSE. Knight has since traded out of its entire erroneous trade position, which has resulted in a realised pre-tax loss of approximately US$440m.

CHAPTER 1 SECTION 4

SETTLEMENT PROCEDURES IN THE UK

SECTION AIMS

By the end of this section, learners should be able to:

- Explain the clearing and settlement procedures for UK exchange-traded securities.

The current standard settlement of London Stock Exchange equity transactions is T+2 (i.e. trade date plus two working days). Settlement is made through CREST, which is a computerised system that allows investors to hold shares in an electronic rather than paper form.

The settlement of gilts is also carried out through CREST, which operates a computerised settlement system for its members, including GEMMS, IDBs, SBLIs and large banks, with a settlement period of T+1.

Since the implementation of MiFID, there has been a rapid growth in equity trading channels (e.g. London Stock Exchange, BATS Chi-X Europe, Turquoise) and trade clearing venues (e.g. LCH.Clearnet, EuroCCP). Trading usually involves an order being placed and executed on a trading platform, which could be an exchange, a multilateral trading facility or a crossing network. These may provide services in addition to trade execution, such as order management. Central counterparties (CCPs) then offer counterparty risk clearing, including preparing transactions for settlement, netting transactions and settlement instruction. Management of failed trades is also provided.

Settlement itself involves pre-settlement positioning (i.e. making sure the buyer has the necessary monies and the seller has the securities available) and the completion of the transaction through transfer of ownership and monies. This process is initiated once the trade has been cleared by the CCP. Such activities are provided directly via central securities depositories (CSDs).

CHAPTER 1 SECTION 5

THE UK LISTING AUTHORITY AND PROSPECTUS REQUIREMENTS

SECTION AIMS

By the end of this section, learners should be able to:

- Explain the role of the FCA as the UK listing authority.
- Identify the listing rules in the Financial Services and Markets Act 2000, and relevant EU directives.
- Explain the main conditions for listing on the Official List, AIM and ISDX.
- Explain the purpose of the requirement for prospectus or listing particulars.
- Identify the main exemptions from listing particulars.

Public companies are defined as those that seek finance from the investing public. Private companies, on the other hand, are generally forbidden to raise capital in this way. A further distinction is that public companies who wish to have their securities listed on the London Stock Exchange must comply with the stock exchange's rules. The advantage of a stock exchange listing is that the shares are freely marketable, which makes them more attractive to an initial investor.

The Financial Conduct Authority (FCA) is the 'competent authority' (or, colloquially, the UK listing authority) to decide on the admission of securities to the Official List. The listing authority makes rules governing admission to listing and the continuing obligation of issuers. These rules are collectively known as the listing rules and the power to create the rules comes from the Financial Services and Markets Act 2000 as amended. The listing rules also implement various EU directives including the Prospectus Directive and the Transparency Directive. Two listing categories exist in relation to admission to the Official List:

- Premium means that a company must meet standards over and above (often described as 'super-equivalent') those set out in the EU legislation, including the UK Corporate Governance Code. A premium listing is only available to equity shares issued by commercial trading companies.
- Standard means a company only has to meet the requirements laid down by EU legislation. This means that their overall compliance responsibilities will be lighter, both in preparing for listing and on an ongoing basis. Standard listings cover the issuance of shares and Depositary Receipts.

A company with either a premium or a standard listing can choose to admit to trading on the main market of the London Stock Exchange.

Under the listing rules, no securities may be admitted unless the listing authority has approved either listing particulars or a prospectus and that these documents have been published. In general, a prospectus is required whenever an application for listing is made and the securities are to be offered to the public prior to admission to listing. Where the securities are not to be offered to the public, a prospectus is not required, but listing particulars still need to be approved and published by the listing authority.

The Prospectus Directive (PD) also requires publication of a prospectus where securities are to be admitted to trading on a regulated market in the EU. This is wider than the normal concept of listing, as it includes securities traded on 'second markets' and on other trading facilities. One of the main consequences of the PD is the 'passport' – that is, the ability to raise capital in any EU member state with the production and approval of a prospectus in one member state.

There are a number of exemptions from the obligation to produce a prospectus, including:

1. Where the offer is made to 'qualified investors'. Qualified investors are those who are, or may elect to become, professional clients or eligible counterparties. Retail clients who elect to become professional clients must meet at least two of the following criteria (called the quantitative test):

   - must have carried out transactions of a significant size (over €1,000) on securities markets at an average frequency of, at least, ten per quarter for the last four quarters;

   - must have a security portfolio exceeding €500,000; and/or

   - must work, or have worked for at least a year, in the financial sector in a professional position which requires knowledge of security investment.

2. Where the offer is made to fewer than 150 persons (other than qualified investors) per European Economic Area (EEA) state.

3. Where the minimum consideration per investor, or the minimum denomination per unit, is equal to or greater than €100,000.

4. Where the total consideration of the offer is less than €5m calculated over a period of twelve months.

5. Where shares representing less than 10% of the number of shares of the same class are already admitted for trading on the same regulated market.

Note that point five only relates to an admission to trading, not to a public offer. Therefore a rights issue to the public, at whatever level, will now require a prospectus.

The prospectus rules specify the content of a prospectus (or the listing particulars), and this varies according to the nature of the company applying for listing. In general, the prospectus should disclose all information that an investor would reasonably require with respect to the assets and liabilities, financial position, profits and losses and prospects of the issuer of the securities and the rights attaching to those securities, so that the investor is able to make an informed assessment.

Finally, the listing authority sets out various conditions for listing. For a premium listing, the most important of these are:

- A company must normally have published accounts which cover at least three years.

- The expected aggregate market value of all the securities to be listed must be:

  - at least £700,000 for shares; and

  - at least £200,000 for debt securities.

- 25% of the listed securities must be held by the public by the date of admission.
- The company must demonstrate it has sufficient working capital to cover at least the next twelve months of business.
- A sponsor is required in connection with the admission for listing.

For companies seeking a standard listing, there is no need for a published three-year trading record so that new companies may apply. Additionally, the twelve-month working capital statement is not required and the company does not require a sponsor. The rules about a 25% public holding and £700,000 minimum market value still apply, however.

Only companies with a premium listing are eligible for inclusion in one of the FTSE UK indices, including FTSE 100 and FTSE 250. This is important for companies seeking liquidity for their listed securities, particularly given that tracker funds' investment are driven by FTSE indexation.

A further segment of the London Stock Exchange main market is the High Growth Segment (HGS). The HGS was launched in March 2013, and is designed to attract high growth, mid-sized UK and European companies aspiring to an Official Listing. An HGS company is larger than a typical AIM company and would normally have aspirations to ultimately join the premium segment of the main market. A HGS company has to meet the following eligibility criteria:

- Be incorporated in the EEA.
- Be a commercial company, issuing equity shares only.
- Have a minimum free float of 10% at IPO.
- Demonstrate historic revenue (on a compound annual growth rate basis) of 20% over three years.

The prospectus and disclosure, and transparency rules, apply to companies in the HGS.

In contrast, AIM does not stipulate minimum criteria for company size, trading record or number of shares held by the public. Companies need a nominated adviser (a 'nomad') from an approved register, who is responsible to the London Stock Exchange for ensuring that all applicants are suitable for admission to AIM and ready to be admitted to a public market. Companies must produce an admission document that includes information about a company's directors, their promoters, business activities and financial position. AIM companies are required to disclose details of their financial performance through scheduled interim and full-year results, together with disclosures on an ongoing basis regarding developments which could affect company performance. AIM is not part of the Official List and is not an EU regulated market but is classified as a MTF (see section 3 of this chapter).

An alternative route to admission to the Official List in the UK is to seek a listing on the ICAP Securities and Derivatives Exchange (ISDX) Main Board. The eligibility for such a listing is the same as for the Official List and companies can choose either a premium or standard listing. ISDX also operates the ISDX Growth Market. The admission criteria for a listing on the ISDX Growth Market are:

- Appoint and retain an ISDX corporate adviser at all times.
- Demonstrate appropriate levels of corporate governance, including having at least one independent non-executive director.
- Have published audited financial reports no more than nine months prior to the date of admission to trading.
- Have at least twelve months' working capital.
- Have no restrictions on the transferability of shares.
- Issue shares which are eligible for electronic settlement.

CHAPTER 1 SECTION 6

INFORMATION DISCLOSURE AND CORPORATE GOVERNANCE REQUIREMENTS FOR UK EQUITY MARKETS

SECTION AIMS

By the end of this section, learners should be able to:

- Explain the disclosures required under the disclosure and transparency rules relating to directors' interests and major shareholdings.
- Explain the purpose of corporate governance regulation and the role of the Financial Reporting Committee in promoting good corporate governance.
- Explain, in outline, the scope and content of corporate governance standards in the UK.
- Explain the London Stock Exchange requirements for listed companies to disclose corporate governance compliance.
- Explain the continuing obligations of London Stock Exchange listed companies regarding information disclosure and dissemination.
- Explain, in outline, the UK company law requirements regarding the calling of general meetings.
- Distinguish between annual general meetings and other types of company meetings.
- Distinguish between the types of resolution that can be considered at company general meetings.
- Distinguish between the voting methods used at company meetings.
- Explain the role and powers of a proxy.

1. DISCLOSURE OF DIRECTORS' INTERESTS IN SHARES

Listed companies are subject to the FCA's disclosure rules and transparency rules (DTR). DTR3 deals with reporting transactions in a company's securities (including derivatives) by PDMRs ('persons discharging managerial responsibilities', including directors). PDMRs and their connected persons must notify the listed company concerned within four business days of a transaction (both sale and purchase of any value). The listed company must notify the market as soon as possible thereafter, and no later than the end of the following business day. This notification must be through a primary information provider.

2. DISCLOSURE OF MAJOR INTERESTS IN SHARES

Major shareholders in listed companies can be in a position to influence company management. The FCA's DTRs apply to disclosure and registration of substantial individual interests in shares carrying unrestricted voting rights. The aim is to ensure that directors, shareholders and employees of a public company can ascertain, for example, the identity of any person who is in the process of buying shares in the company through nominees to gain control of it. Thus an investor must notify a company within two business days when it acquires 3% or more of that company's shares. Further disclosures are required at increments of more than 1% above the initial 3% notified to the company.

A further provision relates to 'concert parties'. Concert parties are groups of individuals acting in agreement for the purpose of acquiring interests in shares. The aim of this provision is to prevent control 'in concert' – to avoid a group of individuals secretly agreeing that, while each person only openly acquires less than the 3% disclosure threshold, they will actually use the combined interest to gain control, or ensure a takeover or a special resolution at the meeting of a company.

The Companies Act requires that each person involved in such an agreement must have the interests of all the other members of the concert party added to their own interest. If the total then exceeds 3%, a disclosure must be made. In addition, each person must notify that they are party to such an agreement and must give the details of it. An individual is also subject to the disclosure rule where they are deemed to personally have control over the exercise of any rights conferred by holding those shares, even where they are not the registered holder. This rule is used to expose any agreement which otherwise might be used to conceal an interest requiring disclosure.

A public company must keep a register of interests in shares disclosed. A company may require a person who is known to have had an interest in a company's shares during the previous three years to indicate whether they hold or have held such an interest. This provides a public company with the power to probe and discover the true beneficial owner of its shares. Such information must also be recorded in the register.

3. REMUNERATION REPORTING REGULATIONS

The Department for Business, Innovation and Skills introduced regulations on remuneration reporting for large and medium-sized companies and groups effective from October 2013. The regulations require the remuneration report of a company to be in two parts:

1. A policy report setting out the company's remuneration policy and key factors that were taken into account in setting that policy.

2. An implementation report setting out actual payments to directors and details on the link between company performance and pay for the financial year.

In particular, the regulations provide detail on how the pay for executive directors is to be calculated. The remuneration policy will include details of the policy on payments to recruit directors and payments made on directors leaving the company. The separate remuneration policy and implementation reports must be put to shareholder vote at the annual general meeting (AGM) held in the first financial year beginning on or after 1 October 2013. Shareholders will have a binding vote on the remuneration policy. The policy should then be put to a shareholder vote at the AGM at least every three years. If shareholders do not approve the policy, a company can:

- continue to operate its previous approved policy even if it is already three years old;
- seek shareholder approval again (at an AGM or other general meeting) for the same (or revised) policy; or
- seek separate shareholder approval for any specific remuneration which is not within a previous approved policy.

The implementation report is published annually.

4. UK CORPORATE GOVERNANCE REGULATIONS

Corporate governance is the system by which companies are directed and controlled; the way in which the affairs of corporations are handled by their corporate boards and officers.

Corporate governance originated in response to the separation of ownership and control following the formation of joint stock companies. The owners or shareholders of these companies – who were not involved in day to day operational issues – required assurances that those in control of the company, the directors and managers, were safeguarding their investments and accurately reporting the financial outcome of their business activities. The corporate governance system in the UK has traditionally stressed the importance of internal controls and the role of financial reporting and accountability rather than external legislation.

5. THE UK CORPORATE GOVERNANCE CODE

Several reports on corporate governance in the UK have been published: the Cadbury (1992) report focused on internal controls, Greenbury (1995) focused on disclosure of directors' remuneration, and Hampel (1998) incorporated the recommendations from both the Cadbury and Greenbury committees and was published as the Combined Code in June 1998. This code was further amended following the Higgs (2003) review of the role and effectiveness of non-executive directors and the Smith (2003) review of audit committees. The new Combined Code was published in July 2003, and contained several main principles of good governance along with supporting principles and detailed code provisions. This code was updated by the Financial Reporting Council (FRC) following the market turbulence in 2008/09. The new code was published in June 2010 (and updated in 2012 and 2014) and is known as the UK Corporate Governance Code.

In addition to the UK Corporate Governance Code, the FRC has also created the UK Stewardship Code. The UK Stewardship Code is a set of principles or guidelines directed at institutional investors who hold voting rights in UK companies. Its principal aim is to make shareholders, who manage other people's money, be active and engage in corporate governance in the interests of their beneficiaries. The UK Stewardship Code adopts the same 'comply or explain' approach used in the UK Corporate Governance Code. This means that it does not require compliance with its principles, but if fund managers and institutional investors do not comply with any of the principles they must explain why they have not done so on their websites. The information is also sent to the FRC, which links to the information provided to it.

The seven principles of the UK Stewardship Code are as follows. Institutional investors should:

1. Publicly disclose their policy on how they will discharge their stewardship responsibilities.
2. Have a robust policy on managing conflicts of interest in relation to stewardship and this policy should be publicly disclosed.
3. Monitor their investee companies.
4. Establish clear guidelines on when and how they will escalate their activities as a method of protecting and enhancing shareholder value.
5. Be willing to act collectively with other investors where appropriate.
6. Have a clear policy on voting and disclosure of voting activity.
7. Report periodically on their stewardship and voting activities.

THE MAIN PRINCIPLES OF THE CODE

Section A: Leadership

- Every company should be headed by an effective board which is collectively responsible for the long term success of the company.
- There should be a clear division of responsibilities at the head of the company between the running of the board and the executive responsibility for the running of the company's business. No one individual should have unfettered powers of decision.
- The chairman is responsible for leadership of the board and ensuring its effectiveness on all aspects of its role.
- As part of their role as members of a unitary board, non-executive directors should constructively challenge and help develop proposals on strategy.

Section B: Effectiveness

- The board and its committees should have the appropriate balance of skills, experience, independence and knowledge of the company to enable them to discharge their respective duties and responsibilities effectively.
- There should be a formal, rigorous and transparent procedure for the appointment of new directors to the board.
- All directors should be able to allocate sufficient time to the company to discharge their responsibilities effectively.
- All directors should receive induction on joining the board and should regularly update and refresh their skills and knowledge.
- The board should be supplied in a timely manner with information in a form and of a quality appropriate to enable it to discharge its duties.
- The board should undertake a formal and rigorous annual evaluation of its own performance and that of its committees and individual directors.
- All directors should be submitted for re-election at regular intervals, subject to continued satisfactory performance.

Section C: Accountability

- The board should present a balanced and understandable assessment of the company's position and prospects.
- The board is responsible for determining the nature and extent of the significant risks it is willing to take in achieving its strategic objectives. The board should maintain sound risk management and internal control systems.
- The board should establish formal and transparent arrangements for considering how they should apply the corporate reporting and risk management and internal control principles and for maintaining an appropriate relationship with the company's auditor.

Section D: Remuneration

- 'Executive directors' remuneration should be designed to promote the long-term success of the company. Performance-related elements should be transparent, stretching and rigorously applied.
- There should be a formal and transparent procedure for developing policy on executive remuneration and for fixing the remuneration packages of individual directors. No director should be involved in deciding his or her own remuneration.

Section E: Relations with shareholders

- There should be a dialogue with shareholders based on the mutual understanding of objectives. The board as a whole has responsibility for ensuring that a satisfactory dialogue with shareholders takes place.
- The board should use the annual general meetings to communicate with investors and to encourage their participation.

6. INFORMATION DISSEMINATION AND DISCLOSURE BY LISTED COMPANIES

When a company is listed on the London Stock Exchange, it agrees to abide by the continuing obligation requirements of listed companies. These requirements are designed to keep shareholders of a listed company properly informed, and require the listed company to submit to the UK listing authority drafts for approval of all meetings and all circulars (except those of a routine nature) to holders of securities. In addition, the company must notify the market of profit announcements, dividend declarations, material acquisitions, change of directors, change in major shareholdings and any other information necessary to enable holders of securities and other members of the public to appraise the position of the company and avoid the establishment of a false market in the securities. Such information is to be given to the market as a whole.

When making an announcement, issuers may use a third-party firm that has demonstrated that it can distribute information in accordance with the Transparency Directive. Issuers using an approved firm to distribute information will not have to make an annual declaration to the FCA about their compliance. Instead, if an issuer decides not to use an approved firm, it has to record how each announcement complies with the Transparency Directive and report on its compliance to the FCA annually or whenever it is required to by the FCA. A number of firms are currently approved by the FCA, including the Regulatory News Service of the London Stock Exchange.

The UK listing authority provides guidance rules on the dissemination of price-sensitive information by companies. These rules are intended to aid compliance with the insider dealing regulations of the Criminal Justice Act 1993, Part V, and the Code of Market Conduct (see chapter 3). In summary, the rules encourage companies to release new information to the market on a regular basis. Companies should have a consistent procedure for determining what information is price-sensitive and for releasing such information. Where companies issue lengthy releases to shareholders or to the market which include comments on current or future trading prospects, this information should be given due prominence. Where price-sensitive information is inadvertently released to, say, analysts or journalists, then a company should take immediate steps to ensure that the whole market has access to the information. Also, a company should correct a public forecast as soon as possible if the outcome is significantly different. However, there is no obligation on a company to tell individual analysts that their forecast is wrong.

7. GENERAL MEETINGS

The Companies Act 2006 sets out requirements relating to the calling and conduct of company general meetings. Every public company is required to hold an AGM within six months of the end of their financial year. The interval between AGMs must not be more than 15 months. The directors of the company must call the meeting, and this must be called by giving not less than 21 calendar days' written notice. Although there are no items of business which the Companies Act require to take place at the meeting, certain items are dealt with by convention, such as:

- Declaring a dividend.
- Consideration of the financial statements.
- Consideration of the reports of the directors and auditors.
- The election of directors in place of those retiring.
- The appointment and remuneration of auditors.

Any meeting of a company other than an AGM is called a 'general meeting'. Such a meeting must be called by giving not less than 14 calendar days' written notice. Companies are now authorised to communicate with their shareholders electronically (by email, posting a note on a website, telephone or any other electronic means). For the purposes of electronic communication, a notice is deemed to be sent when the electronic notice is first transmitted and delivered 48 hours after being sent. Any notice period therefore runs from the delivery date, i.e. 48 hours after being sent.

The directors of a company may call a general meeting whenever they see fit. The directors are also bound to call such a meeting when 5% or more of the shareholders request it, given that twelve months have elapsed since the last general meeting. If the directors fail to call such a meeting within 21 calendar days of such a request, then the shareholders may convene the meeting themselves, providing it is within three months of the request. Directors must also call a general meeting in the event of a serious loss of capital.

Normally, the chairman of the board of directors will act as chairman of a general meeting. It is the duty of the chairman to preserve order, see that the proceedings are regularly conducted, take care that the sense of the meeting is properly ascertained and decide incidental questions arising for decision during the meeting. A resolution put to a meeting is sometimes decided in the first instance by a show of hands. On a show of hands, each member present at the meeting who is entitled to vote has one vote. A more accurate method of ascertaining the wishes of the members of a company is to take a poll. This allows proxy votes to be counted, and pays due regard to a member holding a large number of shares (who would have only one vote on a show of hands). A poll can be demanded by five members having the right to vote, by one or more members having 10% of the total voting rights, or by the chairman. Further, a proxy may demand, or join in demanding, a poll.

Any member entitled to attend and vote at a company meeting may appoint another person (a proxy) to attend and vote on their behalf. A proxy has the right to vote on a show of hands and on a poll. A proxy is appointed in writing in accordance with the articles of the company. A proxy is valid for the general meeting and any adjournment. There are two forms of proxy:

- A general proxy, appointing a person to vote as they think fit, bearing in mind what is said at the meeting.
- A special proxy, appointing a person to vote for or against a particular resolution (termed a 'two-way proxy').

Each person entitled to vote at the meeting must be sent a proxy form when they are sent the notice convening the meeting. The form must state that a shareholder is entitled to appoint a proxy of their own choice. Where a proxy form is returned without an indication as to how the proxy is to vote, then the proxy is deemed to be a general proxy. It is the duty of the chairman of the meeting to decide on the validity of the proxies.

There are two main kinds of resolution that can be considered at a general meeting. An ordinary resolution is the standard type, and requires a simple majority (i.e. over 50%) of those voting to be passed. A special resolution is required before any important constitutional changes can be undertaken, and this requires a 75% vote in favour to be passed.

CHAPTER 1 SECTION 7

INTERNATIONAL MARKETS

SECTION AIMS

By the end of this section, learners should be able to:

- Explain the structure, features, regulatory and trading environment of international markets, including developed markets and emerging markets.
- Explain the structure and operation of the primary and secondary markets for eurobonds.
- Explain the settlement and clearing procedures overseas, including the role of international central securities depositories, and the different settlement cycles and challenges in managing global assets.

1. INTERNATIONAL SECURITIES MARKETS

Both retail and institutional investors have increasingly looked to invest in overseas securities markets in recent years. There are potential diversification benefits where the returns on domestic and overseas securities are less than perfectly correlated. Emerging markets such as Brazil and China outperformed developed markets before 2008. Since then, other emerging markets in South East Asia, such as Thailand, Indonesia and the Philippines, have delivered significantly higher returns than developed economies. One extra risk with overseas investment is foreign exchange risk – investors have to take into account changes in the value of the domestic currency with the currency of the market where the investment has taken place. This can increase or reduce actual returns on the foreign investment.

Retail investors are more likely to achieve international exposure through mutual funds and exchange-traded funds (ETFs). Institutional investors may seek international exposure by buying securities in overseas markets. This brings additional considerations and/or risks as the structure, trading/clearing systems and regulation of overseas markets are likely to be different from the UK market. This is less of an issue in European equity markets where a number of Directives, including MiFiD and the PD, have harmonised regulations across the EU. Most trading of equities on European securities markets takes place on electronic order-matching systems like SETS on the London Stock Exchange. In the US, the largest equity market is the New York Stock Exchange (NYSE), which operates a floor-based specialist system of stock trading. On the trading floor, there are several trading posts, and each stock traded is centralised at that stock's assigned trading post. The designated market makers (DMMs), who are assigned specific trading posts (and thus specific stocks), act in a way that maintains an 'orderly market'. Member firms' floor brokers and 'local' brokers all trade through these DMMs. The specialists sit just outside the post as the floor brokers move around from post to post representing orders in any stock.

The Universal Trading System is the NYSE primary order processing system that supports equity trading on the trading floor and provides the NYSE with the current status of any equity order. NYSE member firms can input orders (in a similar way to SETS) and these go directly to the trading post where the security is traded.

Investing in emerging equity markets presents more challenges. Primarily, the quality of market regulation, corporate governance, transparency, and accounting standards is often below that in developed markets. These factors make it harder to appropriately price securities and as such increase the risk of mispricing. Additionally, there are more likely to be political risks in emerging markets, whether it is from corruption or even coups and civil wars (Ukraine and Syria are two recent examples).

Stock market returns are more volatile partly for the reasons given and also partly because of the amount of foreign ownership of emerging market shares. Emerging markets are seen as risky by overseas investors. Therefore, in strained global macroeconomic situations investors from developed countries will abandon their positions in emerging markets first. This causes volatility in emerging market indices. Due to these factors, emerging market indices tend to rise faster than developed markets during periods of strong global market sentiment, but fall faster when that sentiment turns negative.

Other issues with investing in emerging markets include regulatory limits on overseas investments that can change at short notice, making it difficult to sell a security. More generally, emerging markets may be less liquid than developed stock markets.

2. EUROBOND MARKETS

Eurobonds are bonds that are denominated in a currency other than that of the country in which they are issued. Like most bonds, eurobonds are usually fixed-rate, interest-bearing notes, although many are also offered with floating rates and other variations. Most pay an annual coupon and have maturities of three to seven years. They are also usually unsecured.

The eurobond market consists of several types of participants. First there is the issuer, or borrower, that needs to raise funds by selling bonds. The borrower approaches a bank and asks for help in issuing its bonds. This bank is known as the lead manager and may ask other banks to join it to form a managing group that will negotiate the terms of the bonds and manage issuing the bonds. The managing group will then sell the bonds to an underwriter or directly to a selling group. The three levels—managers, underwriters, and sellers—are known collectively as the syndicate. The underwriter will actually purchase the bonds at a minimum price and assume the risk that it may not be possible to sell them on the market at a higher price. The underwriter (or the managing group if there is no underwriter) sells the bonds to a selling group that then places bonds with investors.

The syndicate companies and their investor clients are considered the primary market for eurobonds; once they are resold to general investors, the bonds enter the secondary market. Participants in the market are organized under the International Capital Markets Association (ICMA). In the secondary market, eurobonds are traded over-the-counter. Major markets for eurobonds exist in London, Frankfurt, Zurich and Amsterdam.

A eurobond may be defined as an international bond issue underwritten by an international syndicate of banks, which is made available for purchase to international investors. Since its beginnings in the 1960s, the market for eurobonds has grown dramatically. By some measures, this market is now the largest capital market in the world. A variety of institutions raise money through the issue of eurobonds, including a wide range of industrial corporations, banks, public sector bodies and supranational organisations. Eurobonds are not regulated by the country of the currency in which they are denominated. Eurobonds are so-called 'bearer bonds', they are not registered anywhere centrally, so whomever holds or bears the bond is considered the owner. Their 'bearer' status also enables eurobonds to be held anonymously. It is difficult to determine the client base for these securities, because eurobonds are bearer bonds. However, it is generally agreed that holders of eurobonds include both private individuals seeking to avoid taxation, and institutional investors who hold these bonds as part of their normal diversified portfolios.

There are currently two systems available to investors for settling eurobond transactions: Euroclear and Clearstream. Both Euroclear and Clearstream provide securities clearance and settlement services, money transfer and banking services associated with securities settlement, custody services and securities lending and borrowing services. ICMA rules currently specify settlement on T+2, but all trades should be confirmed on T+1. Once reported, the trade is validated and then matched to await execution. Euroclear and Clearstream are linked electronically, which allows member organisations to use either system.

3. SETTLEMENT IN OVERSEAS SECURITIES MARKETS

There are many different national features for dealing and settlement in emerging markets. Settlement systems are national, i.e. each country has its own settlement arrangements for different types of instruments, and participation is generally limited to locally regulated participants. As a general rule, government and quasi-government bills, bonds and notes are traded over-the-counter between banks, and settled through settlement systems operated by the central banks. These systems do not provide a guarantee, i.e. they are not linked with a clearing company or a central counterparty, though they do have a link for payment into real time gross settlement systems where they exist. Corporate bonds are generally listed and traded through the central clearing depository systems associated with the exchange. Many of the central securities' depositories are linked with the international depositories.

Some countries (e.g. Korea) settle bond transactions on a rolling basis and T+1 to facilitate use of a delivery versus payment settlement system: obligations are calculated on a gross trade-by-trade basis without netting for both securities and cash. The G30, a consultative group on international economics, has published recommendations for good practice in this area, including T+3 settlement for equities. In some countries (e.g. Thailand) shares are registered in a central depository and a matching system for trading exists to ensure transactions are settled as agreed; settlement is at T+3.

In general, a local custodian is responsible for the safekeeping of securities in a given national market, while a global custodian co-ordinates and supervises the safekeeping of securities in local depositories. Links between the different parties reduce the risk of errors and are not as well developed in emerging markets as in mature ones.

Non-electronic settlement systems are still used in some markets, and securities are physically transferred between buyer and seller. Many emerging markets do not have a central depository. Clearly, ownership rights for securities should be exchanged simultaneously with payment and cannot be reversed; T+3 is the recommended maximum.

CHAPTER 1 SECTION 8

THE PRINCIPAL–AGENT PROBLEM: SEPARATION OF OWNERSHIP AND CONTROL

SECTION AIMS

By the end of this section, learners should be able to:

- Explain how capital markets allow the beneficial ownership, and the control of capital, to be separated.
- Distinguish between beneficial owners (principals) and the various agents involved in the capital allocation process.
- Explain how conflict between the interests of agents and principals gives rise to the 'agency' or 'principal–agent' problem.
- Identify examples of agency costs such as: expropriation, perquisites, self-dealing and higher cost of capital, which arise when the agency problem is known to exist.
- Identify the main reasons why it is argued that reducing the agency problem benefits the investment profession and society as a whole.

Stock markets allow for the separation of ownership of a company from its control. When the owner of a company also manages it, then ownership and control are aligned, but when the ownership of a company is dispersed through the issue of shares it is not possible for the owners to run the company. Instead they appoint managers to manage the company on their behalf. The owners are the principals in the relationship and the managers are the agents of the owners. Generally, the managers do not own significant amounts of shares in the company. This separation of ownership and control leads to the principal–agent problem (also called the agency problem), which arises because owners and managers generally have different interests. The owners want to maximise the value of the firm, while managers want to maximise their own interests such as salary, vanity projects and expenses. It is unlikely that the managers' pursuit of their own interests will lead to maximisation of a firm's value.

Solutions to the agency problem include aligning incentives of managers and owners by compensating managers partly in the form of shares or future shares in the case of stock options. The managers will then have an incentive to make decisions that lead to a rise in the share price as they, along with the owners, will benefit. Other mechanisms to mitigate the principal–agent problem include the board of directors monitoring managers; the board members are appointed by shareholders to look after their interests and can remove under-performing managers.

A further solution to the principal–agent problem comes from external pressure. If the managers are running a company badly, shareholders can sell their shares. If enough shareholders sell shares, the share price will fall, which could make the company a takeover target. The threat of takeover (which often results in the incumbent management losing their jobs) gives managers the incentive to look after the interest of shareholders. Shareholder activism – where groups of shareholders (often large fund managers) voice their concerns to directors – has become more prevalent in recent years. Many of the solutions to mitigate the agency problem introduce costs, e.g. the cost of giving share options to managers. Such costs are referred to as 'agency costs'.

The principal–agent problem occurs in many areas of the investment industry. For example, an investor who appoints a broker to obtain the best price in a trade, or a retail client who appoints an investment adviser to advise on investments. In each case the investor/client is the principal and the broker/adviser is the agent. The principal expects the agent to act in their interest, but the agent may pursue their own self-interest. The broker, on receiving a large order to buy, may place an order to buy for themselves to take advantage of the rise in price anticipated by the large order from the client (a practice known as front-running).

Where a firm operates as both a broker and a dealer they are said to have dual capacity. Such a firm is referred to as a broker-dealer. Firms operating with dual capacity expose themselves to the conflict of interest problem just described. Their duty as broker is to act in the best interest of the client. As dealer, they are acting in their own interest or the interest of their owners.

In most situations, the investment professional will put the interests of the client first but this has not always happened. Many examples of investment professionals pursuing their own interests ahead of their clients have emerged in recent years, including Bernard Madoff turning a wealth management scheme into a Ponzi scheme (where the cash invested by new investors was used to pay the returns to existing investors).

When financial services professionals act in their own interest and cause losses for clients, this can lead to a lack of trust in the products and processes in the industry. This in turn may lead savers to not lend as much thus reducing funds for companies that need to borrow, which will then slow down the rate of growth in the economy. Such unethical behaviour can be mitigated by regulation – for example, a firm should have a conflict of interest policy (see chapter 3). Another approach that has been given more attention in recent years is to raise ethical awareness/ standards in the industry. This is discussed further in chapter 2.

CHAPTER 01 KEY FACTS

1.1

1. The financial services industry provides four main functions: financial intermediation, pooling and managing risk, provision of payment mechanisms and portfolio management.

2. The main types of financial institutions are deposit-taking institutions, including banks, and investment institutions, such as insurance companies, collective investment funds and pension funds.

3. Governments perform a number of important economic functions: the provision of certain goods and services (e.g. defence), regulation of markets to protect consumers, improving the distribution of incomes through taxation and social welfare payments and maintaining economic stability.

1.2

1. Assets are items that have value and include real assets and financial assets. Real assets are physical assets, such as land, buildings and gold. Financial assets are claims representing the right to some return (such as a bank deposit or bond) or could represent ownership of physical assets.

2. Places where buyers and sellers can trade securities are known as securities markets or financial markets.

3. The main functions of markets are:

    - Raising of capital.
    - Transfer of risk.
    - Price discovery.
    - Liquidity creation.

4. Primary markets are where initial sales of securities are made. Subsequent trading takes place in the secondary market.

5. Trading securities incurs transactions costs that include broker commissions, the bid–ask spread, taxation and market impact.

1.3

1. The London Stock Exchange operates an order-driven system called SETS for trading FTSE All-Share constituents. It also operates a quote display system called SEAQ for AIM listed and fixed interest securities. Less liquid stocks, listed on the main market, are traded on SETSqx, which combines a periodic auction book along with quote-driven market-making. International securities are traded through the International Order Book.

2. LCH.Clearnet is the central counterparty to all SETS trades at the point of execution.

3. Dual-listing occurs when two corporations function as a single operating business but retain separate legal identities and stock exchange listings.

4. UK government bonds are known as 'gilts', which pay gross semi-annual coupons and they accrue on an actual/actual basis.

5. The Debt Management Office is the department of the Treasury responsible for gilt issuance, usually via an auction, though occasionally through the 'tap' system.

6. Corporate bonds may be issued via an open offer or private placement. The former can involve a bought deal or fixed price re-offer.

7. An over-the-counter market involves trading in a decentralised way rather than on an exchange; it refers to a bilateral contract, often between an investment bank and a client, and securities not listed on an exchange.

1.4

1. CREST is the London Stock Exchange's electronic (dematerialised) settlement system, which settles on a T+2 basis for equities.

2. CREST operates a computerised settlement system for gilts with a settlement period of T+1.

1.5

1. The FCA decides on securities to be listed and makes the listing rules. A prospectus has to be published, except where the offer is made subject to certain restrictive criteria.

2. Listing on the main market requires at least three years of published accounts, and over £700,000 of listed stock or £200,000 of debt securities.

3. AIM is regulated by the London Stock Exchange, and there is no minimum criterion for size, trading record or shares in public hands.

1.6

1. Directors, major shareholders and concert parties must declare share interests. Governance principles apply to directors, and include their remuneration, accountability and audit procedures, together with their relationship with shareholders and institutional investors. There are also information disclosure and dissemination requirements for listed companies, along with general meetings organisation.

1.7

1. Government bond trading in other countries often involves local banks trading over-the-counter, with settlement via the central bank. Corporate bonds are often listed and traded through central clearing depositary systems associated with local exchanges; these will usually have links to international depositaries.

2. Euroclear and Clearstream are the two main systems currently available for settling eurobond transactions. All trades must be confirmed T+1 and settled T+2.

1.8

1. The separation of ownership and control leads to the principal–agent problem.

2. In capital markets, shareholders act as principals and delegate control to managers, who are agents.

3. Other forms of principal–agent relationship in the investment industry include fund advisers or managers acting as agents for investors.

4. Solutions to the agency problem incur agency costs, and include:

   - Aligning the interests of managers and owners through remuneration of the former in shares or stock options.
   - Boards of directors looking after the interests of shareholders.
   - External control through active groups of shareholders or the threat of takeover.

CHAPTER 01 SELF-ASSESSMENT QUESTIONS

1. **Which of the following is a deposit-accepting institution?**

(a) *A mutual fund.*

(b) *A bank.*

(c) *An investment trust.*

(d) *A pension fund.*

2. **How is the process for trading ordinary FTSE 100 shares best described?**

(a) *Quote-driven.*

(b) *Order-driven.*

(c) *Open outcry.*

(d) *Price-driven.*

3. **UK gilts usually pay:**

(a) *Gross coupons annually.*

(b) *Net coupons annually.*

(c) *Net coupons semi-annually.*

(d) *Gross coupons semi-annually.*

4. **Which body regulates derivatives exchanges in the UK?**

(a) *The Securities and Exchange Commission.*

(b) *The Financial Conduct Authority.*

(c) *The Bank of England.*

(d) *The Prudential Regulation Authority.*

5. **Gilts issuance is managed by which of the following?**

(a) *Gilt-Edged Market Makers.*

(b) *The Central Gilts Office.*

(c) *CRESTco.*

(d) *The Debt Management Office.*

6. The standard settlement time for gilts is:

(a) *Same day.*

(b) *T+1.*

(c) *T+2.*

(d) *T+3.*

7. What term best describes the settlement procedure for CREST?

(a) *Physical settlement.*

(b) *Certified settlement.*

(c) *Paperless settlement.*

(d) *Materialised settlement.*

8. Which organisation is responsible for setting rules for trading in the eurobond market?

(a) *International Capital Markets Association.*

(b) *Euroclear.*

(c) *The Financial Conduct Authority.*

(d) *The Securities and Exchange Commission.*

9. A member who wishes to appoint another person to vote as they think fit on their behalf at a company meeting would appoint:

(a) *Two-way proxy.*

(b) *General proxy.*

(c) *Agent proxy.*

(d) *Special proxy.*

10. The FRC principles which aim to make institutional investors engage actively in corporate governance in the interests of their beneficiaries are known as the:

(a) *The UK Corporate Governance Code.*

(b) *The Agency Code.*

(c) *The Takeover Code.*

(d) *The UK Stewardship Code.*

11. An investor is required to notify the company if their stake goes from:

(a) *3.1% to 4.2% of company shares.*

(b) *3.1% to 3.9% of company shares.*

(c) *1.9% to 2.7% of company shares.*

(d) *10.9% to 10.1% of company shares.*

12. A company wishing to list shares on the main market must ensure these securities have a minimum market capitalisation of at least:

(a) *£200,000.*

(b) *£700,000.*

(c) *£900,000.*

(d) *£1,000,000.*

ANSWERS

1. *(b) Only banks accept deposits to fund their assets. All the other institutions are investment institutions.*

2. *(b) FTSE 100 shares are traded on SETS, an electronic order matching system. Hence trading (pricing) is order driven. The main alternative trading system is one involving market makers – known as quote driven. This kind of system is more used in illiquid markets.*

3. *(d) UK gilts pay interest semi-annually and pay interest gross on new holdings unless the holder indicates otherwise.*

4. *(b) The FCA is the regulator for all recognised investment exchanges in the UK.*

5. *(d) The DMO is the body responsible for gilt issuance and general management of the UK government issued debt.*

6. *(b) The standard settlement time for gilts through CREST is T+1 (i.e. one working day after transaction).*

7. *(c) Settlement through CREST is electronic and hence paperless.*

8. *(a) Eurobonds are normally traded OTC and the rules for trading are set by the ICMA.*

9. *(b) There are two main types of proxy – a general proxy and a special proxy. The general proxy is able to vote as they see fit at the general meeting. The special proxy has to vote in a way specified before the meeting takes place. So a general proxy is the answer.*

10. *(d) The UK Stewardship Code, introduced by the FRC, aims is to make shareholders, who manage other people's money (institutional shareholders), be active and engage in corporate governance in the interests of their beneficiaries.*

11. *(a) Shareholders who already have a stake in the company above 3% are required to notify the company when their stake increases by more than 1%.*

12. *(b) For both a premium and standard listing on the main market the minimum value of the shares listed must be £700,000.*

LINK TO CFA LEVEL 1

The material in this chapter is mainly UK-focused and is therefore not covered in CFA Level 1.

CHAPTER 2

ETHICS AND INVESTMENT PROFESSIONALISM

The 2008 financial crisis and its subsequent impact on both taxpayers and the wider economy drew attention to the ethical responsibility of the entire financial services industry.

This chapter addresses the crucial difference between situations where financial services firms and individuals simply adhere to the letter of compliance regulations, and where they adopt an additional ethical approach.

Candidates will consider ethical obligations towards clients, prospective clients and their employers together with the beneficial outcomes that result from the adoption of rigorously ethical behaviour.

The Code of Ethics and Standards of Professional Conduct sets out the ethical standards that all CFA Institute Members and CFA Candidates registered to take the CFA examinations are required to follow. These standards are designed to promote fair and ethical behaviour, and are set out in seven categories.

Candidates are required not only to familiarise themselves with the categories and subcategories of the Code of Ethics but must also be able to apply the code to a variety of ethical situations. This chapter offers a number of ethical dilemmas and shows how the Code of Ethics provides guidance on the most appropriate behaviour in each situation.

CHAPTER 2 SECTION 1

ETHICAL AND COMPLIANCE DRIVEN BEHAVIOUR

SECTION AIMS

By the end of this section, learners should be able to:

- Describe the need for ethics in the investment industry.
- Identify the ethical obligations to clients, prospective clients, employers and co-workers.
- Identify positive and negative behavioural indicators.
- Critically evaluate the outcomes which may result from behaving ethically – for the industry, individual advisers and consumers.

1. ETHICS VERSUS REGULATIONS

Definitions of ethics vary, but generally they are viewed as a set of basic principles that ensure people behave for the benefit of all.

Regulation addresses some areas of unethical behaviour but there are still grey areas where behaviour, although not prohibited by regulation, does not seem to be in the clients' benefit. The case concerning a major US investment bank (see the case study on Goldman Sachs at the end of this section) shows that, to many, the behaviour of investment professionals can be unacceptable and not in clients' best interests, but still not necessarily prohibited by regulations.

Regulators also have problems keeping pace with the dynamism of the investment industry – new products, instruments and practices are often developed and used before regulations to govern them are even written. Also, if regulations are ambiguous or out of date, there is the risk that they will be exploited by unscrupulous participants in the financial services industry. A further problem is the difficulty of enforcing regulations, given the complexity of transactions and instruments and the requirement to prove rules have been broken.

2. WHY ETHICS ARE IMPORTANT

Ethics are important for a number of reasons, including:

- Building public trust in financial markets, which encourages wider participation in them.
- Promoting trust in investment professionals, encouraging the public to use professionals to manage and advise on their investments.
- Instilling trust in other stakeholders, including providers of capital to the industry such as shareholders or providers of finance for transactions.
- Earning the trust of regulators, allowing greater scope for self-regulation and less restrictive regulation of the participants in capital markets.

3. BEHAVIOURAL INDICATORS

Corporate versus personal ethics

There are two schools of thought regarding unethical behaviour. The first is that unethical behaviour is the result of the environment or the situation a person is in, so a good person in a bad environment may still end up behaving unethically. The second is that unethical behaviour is the result of the attitude or personality of an individual and the environment is less important. Most academic evidence suggests that the environment is the more important of the two factors. In the investment industry, this suggests that the corporate ethics of the firm will be critical in determining the behaviour of its employees. Additionally, a person in authority can have a strong influence on subordinates' behaviour; it is important that a strong ethical culture is led by the behaviour of senior management.

Good corporate ethics can be enhanced by many factors typically found in companies with good corporate governance – independent directors, strong internal procedures, fair remuneration packages that do not overly encourage risk taking and so on. It is also helpful to encourage employees to take some degree of personal responsibility for their actions and not unquestioningly follow instructions or respond to peer pressure that condones unethical activities.

Motivations for unethical behaviour

At a personal level, there are many factors that can lead to unethical behaviour. These include:

- Undue pressure or incentives to perform – bonuses and performance fees give an asymmetric pay-off, arguably increasing risk taking and rewarding short term rather than long term performance.
- Ability to blame others, e.g. 'I was just following instructions'. Also, acting as a member of a team diffuses responsibility rather than forcing an individual to accept personal responsibility for their actions.
- Ability to rationalise unethical behaviour, e.g. the other party is being unethical too.
- Conflicts of interest skewing judgement.
- Lack of rigour due to laziness, i.e. unwillingness to do proper research to understand a product, e.g. investigating who provides capital guarantees for structured products.
- Disregard for clients, which is perhaps more likely to occur when an investment professional is distanced from clients.
- Failure to do something, i.e. being unethical by omission. This is sometimes easier to justify than actively participating in unethical activities.

Cultural issues

Interpretation of ethical behaviour varies between countries; moral standards and value judgments will partly depend on culture and will also vary over time. Is giving a business contact a gift seen as normal hospitality or a bribe? This is one of the challenges of building codes of ethics and standards that are applied globally.

Research by Meir Statman ('Local Ethics in a Global World', *Financial Analysts' Journal*, May/June 2007) looked at how the balance between self-interest and fairness in different countries varies significantly. A test was used where professionals and students in a number of countries were asked whether behaviour in a fictitious insider trading case was fair; the percentage who judged it completely fair or acceptable ranged from 5% to 76% depending on the country and whether they were professionals or students. The responses were examined against stock market participation levels in the respective countries, and there appeared to be a relationship between perception of fairness, levels of trust and the willingness of the public to participate in their stock market.

4. IMPLICATIONS OF UNETHICAL BEHAVIOUR

Industry

When practitioners in an industry are seen to be behaving unethically and putting their own interests ahead of those of their clients (and in some cases ahead of the taxpayers' interests), the industry becomes vulnerable to government intervention. This can take the form of new or higher taxes on the industry, increased regulation, the breaking up of participants' businesses, restrictions on their activities and requirements for greater disclosure. Central regulation by government bodies tends to replace self-regulation by practitioners. Not only does this risk stifling future activity in the industry, but it creates uncertainty, leading to lack of investment and innovation.

A loss of trust in capital markets and investment professionals can lead to reluctance among investors to participate in the markets and to use professionals. When investment firms are perceived to be operating for the benefit of their owners and not their clients then investors will look for alternative ways to manage their money, perhaps preferring tangible assets, such as property or gold, to using investment advisers.

Firm

A poor ethical stance leads to the possibility of prosecution, potentially leading to fines, loss of licence and compensation payments to clients if regulations are broken. However, for individual firms, one of the main risks of unethical behaviour is reputational risk.

Reputation is an asset of a firm, because it should enhance future cash flows. Damage to reputation leads to loss of value of the firm and potentially the collapse of the organisation and/or loss of independence. It will affect the firm's ability to attract new business and may lead to the loss of existing clients. Furthermore, time may be spent responding to client complaints, questions from regulators and rewriting inadequate internal procedures.

Strong, consistent internal procedures should be set in place with the objective of preventing employees from breaking regulations and acting unethically. Procedures need to specifically address activities where there are conflicts of interest and where there are most likely to be occurrences of unethical behaviour, as well as reflecting the individual activities of the firm. Statements on ethical standards should be written clearly and should stand out from the detailed instructions on compliance procedures. They need to be communicated clearly to employees and any violations should be investigated and reported to senior management.

Investment practitioners

While breaking regulations can lead to a trial, fine and possibly a jail sentence, unethical conduct has its own potential penalties: disciplinary action from a professional body, disapproval from clients, colleagues and the industry peer group, negative publicity and potentially the loss of a job.

An example of an investment bank accused of behaving unethically was Goldman Sachs in 2010. The US Securities and Exchange Commission (SEC) filed a complaint against Goldman Sachs in 2010 for 'making materially misleading statements and omissions' in connection with the marketing of ABACUS 2007-AC1. ABACUS was a collateralised debt obligation (CDO) structured and tied to the performance of sub-prime residential mortgage-backed securities. The lawsuit essentially accused Goldman Sachs of selling sub-prime mortgage-backed securities specifically selected by a hedge fund, Paulson and Co, which stood to benefit if and when these securities defaulted. According to the SEC, Paulson and Co paid Goldman Sachs to structure these transactions. This deal was completely unknown to those buying the securities that Goldman Sachs was selling.

The SEC's main accusation was that while Goldman Sachs provided to those firms a detailed list of the assets contained in ABACUS that it built and sold in 2007, it concealed the role of John Paulson, a hedge fund manager who worked with Goldman Sachs to pick what went into the security. Paulson then placed bets that the security would lose value. In essence, the buyers bet that housing prices would go up, while Paulson bet that prices would fall.

At a Senate hearing in April 2010 into the role of Goldman Sachs in the financial crisis, a central line of inquiry was whether it was ethical for Goldman to go short on housing in its own trading positions, while at the same time continuing to market securities on which customers would be on the long side of the market. Goldman's defence was that it shorted the CDOs to manage its own risk exposures.

Goldman Sachs eventually admitted fault and reached a settlement with the SEC, paying $550m. The reputation of Goldman Sachs is likely to have been damaged as its behaviour was widely viewed as unethical.

Customers

The fiduciary duty of investment practitioners is to their clients, and investment decisions should be made for the benefit of the client. Clearly, when these principles are ignored, the clients will be disadvantaged. Financial loss or returns that are less than expected can result from poor or negligent investment advice. This can involve excessive risk taking, the purchase of inappropriate investments and lack of diversification. Financial loss can also result from excessive trading incurring unjustified transaction costs or the purchase of products that charge fees not commensurate with the performance. Needless to say, financial loss can cause extreme stress, particularly in the private client arena where clients may be dependent on their savings to provide income.

CHAPTER 2 SECTION 2

CFA CODE OF ETHICS AND STANDARDS OF PROFESSIONAL CONDUCT

SECTION AIMS

By the end of this section, learners should be able to:

- Identify the elements of the CFA Code of Ethics and Standards of Professional Conduct.
- Explain the professional principles and values on which the CFA Code of Ethics and Standards of Professional Conduct is based.
- Apply the CFA Code of Ethics and Standards of Professional Conduct to a range of ethical dilemmas.

1. CODE OF ETHICS

The Code of Ethics sets out the ethical standards that all CFA Institute Members (Members) and CFA Candidates who are registered to take CFA exams (Candidates) must follow.

There are six elements in the Code of Ethics. Investment professionals must:

- Act with integrity, competence, diligence and respect, and in an ethical manner with the public, clients, prospective clients, employers, employees, colleagues in the investment profession and other participants in the global capital markets.
- Place the integrity of the investment profession and the interests of clients above their own personal interests.
- Use reasonable care and exercise independent professional judgment when conducting investment analysis, making investment recommendations, taking investment actions and engaging in other professional activities.
- Practice, and encourage others to practice, in a professional and ethical manner that will reflect creditably on themselves and the profession.
- Promote the integrity and viability of the global capital markets for the ultimate benefit of society.
- Maintain and improve their professional competence and strive to maintain and improve the competence of other investment professionals.

The Code of Ethics is the underlying philosophy of the Standards of Professional Conduct. The Standards promote fair and ethical behaviour, and are organised into seven broad categories:

I. Professionalism.

II. Integrity of Capital Markets.

III. Duties to Clients.

IV. Duties to Employers.

V. Investment Analysis, Recommendations and Actions.

VI. Conflicts of Interest.

VII. Responsibilities as a CFA Institute Member or CFA Candidate.

2. STANDARDS OF PROFESSIONAL CONDUCT

This section looks at each of the Standards (in italics) followed by some practical situations where the Standards provide guidance on the appropriate behaviour of investment professionals practicing in the UK.

Standard I: Professionalism

A. Knowledge of the law

Members and Candidates must understand and comply with all applicable laws, rules and regulations (including the CFA Institute Code of Ethics and Standards of Professional Conduct) of any government, regulatory organisation, licensing agency, or professional association governing their professional activities. In the event of conflict, Members and Candidates must comply with the more strict law, rule or regulation. Members and candidates must not knowingly participate

EXAMPLE

Situation: Marilyn Barnes is part of the marketing team, whose responsibility is to attract new clients for her employer, a private client investment management firm. She is provided with performance data to use in presentations which she knows have been calculated incorrectly to give the impression that the firm is generating high returns for its clients.

Analysis: Marilyn has been asked to use misleading performance data, and misrepresenting performance violates the Code and Standards. She must bring the situation to the attention of her supervisor or the compliance department and request that the performance data is calculated correctly. She must refrain from using the misleading information and disassociate herself from the activity.

or assist in and must dissociate from any violation of such laws, rules or regulations.

Investment professionals practicing across many countries must adhere to all applicable regulatory requirements, whether they are their own country's laws, rules and regulations or those of foreign countries. When there is a conflict between applicable regulatory requirements and the Code and Standards, they must follow whichever is the strictest. Investment professionals should ensure that they have appropriate knowledge of all relevant regulatory requirements, and should ensure that they are up to date with changes in laws, rules and regulations. If in doubt, they should seek advice from compliance personnel.

If an investment professional suspects that a Standard or regulatory requirement has been violated, they should report it to their supervisor or compliance department (unless they are automatically required to inform the government or any regulatory organisations). If the situation is not remedied, they should disassociate themselves from the illegal or unethical activity, and if necessary resign from their position.

B. Independence and objectivity

Members and Candidates must use reasonable care and judgment to achieve and maintain independence and objectivity in their professional activities. Members and Candidates must not offer, solicit or accept any gift, benefit, compensation or consideration that reasonably could be expected to compromise their own or another's independence and objectivity.

Investment professionals may come under pressure from their employers or be offered free trips or gifts by companies that may influence their recommendations or research. Investment professionals should avoid those situations that would cause, or be perceived as causing, a conflict of interest.

When an investment professional visits a company or issuer, the investment professional should, wherever possible, pay their own transport and accommodation costs. Investment professionals should avoid the issuer regularly acting as host. Investment professionals should decline lavish gifts or benefits and only accept modest ones that will not pose a threat to their independence and objectivity.

EXAMPLE
Situation: Christopher Hilton is a junior fund manager working in London, and is invited to visit a listed company based in Edinburgh by one of the brokers who is recommending the company's shares. The broker pays for Christopher's first class travel, a night in a hotel and for golf the next day.

Analysis: Christopher would be advised to pay (or for his employer to pay) for his own travel costs and golf. Accepting the trip and hospitality from the broker will lead to the accusation that he has compromised his independence by making himself indebted to the broker.

Investment professionals should ensure that corporate relationships between colleagues or their employer are disclosed. If a brokerage company is unwilling to publish a negative opinion in a report on a company that is also a client of a related investment banking operation, then the company should be put on a restricted list and only factual information should be released.

See also chapter 3, section 5 covering FCA rules on inducements.

C. Misrepresentation

Members and Candidates must not knowingly make any misrepresentation relating to investment analysis, recommendations, actions or other professional activities.

A misrepresentation is any untrue statement, or any other statement that is false or misleading. It may also be omission of a fact or a failure to correct a known misunderstanding. The Standard is relevant to misrepresentations in any form, including oral communication, advertisements, emails or written materials. Investment professionals should not misrepresent any aspect of their practice, including:

- Their own or their firm's qualifications.
- Services provided by their firm.
- Their own or their firm's performance record.
- Guaranteeing returns on a risky investment or risky investment product (unless the product is specifically structured with a built-in guarantee).

This Standard also covers plagiarism. Investment professionals shall not copy or use, in substantially the same form as the original, material prepared by another without acknowledging and identifying the name of the author, publisher or source of such material.

Examples of plagiarism include basing a report on another analyst's report, using

EXAMPLE
Situation: Bill Marcus is an investment adviser who tells his clients that equities are guaranteed to recover by at least 10% this year based on his view of the UK economic outlook.

Analysis: Bill is misleading his clients; equities, by their nature, have uncertain returns.

EXAMPLE

Situation: Janet Sands is an investment adviser and has decided that a company, ABC, is attractive. She is anxious to recommend her clients to buy shares as soon as possible. She finds that a brokerage house has recently written a positive research report on the company. She changes headings and a few words in the report, and sends it out to her clients to support her recommendation.

Analysis: Janet should not use another broker's report without acknowledging the source, and must not represent herself as the author of the report.

excerpts from an article, using charts, graphs or proprietary computerised spreadsheets without referring to the original source of the report (or gaining permission, if required). The Standard not only covers plagiarism in written materials, but also in oral communications, such as in client meetings or presentations.

When preparing research reports, analysts should keep copies of sources of information used, acknowledge quotations and cite sources of statistics.

See chapter 3, section 5 for the FCA rules on investment research.

D. Misconduct

Members and Candidates must not engage in any professional conduct involving dishonesty, fraud or deceit, or commit any act that reflects adversely on their professional reputation, integrity or competence.

This Standard addresses compliance with regulations and the upholding of professional integrity. Dishonest personal behaviour reflects badly on the profession. For example, excessive drinking in business hours and the manipulation of expense accounts suggest poor judgment. This Standard addresses professional rather than personal conduct outside of work.

STANDARD II: INTEGRITY OF CAPITAL MARKETS

A. Material non-public information

Members and Candidates who possess material non-public information that could affect the value of an investment must not act or cause others to act on the information.

'Material' means that disclosure is likely to have an impact on the price of a security, or that reasonable investors would want to know the information before making an investment decision. The reliability of the source of the information is also a factor in determining whether it is material; the less reliable the source, the less likely it is to be material.

'Non-public' means that the information has not been disseminated in the market place and investors have not had a chance to react to the information. In the situation that a group of analysts is given information by a company, until it has been disseminated to other investors in the market, it is still non-public information.

However, it is acceptable for an analyst to piece together and analyse public information and non-material non-public information to predict events, which would lead to the same conclusion as receiving

EXAMPLE

Situation: James Welch is a portfolio manager. He was at his son's school party when he overheard another parent saying that she looked at a file in her husband's briefcase and found out that Beckford Corporation is planning to make a bid to purchase a competitor, Easeby Inc, saying, "The company will pay up to two times the current market price for Easeby Inc stock!" James went into the office the next day and immediately purchased Easeby Inc shares for his clients.

Analysis: James has taken an investment action based on material non-public information, which is a violation of Standard II(A).

material non-public information. This is called mosaic theory.

Most investment banking firms with combined brokerage services will set up an information barrier, a 'firewall', to prevent communication of non-public information from one department of a firm to another. For example, the corporate finance department should be separated from the sales and research departments.

See chapter 3, section 7 for a discussion of the law relating to insider dealing.

B. Market manipulation

Members and candidates must not engage in practices that distort prices or artificially inflate trading volume with the intent to mislead market participants.

Market manipulation is often related to:

- Transactions that artificially distort prices or volumes of securities traded.
- Taking a dominant position in a security in order to manipulate the price of a related derivative.
- The dissemination of false or misleading information in order to artificially inflate or decrease a security price.

See chapter 3, section 7 for more information about market abuse.

STANDARD III: DUTIES TO CLIENTS

A. Loyalty, prudence, and care

Members and Candidates have a duty of loyalty to their clients and must act with reasonable care and exercise prudent judgement. Members and Candidates must act for the benefit of their clients and place their clients' interests before their employer's or their own interests.

This Standard confirms that clients' interests must always come first and that the investment professional has a duty of loyalty, prudence and care to clients.

A specific example of the importance of loyalty to clients is dealing (soft) commission. This is when a client's commission is used to purchase research for the benefit of the client's portfolio(s). It is important to remember that commission belongs to the client and should be used for their benefit, not the manager's. The manager should ensure that they get best price and execution for trades, and that any goods or services purchased with dealing commission benefit the client. The voting of proxies is yet another important fiduciary

EXAMPLE

Situation: Dominique Rhynes is a portfolio manager at XYZ Managers and manages a number of pension fund accounts. She directs most of her trades to JNI Brokerage, despite the higher commission rates, because of the close relationship between the executives of the two firms. The quality of research of JNI is considered average, but JNI absorbs overhead expenses of XYZ Managers such as online information services and magazine subscriptions.

Analysis: Dominique violated Standard III(A) by not seeking the best value brokerage services to benefit the pension funds and their beneficiaries. Dealing commission should not be used to pay for the firm's operating expenses, only for service related to the investment decision making process.

duty. Unless the client instructs otherwise, the investment manager must always vote on a proxy issue – it cannot be ignored.

See chapter 3, section 5 for the FCA rules regarding dealing commission.

B. Fair dealing

Members and Candidates must deal fairly and objectively with all clients when providing investment analysis, making investment recommendations, taking investment action or engaging in other professional activities.

Fair dealing means that the investment professional does not favour one client above any other when disseminating recommendations or taking investment action. Material changes must be announced, as far as it is practical, to all clients at the same time.

Discretionary and non-discretionary clients must be treated equally. New issues should be offered to all clients for whom the issue is an appropriate investment, and if an issue is over-subscribed, or is a block trade, it should be distributed on a pro rata basis.

See chapter 3, section 5 for FCA rules on client order handling.

EXAMPLE

Situation: Monica Cross works in the investment management department of a private client firm. She learns that the research department has just issued a 'buy' recommendation for ABC Housing Ltd. She promptly buys a large quantity of ABC Housing shares and allocates it to the collectives that are managed internally, since these accounts are particularly performance-sensitive. She then reviews the firm's other clients and purchases additional shares where appropriate.

Analysis: Monica's activities clearly violate Standard III(B) by giving the collectives preferential treatment over other clients.

C. Suitability

1. *When Members and Candidates are in an advisory relationship with a client, they must:*

   (a) Make a reasonable inquiry into a client's or prospective client's investment experience, risk and return objectives and financial constraints prior to making any investment recommendation or taking investment action, and must reassess and update this information regularly.

   (b) Determine that an investment is suitable to the client's financial situation and consistent with the client's written objectives, mandates and constraints before making an investment recommendation or taking investment action.

   (c) Judge the suitability of investments in the context of the client's total portfolio.

2. *When Members and Candidates are responsible for managing a portfolio to a specific mandate, strategy or style, they must only make investment recommendations or take investment actions that are consistent with the stated objectives and constraints of the portfolio.*

This list of requirements means that advisers must know their clients prior to giving them advice. In order to comply with the Standard, an investment professional should undertake a fact-find for each client. The fact-find should establish:

- The type and nature of the client and the client's attitude to risk.
- Investment objectives in terms of risk and return.

EXAMPLE

Situation: David Hands, CFA, an investment adviser, has been advising Delia Chandler, a risk-averse client, on the use of covered call options in her equity portfolio. The purpose is to generate income in the portfolio. David explains to Delia the risks and tax implications involved.

Analysis: When determining the suitability of particular investments, the primary consideration is the characteristics of the client's entire portfolio, i.e. not looking at it on an issue-by-issue basis. Although writing options is potentially very risky, in this case David appears to have properly considered the investment in the context of the entire portfolio and has thoroughly explained the investment to the client, making him compliant with Standard III(C).

- Investment constraints, such as liquidity, legal requirements, time horizon, tax position and unique circumstances.
- Performance measurement benchmarks.

See chapter 5 on determining client objectives.

D. Performance presentation

When communicating investment performance information, Members or Candidates must make reasonable efforts to ensure that it is fair, accurate and complete.

The CFA Institute has developed the Global Investment Performance Standards (GIPS)

EXAMPLE

Situation: Terry Arbuckle is preparing marketing material for his firm's portfolio management services and decides to use the performance of a model portfolio to illustrate his firm's performance record.

Analysis: Terry should make it clear in his marketing materials that these are the results of a model portfolio and not actual results achieved for clients.

as a common, accepted set of standards for the investment management industry. Although compliance is voluntary, investment professionals and their firms are encouraged to adopt the standards, and they are becoming increasingly widely used.

All performance statements must be fair, accurate and complete.

See chapter 3, section 5 for FCA rules on the presentation of performance information in financial promotions.

E. Preservation of confidentiality

Members and Candidates must keep information about current, former and prospective clients confidential unless:

1. *The information concerns illegal activities on the part of the client or prospective client;*
2. *Disclosure is required by law; or*
3. *The client or prospective client permits disclosure of the information.*

In general, investment professionals should avoid disclosing any information about a

EXAMPLE

Situation: Roger Warner is a portfolio manager and manages an endowment plan of a university. The university has given Roger a confidential review of the future plans for expansion so he can better understand the fund's objectives. Roger's friend owns a local construction firm and is interested in making a contribution to the endowment plan, with the understanding that his company would be favourably considered when bidding for construction work at the university. He asks Roger for information about the expansion plans.

Analysis: Roger owes confidentiality to the endowment fund and its trustees, and therefore should refuse to divulge any information to his friend without his client's agreement.

client except to authorised fellow employees who are working for the benefit of the client. However, an investment professional may want to disclose information of a non-confidential nature, in this case they should check if the information is relevant to the work being performed for the client and whether disclosure enables the investment professional to provide a better service to the client.

STANDARD IV: DUTIES TO EMPLOYERS

A. Loyalty

In matters related to their employment, Members and Candidates must act for the benefit of their employer and not deprive their employer of the advantage of their skills and abilities, divulge confidential information or otherwise cause harm to their employer.

The employer's interests must come above the employee's own interest in matters relating to employment. This covers issues such as independent practice – investment professionals should not enter into independent practice if it is in conflict with their employer's interests. However, independent practice is not explicitly prohibited, but investment professionals need to obtain prior permission from their employer and any other party. Investment professionals can make preparations to undertake independent practice prior to leaving their employer, but care must be taken to ensure that the employer's interests are maintained.

When investment professionals plan to leave their current employers, there is scope for conflicts to arise, but they still have a duty to act in their employer's best interests until their resignation becomes effective. For example, the investment professional must be careful not to misappropriate trade secrets or misuse confidential information, solicit the employer's clients or misappropriate client lists.

EXAMPLE

Situation: Joanna Reilly is an independent investment adviser, and runs her own advisory business advising five high net worth clients. A local stockbroker asks Joanne to join his firm as a portfolio manager. She accepts the offer, but keeps her five clients.

Analysis: Joanna must seek written consent from her new employer to comply with Standard IV(A).

EXAMPLE

Situation: Prior to his departure from AT Advisers, Brian Matthews took certain steps to begin his new business, including talking confidentially with the clients of AT Advisers regarding his intention to start his own advisory firm. He also mentioned his planned fee structure, which would be more competitive than that of AT Advisers. He copied client records to use at his new firm.

Analysis: Brian violated Standard IV(A) by soliciting his employer's clients while still in their employment. He is free to contact clients after his departure, as long as the contact information has not come from AT Advisers records (if there is no non-compete agreement with AT Advisers). He should not take client records with him.

B. Additional compensation arrangements

Members and Candidates must not accept gifts, benefits, compensation or consideration that competes with, or might reasonably be expected to create a conflict of interest with, their employer's interest unless they obtain written consent from all parties involved.

Employers have a right to know if their employees are subject to any conflict of loyalties. Additional compensation includes payments from clients or from third parties.

EXAMPLE

Situation: Tony Spencer is a manager in a regional stock broker. He also sits on the board of a publicly listed resort chain. In addition to receiving an annual payment as a non-executive director, he is given membership privileges for his family at all the resort facilities. Although Tony discloses the payment, he does not disclose receiving the membership privileges, because he believes that he is only obliged to report monetary compensation, not benefits in kind.

Analysis: Tony violated Standard IV(B) by failing to disclose the total compensation as a member of the board of directors. When dealing with the securities of the resort chain, he may be obligated to disclose this arrangement to clients and prospective clients under Standard VI(A).

C. Responsibilities of supervisors

Members and candidates must make reasonable efforts to ensure that anyone subject to their supervision or authority complies with applicable laws, rules, regulations, and the Code and Standards.

Supervisors are responsible for their subordinates' ethical behaviour, even if the subordinate is not a CFA Institute Member. Supervisors can rely on reasonable compliance procedures designed to avoid and detect any wrongdoing. Moreover, if a compliance system is not in place, then the investment professionals should not accept the supervisory responsibility until reasonable procedures are in place.

Ideally, compliance procedures should:

- Be contained in a clearly written and accessible manual that is easy to understand.
- Outline permissible conduct.
- Outline the scope of the procedures.
- Implement a system of checks and balances.
- Designate a compliance officer and specify their authority.
- Outline procedures for reporting violations and sanctions.
- Outline procedures to document and test compliance procedures.
- Describe the hierarchy of supervision and assign duties to supervisors.

Compliance rules should be communicated to all employees and updated periodically. If a violation occurs, then a supervisor must respond promptly, conduct a thorough investigation and put limits on the relevant employee's/employees' activities until the investigation is complete.

STANDARD V: INVESTMENT ANALYSIS, RECOMMENDATIONS AND ACTIONS

A. Diligence and reasonable basis

Members and Candidates must:

1. *Exercise diligence, independence and thoroughness in analysing investments, making investment recommendations and taking investment actions.*

2. *Have a reasonable and adequate basis, supported by appropriate research and investigation, for any investment analysis, recommendation or action.*

This applies to primary research, secondary research (research conducted by someone else in the same firm) or third party research. Investment professionals must make reasonable and diligent efforts to ensure that the research is sound. If any information is suspected of being inaccurate, then it cannot be used.

> **EXAMPLE**
>
> **Situation:** Innes Kod follows Widget Ltd as a research analyst. All the information she has accumulated and documented suggests that the outlook for the company's existing products is poor and the launch of new products has been delayed. Innes overhears a financial analyst during lunch say that Widget's new products will be superior to those of its competitors. Upon returning to her office, Innes immediately changes her recommendation from 'sell' to 'buy'.
>
> **Analysis:** Innes violated Standard V(A), as she should have conducted her own thorough research as an adequate and reasonable basis for her recommendation.

See chapter 3, section 5 for FCA rules relating to investment research.

B. Communication with clients and prospective clients

Members and Candidates must:

1. *Disclose to clients and prospective clients the basic format and general principles of the investment processes they use to analyse investments, select securities and construct portfolios, and must promptly disclose any changes that might materially affect those processes.*

2. *Disclose to clients and prospective clients significant limitations and risks associated with the investment process.*

3. *Use reasonable judgment in identifying which factors are important to their investment analyses, recommendations or actions, and include those factors in communications with clients and prospective clients.*

4. *Distinguish between fact and opinion in the presentation of investment analysis and recommendations.*

This is a very important standard. It establishes the importance of clients understanding the information sent to them (via any means of communication), allowing them to make informed decisions. Analysts must provide information on the basic characteristics of an investment, which are

EXAMPLE

Situation: Judy Wiencek is a mining analyst and has written a research report on NB Minerals. Included in her report is her own assessment of the extent of mineral reserves likely to be found on the company's land. Based on preliminary core sample results from the company's latest drilling and her own calculations, Judy writes, "Based on the fact that the company has in excess of 200,000 ounces of gold, we rate NB Minerals a 'buy'". She omitted to state that a potentially serious environmental litigation case has just been filed by local residents living adjacent to the mining sites.

Analysis: Judy violated Standard V(B), as her calculation of the total reserves is an opinion, not a fact, and her omission of the relevant legal case is not reasonable.

the key factors supporting a recommendation, and differentiate between opinion (often on the investment's future prospects) and fact.

C. Record retention

Members and Candidates must develop and maintain appropriate records to support their investment analysis, recommendations, actions and other investment-related communications with clients and prospective clients.

Investment professionals should maintain files to support their work, including sources of information and methodology by which recommendations or conclusions were made. Generally, these remain the property of the firm, not the employee. Records can be maintained in either hard copy or electronically. The Standard does not stipulate a minimum holding period, but local regulatory requirements must be followed.

See chapter 3, section 5 for FCA rules on record keeping.

STANDARD VI: CONFLICTS OF INTEREST

A. Disclosure of conflicts

Members and Candidates must make full and fair disclosure of all matters that could reasonably be expected to impair their independence and objectivity or interfere with respective duties to their clients, prospective clients and employer. Members and Candidates must ensure that such disclosures are prominent, are delivered in plain language and communicate the relevant information effectively.

This Standard considers potential conflicts between investment professionals, their employer, clients and prospective clients. The emphasis is on full disclosure of conflicts, so that all the parties can evaluate the objectivity of advice or investment actions being taken. The investment professional cannot decide for themselves whether an actual or potential conflict exists – only clients and employers can make this decision.

Investment advice to clients could be biased for a number of reasons, including where the investment professional has beneficial ownership (a direct or indirect personal interest) of a security. Other issues causing a conflict of interest include an investment professional or their firm providing directors or acting as consultant to an issuer, acting as underwriter and broker-dealer relationships.

Investment professionals should report any beneficial ownership that they have in securities and any corporate directorships or similar positions that could reasonably be considered to produce a conflict of interest to their employer. If in doubt about whether any action could provide a conflict of interest, they should discuss the issue with a compliance officer or supervisor.

See chapter 3, section 5 for FCA rules on personal account dealing.

B. Priority of transactions

Investment transactions for clients and employers must have priority over investment transactions in which a Member or Candidate is the beneficial owner.

A beneficial owner means the investment professional owns the shares directly or has an indirect interest in the security. Note, however, that family accounts that are also client accounts should be treated equally with other clients.

In many cases, conflicts arise in initial public offerings (IPOs) where there is a shortage of stock available and a rise in price is anticipated. Conflicts can be avoided if investment professionals do not participate in IPOs. Similar conflicts arise with private placements; investment professionals should not be involved in these transactions if they could influence their judgment.

EXAMPLE

Situation: Bruce Trafford is an assistant on the dealing desk at a brokerage firm. Whenever a 'buy' recommendation is about to be made by the firm, Bruce buys the recommended shares for his wife ahead of the recommendation being circulated to clients.

Analysis: Bruce must allow clients to buy shares first, ahead of buying them for his wife, so he is in violation of Standard VI(B).

All individuals involved in investment decision making should observe a blackout or restricted period prior to trading for clients so they cannot front-run client trades.

See chapter 3, section 5 for FCA rules on investment research, particularly those relating to front-running.

C. Referral fees

Members and Candidates must disclose to their employer, clients and prospective clients, as appropriate, any compensation, consideration or benefit received from, or paid to, others for the recommendation of products or services.

The disclosure should be before any arrangement is entered into and should include the nature of the benefit together with an estimate of the monetary value. Investment professionals should consult a supervisor and legal counsel concerning any such prospective arrangements.

EXAMPLE

Situation: Hans Lindberg is a portfolio manager with ABC Investment Management, responsible for the management of private client investments. He is often requested by his clients to recommend a solicitor to establish trusts on their behalf. Hans recommends a local solicitor's firm and in return he receives referral fees.

Analysis: Hans is obliged to disclose any such arrangement to his clients in order to comply with Standard VI(C). The disclosure enables clients to determine if there was any partiality in the referral and the true cost of the referred services.

STANDARD VII: RESPONSIBILITIES AS A CFA INSTITUTE MEMBER OR CFA CANDIDATE

A. Conduct as Members and Candidates in the CFA programs

Members and Candidates must not engage in any conduct that compromises the reputation or integrity of the CFA Institute or the CFA designation, or the integrity, validity or security of the CFA Institute programs.

B. Reference to CFA Institute, the CFA designation, and the CFA Program

When referring to CFA Institute, CFA Institute membership, the CFA designation or candidacy in the CFA Program, Members and Candidates must not misrepresent or exaggerate the meaning or implications of membership in CFA Institute, holding the CFA designation or candidacy in the CFA Program.

CHAPTER 02 KEY FACTS

2.1

1. Ethics is generally viewed as a set of basic principles that ensure people behave for the benefit of all.

2. Ethics is important for a number of reasons, including:

   - Building public trust in markets, which encourages wider participation in markets.
   - Promoting trust in investment professionals, encouraging the public to use professionals to manage and advise on their investments.
   - In a broader sense, instilling trust in other stakeholders, including providers of capital to the industry such as shareholders or providers of finance for transactions, etc.
   - Earning the trust of regulators, allowing greater scope for self-regulation and less restrictive regulation of the participants in capital markets.

3. When practitioners in an industry are seen to be behaving unethically and putting their own interests ahead of those of their clients (and in some cases ahead of the taxpayers' interests), the industry becomes vulnerable to government intervention.

4. Where a firm behaves unethically, it risks prosecution and payment of compensation to clients. However, one of the main risks of unethical behaviour is reputational risk.

5. For individual investment professionals, while breaking regulations can lead to a trial, fine and possible jail sentence, unethical conduct has its own potential penalties: disciplinary action from a professional body, disapproval from clients, colleagues and the industry peer group, negative publicity and potentially loss of job.

2.2

1. The CFA Code of Ethics sets out the ethical standards that all CFA Institute Members and CFA Candidates who are registered to take CFA exams must follow.

2. There are six elements to the CFA Code of Ethics.

3. The Code of Ethics is the underlying philosophy of the Standards of Professional Conduct. The Standards promote fair and ethical behaviour, and are organised into seven broad categories:

I. Professionalism.

II. Integrity of Capital Markets.

III. Duties to Clients.

IV. Duties to Employers.

V. Investment Analysis, Recommendations and Actions.

VI. Conflicts of Interest.

VII. Responsibilities as a CFA Institute Member or CFA Candidate.

CHAPTER 02 SELF-ASSESSMENT QUESTIONS

1. Which of the following is not one of the elements of the CFA Code of Ethics, relating to investment professionals?

(a) *Act with integrity, competence, diligence and respect, and in an ethical manner with the public, clients, prospective clients, employers, and employees, colleagues in the investment profession and other participants in the global capital markets.*

(b) *Communicate clearly with the public, clients and prospective clients, ensuring additional care is taken when recommending on derivative related products.*

(c) *Promote the integrity of, and uphold the rules governing, capital markets.*

(d) *Maintain and improve professional competence and strive to maintain and improve the competence of other investment professionals.*

2. The CFA Code and Standards requires investment professionals to adhere to all applicable regulatory requirements in the country in which they are working. When there is a conflict between these country requirements and the CFA Code and Standards, which should be followed?

(a) *The CFA Code and Standards.*

(b) *The applicable regulatory requirements in that country.*

(c) *Whichever is the stricter of the CFA Code and Standards, and the applicable regulatory requirements in that country.*

(d) *Whichever the investment professional feels most appropriate, once all factors have been considered.*

3. An investment professional who is an employee at a large investment firm also wishes to undertake independent practice away from their employer. What requirements are laid down by the CFA Code and Standards?

(a) *The investment professional must obtain prior permission from their employer before undertaking independent practice.*

(b) *The investment professional is forbidden from undertaking independent practice.*

(c) *The investment professional must obtain prior permission from the financial regulator before undertaking independent practice.*

(d) *The investment professional may undertake independent practice without notifying their employer, so long as their employer's best interests are always put first.*

4. An analyst writing a research report covering the aerospace industry is focusing on a company which produces wing components for the passenger planes and which they believe is about to win a huge contract with a major plane manufacturer. They write, 'Given the fact that the company will soon sign a major contract with a major manufacturer, the company is rated as a "buy".' In writing this the analyst has:

(a) *Not violated any CFA Standards of Professional Conduct.*

(b) *Violated CFA Standard II(B).*

(c) *Violated CFA Standard V(B).*

(d) *Violated CFA Standard III(C).*

5. Jack requests that his broker, Sarah, buys shares in ABC plc. Before placing the order, Sarah purchases ABC shares for her own personal dealings. In doing so she has:

(a) *Not violated any CFA Standards of Professional Conduct.*

(b) *Violated CFA Standard II(A).*

(c) *Violated CFA Standard IV(A).*

(d) *Violated CFA Standard VI(B).*

6. Mike is a broker who believes that a major client is embezzling money from his employers and investing it in securities for a personal account. Under CFA Standard III(E), Mike should:

(a) *Not report his suspicions to anyone as he has a duty of confidentiality.*

(b) *Freeze all funds and assets belonging to his client.*

(c) *Complete all outstanding trades but decline to carry out any further trades.*

(d) *Consult his compliance department to determine what regulatory action is required.*

ANSWERS

1. *(b) Although (b) is a requirement for firms under FCA rules, it is not an element of the CFA Code of Ethics.*

2. *(c) Investment professionals practicing across many countries must adhere to all applicable regulatory requirements, whether they are their own country's laws, rules and regulations or those of foreign countries. When there is a conflict between applicable regulatory requirements and the Code and Standards, they must follow whichever is the strictest.*

3. *(a) Investment professionals should not enter into independent practice if it is in conflict with their employer's interests. However, independent practice is not explicitly prohibited, but investment professionals need to obtain prior permission from their employer.*

4. *(c) CFA Standard V: Investment Analysis, Recommendations And Actions, part B: Communication with clients and prospective clients is relevant here. In part 4, there is a requirement to distinguish between fact and opinion in the presentation of investment analysis and recommendations. In the case presented in the question, the recommendation to buy is based on opinion rather than fact and so should not have occurred.*

5. *(d) Standard V1 B states that investment transactions for clients and employers must have priority over investment transactions in which a member or candidate is the beneficial owner. Sarah has clearly breached this standard by placing her order ahead of that of her client.*

6. *(d) CFA Standard III(E) states that Members and Candidates must keep information about current, former and prospective clients confidential unless:*

1. *the information concerns illegal activities on the part of the client or prospective client;*
2. *disclosure is required by law; or*
3. *the client or prospective client permits disclosure of the information.*

The duty of confidentiality to the client is overridden by (1).

LINK TO CFA LEVEL 1

Ethical and professional standards are covered extensively at CFA Level 1 in Program curriculum volume 1.

CHAPTER 3

THE REGULATION OF FINANCIAL MARKETS AND INSTITUTIONS

Firms and individuals operating within the UK financial services industry come under a regulatory framework that is implemented by a number of bodies. Their powers arise from various pieces of legislation including the Financial Services and Markets Act 2000, subsequently amended by the Financial Services Act 2012.

This chapter describes the role of the Financial Conduct Authority, Prudential Regulation Authority, Bank of England, Financial Policy Committee and HM Treasury, together with other bodies such as the Competition and Markets Authority and the Panel on Takeovers and Mergers. While all of these bodies play their own role, it is the actions of the FCA that have the highest profile in this chapter.

The FCA has three statutory objectives, perhaps the most significant of which is that of offering protection to consumers. The FCA aims to achieve this by a number of measures, including the regulation of both individual finance professionals and firms. The FCA Handbook collects these principles and rules together alongside guidance on how they should be applied.

The examination requires that candidates know the structure of the FCA Handbook and have a detailed knowledge of certain key sections. An understanding of the FCA rules and their application is needed for client marketing, client categorisation, dealing, advising and the management of assets in addition to areas such as investment research, record keeping and safekeeping client assets and money.

The rights of consumers to complain and the processes which firms must have in place, together with protection offered to consumers when firms fail are also addressed in this chapter.

The section on financial crime and the implications of associated legislation address the key concerns of money laundering and associated anti-terrorism measures, insider dealing, bribery and market abuse.

CHAPTER 3 SECTION 1

INTERNATIONAL AND EUROPEAN UNION DIRECTIVES, REGULATION AND GUIDANCE

SECTION AIMS

By the end of this section, learners should be able to:

- Explain the legal status of EU directives and regulations within the UK.
- Explain the role and powers of the European Securities and Markets Authority.
- Explain the purpose and scope of the Markets in Financial Instruments Directive (MiFID) with respect to: passporting; roles of the home and host state; core and non-core investment services; financial instruments covered by the legislation.
- Explain the purpose and scope of the Undertakings for Collective Investment in Transferable Securities (UCITS) Directives.
- Explain the purpose, scope and the requirements of the Alternative Investment Fund Managers Directive (AIFMD).
- Explain the purpose and scope of the European Market Infrastructure Regulation (EMIR).
- Explain the purpose and scope of the Foreign Account Tax Compliance Act enacted in March 2010 under US federal law.

1. HARMONISATION OF FINANCIAL SERVICES IN EUROPE

There have been a number of measures taken by the EU to harmonise the company and financial services laws of member states. This is part of the project of promoting a single market in the EU.

A major development in achieving financial services harmonisation within the EU occurred in 1999, when the Financial Services Action Plan (FSAP) was launched. It consisted of 42 measures, including 24 EU directives that were transposed into the law of each member state, and regulations that apply directly in all member states.

The FSAP has three specific objectives:

- To create a single EU wholesale market.
- To achieve open and secure retail markets.
- To create state of the art prudential rules and structures of supervision.

These objectives are designed to promote Europe's wider economy by removing barriers and increasing competition among financial services firms, thereby making markets more efficient and reducing the cost of raising capital to industry generally.

Since 1999, the EU has adopted or updated requirements concerning, among other things:

- The amount of capital firms should hold.
- The rules companies must comply with when carrying on business with their customers.
- The controls companies must apply to counter the risk of money laundering and terrorist financing.
- The tests to apply when assessing the suitability of new controllers or large shareholders.
- The requirements companies must impose to counter the risk of market abuse.
- The disclosures companies must make when seeking new capital.

Completion of the FSAP within a tight deadline was accompanied by a new legislative approach called the Lamfalussy approach. This approach is based on the recommendations of the Committee of 'Wise Men', chaired by Baron Alexandre Lamfalussy. It comprises a four-level procedure that speeds up the legislative process by dividing the legislation into high level framework provisions and implementing measures. The arrangements also make provision for legislation to be modified in order to keep pace with market and supervisory developments. The Committee of European Securities Regulators (CESR) was also established at this time.

Since its formation, a number of FSAP measures have been adopted using this new process. The first directives to be adopted in line with this approach were the Market Abuse Directive and the Prospectus Directive. The Markets in Financial Instruments Directive (MiFID) and the Transparency Directive also followed this approach, and Solvency 2, the fundamental review of the capital adequacy regime for the European insurance industry, is currently being developed through the Lamfalussy framework.

The Alternative Investment Fund Managers Directive was implemented in July 2013 and affects regulation of hedge funds and private equity. It creates a passport for EU Alternative Investment Fund (AIF) managers to market units or shares in their EU AIFs to professional investors in all EU member states without needing to comply with any further local requirements.

On 1 January 2011, three European authorities for the supervision of financial activities were established. This followed a review of financial market regulation after the 2008 financial crisis. The crisis highlighted the failings of the supervision system in Europe: the accumulation of excessive risk was not detected; surveillance and supervision were not effective in time; and when transnational financial institutions faced problems, the co-ordination between national authorities was far from optimal.

The three European supervisory authorities are:

1. The European Securities and Markets Authority (ESMA).
2. The European Banking Authority (EBA).
3. The European Insurance and Occupational Pensions Authority (EIOPA).

The European Systemic Risk Board (ESRB) monitors the entire financial sector to identify potential problems that could contribute to a crisis in the future. These bodies do not replace national supervisory authorities. The aim is to create a network of authorities where the national bodies are responsible for daily surveillance, while the European bodies are responsible for co-ordination, monitoring and, if need be, arbitration between national authorities, contributing to the harmonisation of technical rules applicable to financial institutions.

The ESMA aims to ensure the integrity, transparency, efficiency and orderly functioning of securities markets in Europe, as well as enhancing investor protection. Its main powers are:

- The ability to draft technical standards that are legally binding in EU member states.
- The ability to launch a fast track procedure to ensure consistent application of EU law.
- New powers in resolving disagreements between national authorities.
- Additional responsibilities for consumer protection (including the ability to prohibit financial

products that threaten financial stability or the orderly functioning of financial markets for a period of three months).

- Emergency powers.
- Participating in Colleges of Supervisors and on-site inspections.
- Monitoring systemic risk of cross border financial institutions.
- A new supervisory role (in particular for credit rating agencies).
- The ability to enter into administrative arrangements with supervisory authorities, international organisations and the administrations of third countries.

In general, ESMA works at a high level setting standards, while day-to-day supervision is carried out by national supervisory authorities.

The EU supervisory system has resulted in some changes regarding how the four-level legislative procedure, introduced under the Lamfalussy approach, operates.

Level 1 directives and regulations set the high-level political objectives on the area concerned. Occasionally, at this early stage, ESMA may be asked for technical advice by the Commission as it develops its legislative proposal.

However, ESMA has a greater role in Level 2 in drafting 'subordinate acts' (known as delegated acts and implementing acts). Delegated acts are concerned more with the substantive content of the legislative requirement, for example setting out what authorisation information firms must provide to competent authorities, while implementing acts are similar to executive measures, giving effect to the substantive requirements. This might include, for example, standard forms, templates and procedures for communicating information or processes between competent authorities.

At Level 3, ESMA develops guidelines and recommendations with a view to establishing consistent, efficient and effective supervisory practices within the European System of Financial Supervision, and to ensure the common, uniform and consistent application of Union law.

The guidelines and recommendations are addressed to competent authorities or financial market participants. While not legally binding, these have been strengthened under ESMA and competent authorities must now make every effort to comply and must explain if they do not intend to comply. Financial market participants can also be required to report publicly whether they comply. ESMA will also take steps under Level 3 to ensure supervisory convergence.

At Level 4, a fast track procedure has been introduced by the regulation establishing ESMA. On this basis, ESMA has a new role. At the request of a national competent authority, the European

Parliament, Council, Commission or the Stakeholder Group, ESMA can be requested to launch an enquiry and can issue a recommendation addressed to the national authority within two months of launching its investigation. ESMA will also be able to launch investigations on its own initiative. The Commission will also be able to follow its usual procedures for referring a case against the member state to the Court of Justice.

2. THE LEGAL STATUS OF EU DIRECTIVES WITHIN THE UK

In general, the programme of harmonisation consists mainly of a series of directives issued under article 58 of the European Treaty. These directives require member states to amend their law to comply with them if necessary. Directives can be implemented by primary legislation, or by the more recent tendency of delegated legislation under section 2(2) of the European Community Act 1972. This latter method may only alter a statute in so far as it is necessary to implement a directive.

Problems can arise when a directive has not been implemented by the due date, or the implementing legislation does not properly comply with the terms of the directive. In such cases, the European Court has held that the directives have a vertical direct effect. This means that, between a member state and a company or individual, the provisions of the directive must be given precedence over national law. Between two companies and/or two individuals (known as the horizontal–direct effect), this does not apply. However, in applying national law in this situation, the court should interpret the law in such a way as to achieve the result required by the directive.

Regulations are the most direct form of EU law – as soon as they are passed, they have binding legal force throughout every member state, on a par with national laws. They are different from directives, which are addressed to national authorities, who must then take action to make them part of national law, and decisions, which apply in specific cases only, involving particular authorities or individuals. Regulations are passed either jointly by the EU Council and European Parliament, or by the Commission alone.

3. THE MARKETS IN FINANCIAL INSTRUMENTS DIRECTIVE

One important objective of harmonisation has been to give firms the right to trade financial services throughout the EU on the basis of a single authorisation 'passport' from their home regulator. To ease doubts about the rigour of home country regulation, a parallel development has focused on harmonising key prudential standards.

The Investment Services Directive (ISD) created a 'single passport', under which an authorised firm incorporated in one member state (i.e. the 'home state') may engage in investment services throughout the European Economic Area (EEA) without separate authorisation by other member states ('host states'). The passport only allows a firm to provide those investment services that have been authorised by its home member state authority in a host member state.

The ISD was superseded by the Markets in Financial Instruments Directive (MiFID) in the UK in November 2007. MiFID has the same basic purpose, but it makes changes to the regulatory framework to reflect developments in financial services and markets. Firstly, MiFID widened the range of 'core' investment services and activities that can be passported. In addition to the services covered by the ISD, MiFID:

- Upgraded advice that involves a personal recommendation to a core investment service that can be passported on a stand-alone basis.
- Clarified that operating a multilateral trading facility (MTF) is covered by the passport.
- Extended the scope of the passport to cover commodity derivatives, credit derivatives and financial contracts for differences.

Under MiFID, a company, whether offering services in another member state through a branch or cross-border may follow the rules of the home state. The exception to this is where a firm operates from a branch in another member state, the host state conduct of business rules will normally apply.

MiFID distinguishes between 'investment services and activities' and 'ancillary services'. If a firm performs investment services and activities, it is subject to MiFID in respect of both these and also ancillary services (and it can use the MiFID passport to provide them to member states other than its home state). However, if a firm only performs ancillary services, it is not subject to MiFID (but nor can it benefit from the MiFID passport).

Investment services and activities are:

- Reception and transmission of orders in relation to one or more 'financial instruments'.
- Execution of orders on behalf of clients.
- Dealing in any financial instrument for an investment firm's 'own account', including market making and principal dealing.
- Managing portfolios of investments in financial instruments.
- The making of personal recommendations.
- Underwriting in respect of issues of any financial instruments and/or the placing of such issues on a firm commitment basis.
- The placing of financial instruments without a firm commitment basis.
- The operation of MTFs.

Ancillary services are:

- Safekeeping and administration of financial instruments for the accounts of clients, including custodianship and related services such as cash/collateral management.
- Granting credits or loans to an investor to allow the investor to execute a transaction, where the firm granting the credit or loan is involved in the transaction.
- Advice to undertakings on capital structure, industrial strategy and related matters, and advice and services relating to mergers and the purchase of undertakings.
- Foreign exchange services where these are connected to the provision of investment services.
- Investment research and financial analysis or other forms of general recommendation relating to transactions in financial instruments.
- Services relating to underwriting.
- Investment services and ancillary services related to the underlying of derivative instruments covered by MiFID.

A further directive, MiFID II, which will extend the scope of MiFID, is being implemented by the FCA in January 2017.

4. THE UCITS DIRECTIVES

The FCA gives 'automatic' recognition to certain collective investment schemes constituted in a member state of the EU other than the UK. This follows from the UK's obligations under the EU directive on Undertakings for Collective Investment in Transferable Securities (UCITS). Under this 1985 directive, a collective investment scheme which complies with its conditions, and which is authorised in any member state of the EU, can be marketed without further authorisation in any other member state subject only to the local marketing laws.

The FCA is responsible for recognising a scheme under UCITS. The original UCITS Directive (termed UCITS I) was amended in 2002 by a directive known as UCITS III. UCITS III is split into two parts: the Management Directive and the Product Directive.

The Management Directive increases the scope of management companies' activities that can be passported to include discretionary management, safekeeping and fund administration. The directive also aims to protect investors by ensuring that management companies are suitably capitalised, and that they have appropriate measures in place for risk management and reporting. The directive introduced the simplified prospectus, which is a document that is designed to provide investors with a shortened 'core' version of the current prospectus, while introducing additional features such as performance figures.

The simplified prospectus does not replace the current prospectus, and the current prospectus will still be available for all investors. The Product Directive expanded the range and type of financial instruments that are permitted within UCITS funds, in particular allowing investment in derivatives for investment as well as for existing risk reduction purposes (subject to certain risk controls), and investment in other funds. The directive also increases the investment limits for particular types of financial instruments, and puts in place a combined investment limit on all of a fund's exposure to any one group of companies.

A newer UCITS Directive (UCITS IV) was implemented in July 2011. The main changes in are:

- A passport for management companies (which is subject to prudential and conduct of business measures broadly similar to those in MiFID).
- A procedure for cross-border fund mergers.
- Introduction of master feeder structures to permit asset pooling.
- Replacement of the simplified prospectus with a key investor information document (see section 5 of this chapter for more information).
- A notification procedure for cross-border marketing.
- Strengthening of supervisory co-operation.

UCITS V, which aims to enhance the rules on the responsibilities of depositaries and introduces remuneration policy requirements for UCITS fund managers, has to be implemented into UK law by March 2016.

5. THE ALTERNATIVE INVESTMENT FUND MANAGERS DIRECTIVE

The Alternative Investment Fund Managers Directive (AIFMD) was implemented in 2013 and covers the management, administration and marketing of alternative investment funds (AIFs). Its focus is on regulating the AIF managers (AIFMs), rather than AIFs.

An AIF is a 'collective investment undertaking' that is not subject to the UCITS regime and includes hedge funds, private equity funds, retail investment funds, investment companies and real estate funds.

Requirements under the AIFMD include authorisation of an AIFM with the home state regulator if they have assets under management in AIFs above:

- €100m if any of the AIF uses leverage; or
- €500m if the AIFs do not use leverage and do not give their investors a right of redemption within five years of initial investment in each AIF.

AIFMs with assets under management that do not meet these criteria are deemed to be subthreshold and lighter regulation applies – see below. The AIFMD includes capital obligations, organisational and governance requirements, and the regular disclosure of information to investors.

The AIFMD's reporting regulations assert that each AIF should be named using a series of codes. It also requires AIFMs to select only brokers and counterparties that:

- are subject to regulatory supervision;
- are financially sound; and
- have the necessary organisational structure to provide services to the AIFM or the AIF.

Finally, all AIFMs must submit quarterly, semi-annual, or annual reports to their respective member state regulator with information about the AIFM and its AIFs. AIFMs must also submit an annual report with information such as the fund's financial statements, activities, and information about the total amount of remuneration paid by the AIFM to its staff.

Under the AIFMD, special requirements apply to AIFMs using leverage. AIFMs are required to disclose the extent of the leverage employed within their funds, and prove that leverage in any fund has been limited to a reasonable amount. The scope of AIFMD requirements that apply to AIFMs differ, according to whether the AIFM is engaged in portfolio or risk management activities within the EU or markets its funds to EU investors. Under the AIFMD, each fund can only have one AIFM, though the AIFM can delegate certain functions to other entities. Authorised fund managers located within the EU are permitted to market their EU funds to professional investors in any EU member state under an AIFMD passport.

There are two types of sub-threshold AIFM:

- A Small Authorised UK AIFM is an AIFM that is sub-threshold, FCA authorised and has not opted in to the AIFMD. This will be the relevant categorisation for most small private fund managers.
- A Small Registered UK AIFM is an AIFM that is sub-threshold and either:
    i) an internal AIFM of a corporate body, such as an investment trust;
    ii) the unauthorised manager of property funds which are operated by an FCA authorised operator; or
    iii) a fund manager which has applied for registration under the European Venture Capital Funds Regulation or the European Social Entrepreneurship Funds Regulation.

For sub-threshold AIFMs, the FCA SYSC and COBS rules generally apply. In addition, a UK sub-threshold AIFM cannot benefit from the EU marketing passport under the AIFMD. This means that any marketing in the EU must comply with local private placement regimes.

6. THE EUROPEAN MARKET INFRASTRUCTURE REGULATION

The European Market Infrastructure Regulation (EMIR) came into force on 16 August 2012 and covers over-the-counter (OTC) derivatives, central counterparties and trade repositories. The regulation requires anyone who has entered into a derivatives contract to report and risk manage their derivative positions. The technical standards on OTC derivatives, reporting to trade repositories and requirements for trade repositories and central counterparties came into force on 15 March 2013.

In the UK, HM Treasury has implemented EMIR through the Financial Services and Markets Act 2000 (Over the Counter Derivatives, Central Counterparties and Trade Repositories) Regulations 2013. The regulations repeal provisions in UK domestic law which are either inconsistent with EMIR or are no longer required. By doing so, the regulations are intended to ensure that EMIR is fully effective and enforceable in the UK. These regulations came into force on 1 April 2013.

EMIR imposes three requirements on those who trade derivatives:

1. To clear OTC derivatives that have been declared subject to the clearing obligation through a central counterparty.

2. To put in place certain risk management procedures for OTC derivatives transactions that are not cleared.

3. To report derivatives to a trade repository.

7. THE FOREIGN ACCOUNT TAX COMPLIANCE ACT

The Foreign Account Tax Compliance Act (FATCA) is a US law to prevent tax evasion by US citizens using offshore banking facilities. FATCA created a new tax information and reporting and withholding regime, designed to gain information about US persons rather than to raise revenue.

FATCA applies to non-US financial institutions and imposes a 30% withholding tax on payments of US source income made to non-US financial institutions. Non-US financial institutions can, however, enter into an agreement with the US Internal Revenue Service (IRS) and disclose information about their US account holders.

The UK and the US entered into an inter–governmental agreement in September 2012, meaning that UK financial institutions can meet their FATCA obligations by reporting information to HMRC. HMRC will supply the information received to the US. For non-UK clients, e.g. Irish UCITS funds, FATCA reporting will be done via the Irish tax authority.

FATCA requires all foreign financial institutions (FFIs) to provide information about their US customers to the IRS in accordance with the terms of an FFI agreement entered into between the FFI and the IRS. If it does enter into an FFI agreement, the FFI is known as a 'participating FFI' and if it does not, it is deemed to be a 'non-participating FFI' and a 30% withholding tax charge is applied to certain payments made to it. 'FFI' is defined very widely and includes:

- an entity that accepts deposits in the ordinary course of a banking or similar business;
- holds financial assets for the account of others as a substantial portion of its business;
- engages primarily in the business of trading in financial instruments, managing portfolios or otherwise administering or managing funds or money; or
- conducts certain business as an insurance company.

The basic obligation is to disclose details of all 'reportable accounts'. Reportable accounts are financial accounts maintained by the FFI where the account holder is either a specified US person (which includes any individual who is a citizen or resident of the US) or is a non-US entity where the 'controlling persons' include one or more specified US persons. Controlling persons are individuals who exercise control over an entity. In the case of a trust, this will mean the settlor, the trustees, the protector (if any), the beneficiaries or class of beneficiaries, and any other individual exercising ultimate effective control over the trust. Financial accounts include any depositary or custodial accounts maintained by an FFI, any equity or debt holdings in the FFI (although this does not include shares or debt regularly traded on an established securities market) and cash value insurance contracts.

The reporting to the IRS takes the form of an annual report on each US reportable account and includes an obligation to provide any further information about those accounts that the IRS may request. The information that must be provided includes:

- the name, address and US taxpayer identification number of each specified US person that is an account holder;
- the year end account balance or value;
- the total gross amount of interest credited to the account; and
- the total gross amount paid or credited to the account holder in the case of any other account.

CHAPTER 3 SECTION 2

UK REGULATION

SECTION AIMS

By the end of this section, learners should be able to:

- Describe and distinguish between the roles of the Financial Conduct Authority, Prudential Regulation Authority, Bank of England, Financial Policy Committee and HM Treasury.
- Explain the different roles of the FCA and PRA for dual-regulated investment firms.
- Explain the scope of the Financial Services and Markets Act (FSMA) 2000 (as amended by the Financial Services Act 2012).
- Explain the scope of the Regulated Activities Order 2001 (as amended) in terms of regulated activities and specified investments.
- Explain the purpose and scope of the FCA's rules regarding Senior Management Arrangements, Systems and Controls (SYSC).
- Explain the function of the following bodies/persons: the Panel on Takeovers and Mergers, the Department for Business, Innovation and Skills, the Competition and Markets Authority and the Information Commissioner's Office.
- Explain the make-up of the Panel on Takeovers and Mergers (the Takeover Panel) and how it is financed.
- Explain the regulatory status of the City Code on Takeovers and Mergers.
- Explain the main provisions of the City Code, including the bid timetable.
- Explain the purpose and scope of the Trustees Act 2000: the rights and duties of the parties involved, the nature of the trust deed and the investment powers of trustees.
- Explain the significance of the Pensions Act 2004: scheme specific funding requirement, The Pensions

CHAPTER 3 SECTION 2 cont...

UK REGULATION

Regulator, the Pension Protection Fund.

- Explain the significance of the Pensions Act 2008 and the reforms to pension rules in March 2014: automatic enrolment, National Employment Savings Trust, freedom of choices in pensions.
- Explain the purpose of a Statement of Investment Principles.

1. THE UK REGULATORY STRUCTURE

The Financial Services Act 2012, which came into force on 1 April 2013, amended the Financial Services and Markets Act 2000 (FSMA) and contains reforms of the UK financial services regulatory structure. It created a new regulatory framework for the supervision and management of the UK's banking and financial services industry. The new regulatory structure involved:

- Establishing a macro-prudential regulator, the Financial Policy Committee (FPC), within the Bank of England to monitor and respond to systemic risks.
- Transferring responsibility for prudential regulation of banks, insurers and systemically important investment firms to a new regulator, the Prudential Regulation Authority (PRA), established as a subsidiary of the Bank of England.
- Creating a focused conduct of business regulator, the FCA. This body regulates both retail and wholesale markets with an emphasis on promoting consumer protection.

The various roles and accountabilities of the new regulatory bodies are shown in Figure 3.1.

FIGURE 3.1: ROLES IN THE REGULATORY ARCHITECTURE

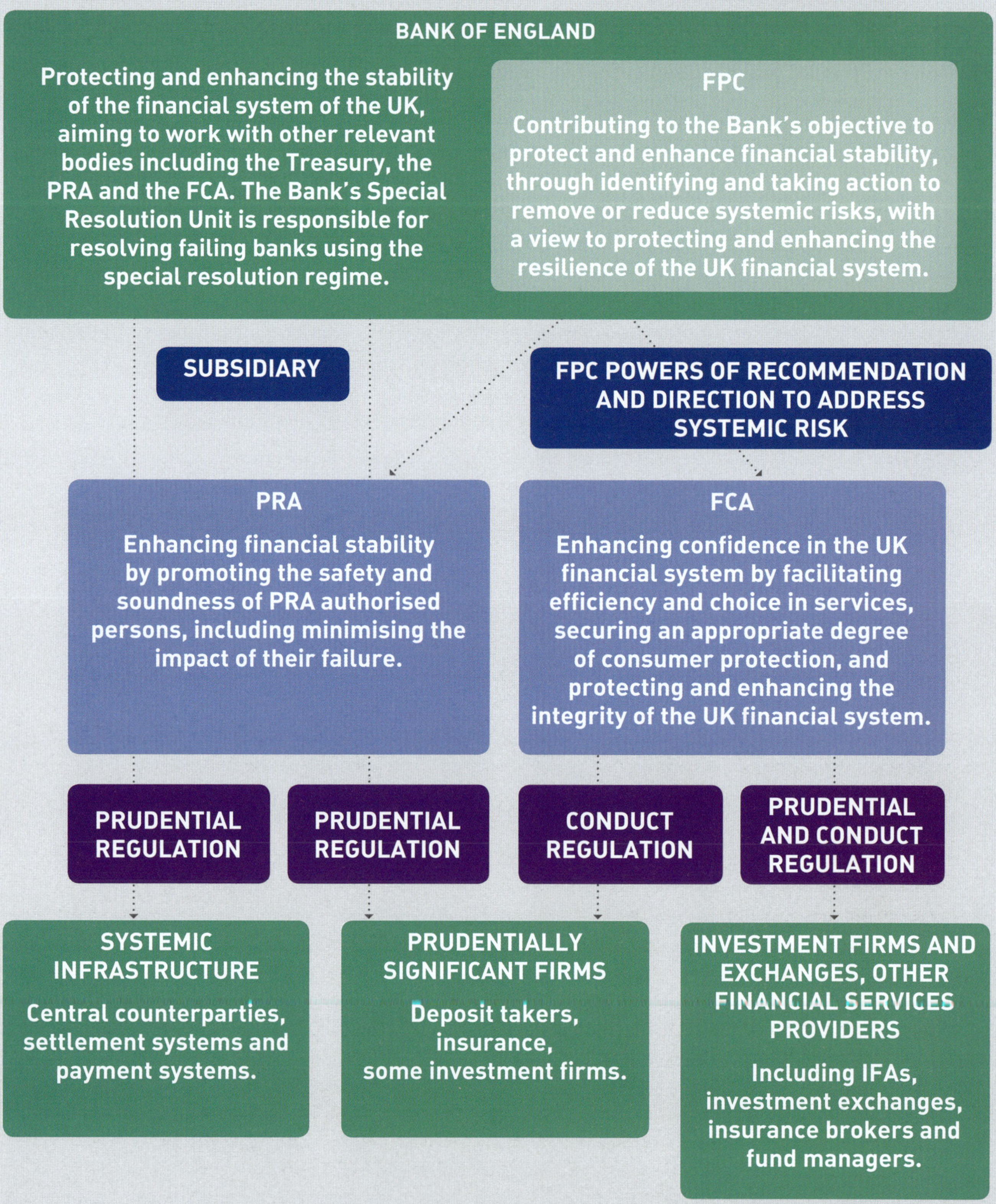

Source: HM Treasury 'A new approach to financial regulation: building a stronger system', 2011

The Financial Conduct Authority

The FCA is the conduct of business regulator, charged with the strategic objective of ensuring that relevant markets function well. 'Relevant markets' are defined as:

1. The financial markets.
2. Markets for regulated financial services (as defined in a new section of FSMA).
3. The markets for services that are provided by unauthorised persons in carrying on regulated activities without contravening the general prohibition.

The FCA has three operational objectives:

1. To secure an appropriate degree of protection for consumers.
2. To protect and enhance the integrity of the UK financial system.
3. To promote effective competition in the interests of consumers in the markets for regulated financial services and services provided by recognised investment exchanges in carrying on certain regulated activities.

The scope of the FCA's activities include:

- Conduct of business regulation for all firms in both retail and wholesale markets. The FCA is responsible for the conduct of business regulation of all regulated firms, including PRA-authorised firms and firms passporting into the UK.
- Acting as the lead regulator for firms other than PRA-authorised firms, including in respect of prudential supervision. The Financial Services Act 2012 refers to these firms as 'FCA-authorised firms'. In its October 2012 'Journey to the FCA' paper, the FSA stated that the FCA will be the conduct supervisor for approximately 26,000 firms across all industry sectors and the prudential supervisor for approximately 23,000 firms not regulated by the PRA.
- The FCA inherited the FSA's roles relating to markets regulation, with the exception of the FSA's responsibilities for settlement systems and recognised clearing houses (RCHs), which transferred to the Bank of England (BoE). Institutions that provide both exchange services and central counterparty clearing services are regulated by the BoE with respect to their activities as RCHs and by the FCA as Recognised Investment Exchanges (RIEs).
- The FCA also inherited the FSA's responsibilities for the regulatory oversight of client assets and countering financial crime.
- The FCA also inherited the FSA's responsibilities for certain institutions operating outside the FSMA regulatory perimeter, including:

- E-money firms;
- Payment service providers; and
- Mutual societies.

The current framework separates the responsibility for prudential and conduct of business regulation for systemically important firms. The PRA is responsible for prudential supervision of banks, insurers and large investment firms and the FCA is responsible for conduct regulation of these firms. This separation of responsibilities is known as the 'twin peaks' approach to regulation. Of course, many fundamental principles of regulation are common to the PRA and FCA.

The Financial Services Act sets out the power of HM Treasury to place the boundary between the PRA and FCA and the power of the PRA to require the FCA not to take a specific action in closely defined circumstances. Both regulators must consult each other, other regulators, appropriate panels and the public on specific issues. There are a series of memoranda of understanding between the PRA, FCA, the BoE and the Treasury, dealing with general co-operation and specific issues such as crisis management.

The FCA uses its general rule-making and supervisory toolkit to promote transparency in the provision of services, removing barriers to entry, or to take other action in pursuit of its competition duty. It also has a specific new competition power to require the Competition and Markets Authority to consider whether structural barriers or other features of the market are creating competitive inefficiencies in specific markets.

The FCA takes a more proactive approach to dealing with the conduct of financial firms, and has a lower risk threshold for potential consumer detriment. This follows numerous mis-selling scandals whereby financial firms – and banks in particular – have sold inappropriate products to consumers, from endowment policies to payment protection insurance. In this regard, the FCA has been given powers to intervene to impose requirements on (or even to ban) products, the ability to disclose the commencement of formal enforcement action against a firm, and a strengthening of the FCA's ability to tackle misleading financial promotions. The product intervention rules are covered in more detail later in this chapter.

The FCA has the power to ban misleading financial promotions, which means it can remove promotions immediately from the market or prevent them from being used in the first place without going through the enforcement process.

From April 2014, the FCA took over supervision of some new activities from the Office of Fair Trading:

- Lending or brokering credit, whether or not secured on land.
- Being a credit reference agency or providing credit information services.

- Debt collection and debt administration services.
- Carrying out activities in relation to contracts for the hire of goods.

Key changes include:

- The two separate activities of 'credit brokerage' (introducing individuals to businesses that are lenders or other credit brokers) and 'credit intermediation' (certain other activities to arrange a loan) are combined into a single 'credit brokering' activity, for which businesses will need to be authorised.
- A new activity of 'providing credit references' will replace the current activity of operating a credit reference agency. However, only where this is a firm's main business is it likely to meet the criteria which would mean that it is required to hold permission for the activity.
- A firm will be categorised based on certain criteria, such as its size, number of customers and the perceived risk to consumers. The category a firm is placed in will determine the way it is supervised by the FCA and the intensity of this supervision.

The Prudential Regulation Authority

The PRA is a subsidiary of the BoE that conducts prudential regulation of firms that manage significant balance sheet risk as a core part of their business – such as banks, insurers and the larger, more complex investment firms. The PRA's core objective is to promote the safety and soundness of the firms it regulates.

The PRA's approach combines regulatory policy – relating to both firm resilience (e.g. capital, liquidity and leverage) and to resolution of firms when they fail – with the application of that policy through effective and, where necessary, intensive supervision. The PRA's approach to supervision is judgment-led. The nature and intensity of supervision depends on the risks posed by each firm. While every firm is subject to a baseline level of supervision to promote and support their soundness and resilience, supervisory efforts and resources will focus particularly on 'big picture' issues with potential systemic impact.

In contrast to the light touch regulation of the past, the PRA seeks to challenge where appropriate. Supervision is undertaken by senior, expert teams, whose role is to make forward-looking judgments about these issues and, where necessary, decide on the appropriate intervention. In carrying out this function, the PRA's supervisors co-ordinate with other authorities, such as the FCA, but also those in other jurisdictions where the most complex, multinational firms operate.

The Financial Policy Committee

One of the main failings of the previous regulatory framework was the lack of a single body with responsibility for monitoring the stability of the whole financial system. The FPC aims to fill this gap, ensuring that a single body, situated within the BoE, has the expertise to monitor the financial system and identify risks to its stability; the authority to make recommendations and offer advice to institutions responsible for day-to-day oversight and policy; and the power to intervene to ensure appropriate action is taken to ensure stability where needed.

The FPC is a committee of the Court of the BoE, made up of the Governor (as Chair) and three Deputy Governors, two BoE executive directors, the Chief Executive of the FCA, four external members and a non-voting Treasury representative. The FPC's role is to contribute to the BoE's financial stability objective by identifying and monitoring systemic risks and taking action to address them. The government requires the FPC to take economic growth into account in pursuing financial stability, recognising that stability is generally an important enabler of growth.

In order to create a transparent and accountable body, the FPC must publish two financial stability reports each year and a record of its meetings. The FPC is responsible for periodic monitoring of risks to financial stability, meeting at least quarterly. Where it identifies risks, it can offer advice and recommendations to bodies with responsibilities in relation to oversight of the financial system – not only the regulators, but also the Treasury and other relevant bodies, such as the Financial Reporting Council. It has formal powers of direction over the PRA and FCA, where such powers have been granted by the Treasury in the form of a specific macroprudential tool.

Dual-regulated firms

The FCA and PRA have separate authorisation functions, but have a single administrative process for dual-regulated firms. Firms that are dual-regulated apply to the PRA unless directed otherwise. Applications from dual-regulated firms are considered by both the FCA and the PRA and follow one of two processes:

1. Consent: When a firm applies to the PRA for authorisation or voluntary variation of permission or approved persons, the role of the FCA can give or refuse consent to the PRA. If the FCA does not give consent, the PRA must refuse the application. Of course, the FCA's focus in the authorisation process is on the issues that have conduct implications. The PRA focuses on the financial soundness of the firm.

2. Consult: When a firm applies for a change in control, a waiver which is materially important to the FCA's objectives, passporting, transfer of insurance business or cancellation of permission, the PRA must consult the FCA. The PRA must consider the response of the FCA but is not bound by it.

Both regulators have their own threshold conditions that are used to assess authorisation. The FCA threshold conditions are set out in section 3 of this chapter. The PRA threshold conditions, in broad terms require firms to have an appropriate amount and quality of capital and liquidity, to have appropriate resources to measure, monitor and manage risk, to be fit and proper, and to conduct their business prudently. Dual-regulated firms must meet both sets of threshold conditions.

In relation to the approved persons regime the significant influence functions are split between the PRA and FCA in the following way.

PRA SIGNIFICANT INFLUENCE FUNCTIONS		FCA SIGNIFICANT INFLUENCE FUNCTIONS	
PRA GOVERNING FUNCTIONS		**FCA GOVERNING FUNCTIONS**	
		CF1	Director
CF2	PRA Non-executive director (PRA)*	CF2	FCA Non-executive director (FCA)*
CF3	Chief executive	CF4	Partner
		CF5	Director of an unincorporated association
		CF6	Small friendly society
PRA REQUIRED FUNCTIONS		**FCA REQUIRED FUNCTIONS**	
CF12	Actuarial	CF8	Apportionment and oversight
CF12A	With-profits actuary	CF10	Compliance oversight
CF12B	Lloyd's actuary	CF10a	Client assets
CF28	Systems and controls	CF11	Money laundering reporting
		Significant management function	
		CF29	Significant management
		Customer functions	
		CF30	Customer function

* New controlled function

Even where an individual carries on both PRA and FCA significant influence functions (SIFs), an application needs to only be made to the PRA, and not to the FCA, under specified circumstances (effectively where two functions overlap). For example, where the chief executive of a firm (controlled function CF3) is also carrying out the apportionment and oversight function (CF8) they need to apply to the PRA.

In relation to enforcement, before taking action against dual-regulated firms, the FCA consults with the PRA. If an issue is relevant to both regulators, they decide whether it is best for them to pursue a joint investigation or for one of them to act on their own, keeping the other informed during the investigation. In limited circumstances, there may be separate but co-ordinated investigations.

2. THE PAYMENTS SYSTEMS REGULATOR

The Payment Systems Regulator (PSR) is the new economic regulator for the payment systems industry in the UK. It was established in April 2015 and is a subsidiary of the FCA. The PSR adopts a utility-style approach, distinctive from the FCA's existing remit. The PSR regulates systems designated by HM Treasury, which are:

- BACS;
- Cheque and Credit Clearing Company;
- CHAPS;
- Faster Payments Service (FPS);
- LINK;
- MasterCard; and
- Visa Europe.

Payment systems that are embedded in securities trading systems, clearing houses or central counterparties are excluded from the scope of PSR regulation, as is the Bank of England in its role as payments provider and operator of the real-time gross settlement infrastructure. The Bank of England is responsible for supervising financial market infrastructures (FMIs) as part of its remit to ensure financial stability – see section 4 of this chapter.

The statutory objectives of the PSR are:

- to ensure that payment systems are operated and developed in a way that considers and promotes the interests of all the businesses and consumers that use them;
- to promote effective competition in the markets for payment systems and services – between operators, payment system participants and infrastructure providers; and
- to promote the development of and innovation in payment systems, in particular the infrastructure used to operate those systems.

3. THE COMPETITION AND MARKETS AUTHORITY AND THE DEPARTMENT FOR BUSINESS, INNOVATION AND SKILLS

The majority of acquisitions in the UK involve the change of ownership of small, private companies. Such transactions are rarely of concern to either the official bodies responsible for competition policy or the securities markets regulators. These bodies tend to be concerned with takeovers of publicly quoted companies, which, although less frequent, are typically much larger and have on occasion been thought to involve issues affecting the public interest.

Merger policy in the UK comes largely from the Competition Act 1998 and the Enterprise Act 2002. The Competition Act established the Competition Commission, and the Enterprise Act established the Office of Fair Trading (OFT). From 1 April 2014, the Competition Commission and the OFT closed and their main functions were passed to a new body, the Competition and Markets Authority (CMA).

The CMA was established under the Enterprise and Regulatory Reform Act 2013. The framework of control of mergers in the UK involves the CMA acting as an independent competition authority. Only in exceptional cases – where there are public interest issues – will the Secretary of State at the Department for Business, Innovation and Skills intervene and take decisions in place of the CMA.

National security is the only currently defined public interest consideration. The CMA has a duty to investigate all mergers which meet the 'turnover test' or the 'share of supply test'. The turnover test is met if the target company has a UK turnover of £70m or more. The share of supply test is met if the merging parties will together supply at least 25% of goods or services of a particular description either in the UK as a whole or in a substantial part. The CMA has up to 40 days to undertake an initial (phase one) study of a merger. If the CMA believes the merger will lead to a 'substantial lessening of competition', then it will normally move to a phase two investigation.

If the phase two investigation finds that the merger will substantially reduce competition, the CMA has the power to either prohibit the merger or impose remedies if the merger has taken place.

4. THE PANEL ON TAKEOVERS AND MERGERS

The other main organisation relevant to the takeover process in the UK is the Panel on Takeovers and Mergers (the Takeover Panel), which is responsible for operating and enforcing the City Code on Takeovers and Mergers (the Takeover Code).

The Takeover Panel is partly financed by a levy on share transactions, and its rules apply to all publicly quoted companies. The levy (known as the PTM levy) is payable on trades in securities of companies which are incorporated in the UK, the Channel Islands or the Isle of Man and whose shares are admitted to trading on a UK regulated market or MTF. The current levy rate is 100p per contract where the total consideration of the relevant trade is greater than £10,000 (or the equivalent in any other currency). The PTM levy is payable on trades in:

- Equity share capital, whether voting or non-voting. For these purposes, equity share capital is share capital that has an unlimited right to participate in the profits of the company.
- Securities convertible into equity share capital.
- Transferable securities that give the holder the right to subscribe for equity share capital, including warrants, provisional allotment letters and nil paid rights.

- American depository receipts and global depository receipts in respect of any of the securities described above.

The PTM levy is not payable on trades in:

- covered warrants;
- debentures and other debt securities;
- preference shares;
- permanent interest bearing securities;
- contracts for differences and total return swaps;
- spread bets; or
- option contracts.

Additional funding for the Takeover Panel comes from charging fees relating to things such as offer documents. The role of the Panel is to act as the referee of the fair conduct of takeover bids, and in particular to ensure that all shareholders involved in a bid are treated fairly. It does not consider the broad questions of competition policy and the public interest.

The Takeover Panel has a statutory role and hence the takeover code has statutory force. The statutory basis for the Takeover Panel is set out by the Companies Act 2006. The need for companies, and particularly their advisers, to gain continued access to the facilities of the financial markets ensures that major firms would not contemplate public defiance of the rules of the Takeover Panel. However, this does not provide any protection against concealed breaches of the rules.

The Takeover Code regulates the conduct of bids and restricts the actions of predator companies, target companies and third parties. It aims to provide protection for shareholders and to allow a reasonable period in which a bid may be considered. Its flexibility has ensured that the UK has not experienced the proliferation of defensive measures that has occurred in the US. Despite this, the code has its drawbacks. Once a takeover has actually occurred, the Panel is unable to impose sanctions retrospectively, and it is argued that this limits the Panel's effectiveness.

As a referee, the Panel is careful not to favour either the offeror or the offeree, but by applying the principle of fairness to shareholders it does constrain what each can do. A fundamental principle is that there should be equal treatment of all shareholders in a particular class; therefore, any bidder who acquires 30% or more of the voting rights of company is required to make a cash offer to all other shareholders at the highest price they paid in the previous year. Any offer must remain open for a minimum period of 21 days after its initial posting. If the bidder's stake in a company reaches 50%, the company is required to keep the offer open for acceptance by the remaining shareholders.

A shareholder may therefore decide whether to accept a bid or not on merits, without risking loss because other shareholders have chosen to sell. However, if the predator company reaches a position where it owns a 90% or more stake of the target company, the predator company can force the minority shareholders to sell their shares. A further requirement of the Code is that the management of a target company should not deny shareholders the opportunity of considering a bid for the company.

5. THE INFORMATION COMMISSIONER'S OFFICE

The Data Protection Act 1998 (DPA) requires anyone who handles personal information (to fall within the scope of the DPA the information must be about a living person) to comply with eight principles, and gives rights to individuals over their personal information. The eight principles are to ensure that personal information is:

- Fairly and lawfully processed.
- Processed for limited purposes.
- Adequate, relevant and not excessive.
- Accurate and up to date.
- Not kept for longer than is necessary.
- Processed in line with an individual's rights.
- Secure.
- Not transferred to other countries without adequate protection.

Under the DPA, anyone handling personal information (a data controller) must notify the Information Commissioner's Office (ICO), unless they are exempt. Failure to notify is a criminal offence. Certain details must be provided, which the ICO uses to compile the Public Register of Data Controllers.

The DPA allows individuals to make a written request for access to information being held about them by a firm/organisation. This is referred to as a subject access request. The individual may be charged a maximum of £10 for access to their records (£2 in the case of credit reference agency records). This request is submitted to the firm/organisation, which must normally respond to it within 40 days.

If the ICO considers that a data controller is in breach of any of the data protection principles, the ICO can serve an enforcement notice. If the data controller fails to comply with the enforcement notice, they are committing an offence and can be fined up to £500,000.

6. THE FINANCIAL SERVICES AND MARKETS ACT 2000

Before the passing of the Financial Services Act 2012, the FSMA provided the main framework for the regulation of investment business in the UK. The Financial Services Act substantially modifies many of the provisions of the FSMA. Anyone who undertakes investment business in the UK is required to be an authorised person or an exempt person (exempt from the provisions of the FSMA). A 'person' includes both a legal person, e.g. a body corporate, and an individual.

There are two main kinds of authorised person: a person who is authorised because of a Part 4A permission, and a person who qualifies for authorisation. The former must apply to the FCA (unless they are a systemically important firm that must by authorised by the PRA) under Part 4A of FSMA. The requirements for authorisation under Part 4A, along with the continuing relationship between the FCA (and PRA where appropriate) and the authorised firm, are described in chapter 3, section 3. The latter will be a person from another EEA state who is authorised in their home state but who is able to carry on investment business in the UK under the MiFID, AIFMD and UCITS Directives. This is often referred to as 'passporting'.

There are three main factors that determine whether a particular kind of investment business requires authorisation:

- Whether the investments come within the scope of the system of regulation.
- Whether the activity carried out in relation to those investments is regulated.
- Whether any exemption is available.

Both investments and activities that are regulated are defined in the Regulated Activities Order 2001 (as amended), made by the Treasury.

7. SPECIFIED INVESTMENTS

In general terms, regulated investments include all investment instruments and rights to those instruments, but exclude physical assets. Therefore, assets that are not covered include land, antiques and commodities. Provision of credit is also currently regulated by the FCA, as well as regulated mortgages. This will extend in 2016 to other forms of lending where the dwelling is not intended to be the residence of the borrower, such as buy to let.

The following list summarises the specified regulated investments:

- Deposits.
- Electronic money.

- Rights under a contract of insurance – both general and life policies.
- Shares in companies.
- Debt instruments – both public and private issues.
- Alternative finance investment bonds – sharia compliant debt instruments.
- Warrants, i.e. instruments that confer a right to subscribe to shares, debentures or government securities.
- Certificates representing securities, e.g. depository receipts.
- Units – units in collective investment schemes, which include both unit trusts and shares in open ended investment companies (OEICs).
- Rights under a pension scheme – both stakeholder and personal pension schemes.
- Greenhouse gas emissions allowances.
- Options, futures and contracts for differences – applies to contracts for investment purposes, but does not apply where the contracts are used for risk management.
- Lloyds investments.
- Rights under a funeral plan.
- Rights under a regulated mortgage contract.
- Rights under a home reversion plan.
- Rights under a home purchase plan.
- Rights under a regulated sale and rent-back agreement.
- Rights under a credit agreement or consumer hire agreement.

8. REGULATED ACTIVITIES

There are several regulated activities specified in the Regulated Activities Order 2001 (as amended). Authorisation (or exemption) is required if the activity is carried out in relation to one or more of the investments listed above. The regulated activities are as follows:

- Accepting deposits.
- Issuing electronic money.
- Effecting or carrying out contracts of insurance as principal.

- Dealing in investments – this refers to buying, selling, subscribing for or underwriting investments, whether as an agent or principal.
- Arranging deals in investments and arranging a home finance transaction – this refers to the process of matching buyers and sellers and arranging a mortgage or other home finance transaction.
- Managing investments – where a person exercises discretion over investment decisions.
- Operating a multilateral trading facility.
- Safeguarding and administering investments – safeguarding covers acting as a custodian of investments on behalf of another. Administering covers services provided to the owner or manager of investments, such as settlement.
- Sending dematerialised instructions – this relates to the activity of electronic transfer of title to securities set up by the Uncertificated Securities Regulations (1995) currently operated by Euroclear.
- Establishing, operating or winding up a collective investment scheme or a pension scheme (a stakeholder or personal pension scheme) – this includes acting as a trustee of an authorised unit trust and acting as a depository of an OEIC.
- Providing basic advice on stakeholder products.
- Advising on investments, where the advice relates to securities and contractually based investments (i.e. not deposits).
- Advising on regulated mortgages, home reversion plans, home purchase plans and regulated sale and rent back agreements.
- Lloyds activities – certain activities in relation to Lloyds are regulated activities, e.g. managing the underwriting capacity of a Lloyds syndicate.
- Providing funeral plan contracts.
- Entering into and administering a regulated mortgage, home reversion plan, home purchase plan or a regulated sale and rent back agreement.
- Assisting in the administration and performance of a contract of insurance.
- Agreeing to carry on most regulated activities.
- Bidding in emissions auctions.

- Dormant account funds – being a dormant account operator for meeting repayment claims and managing dormant accounts.

9. EXEMPT PERSONS

There are certain categories of persons carrying on regulated activities that do not need authorisation. The most important exempt persons are:

- Appointed representatives of an authorised person.
- Recognised investment exchanges and clearing houses.
- Members of the professions – where a person is a member of a designated professional body (e.g. an accountant or solicitor) and is carrying on certain regulated activities in a manner that is incidental to the normal business of the profession. Where the activity is a distinct and separate business, then authorisation must be obtained from the FCA.
- Members of Lloyds.

10. CONTROLLED ACTIVITIES AND INVESTMENTS AND FINANCIAL PROMOTIONS

A financial promotion is an invitation or inducement to engage in investment activity. 'Investment activity' is defined under section 21 of FSMA as:

- Entering or offering to enter into an agreement, the making or performance of which by either party constitutes a controlled activity; or
- Exercising any rights conferred by a controlled investment to acquire, dispose of, underwrite or convert a controlled investment.

Promotion of controlled activities and controlled investments is prescribed under Schedule 1 to the FSMA 2000 (Financial Promotion) Order 2005 (FPO). This generally relates to invitations or inducements about providing or advising on the following products:

- Stakeholder pensions.
- Personal pensions.
- Investments such as:
  - bonds or gilts;
  - shares/stock in a company;
  - units in collective investment schemes;
  - endowment plans;

- options, futures and contracts for differences;
- individual savings accounts (ISAs);
- stakeholder and non-stakeholder investment child trust funds; and
- funeral plan contracts.

- Cash savings and bank accounts.
- Insurance such as:
  - household and motor;
  - travel;
  - payment protection or critical illness;
  - private medical insurance; and
  - extended warranties (but not general insurance mediation services).
- Most mortgages and other home finance products.

Under section 21 of FSMA, an unauthorised person may not communicate a financial promotion in the UK, in the course of business, unless either:

- its contents are approved for the purposes of section 21 by an authorised person; or
- it is subject to an exemption under the FPO.

11. OFFENCES

Criminal offences under the FSMA (as amended by the Financial Services Act) include:

- A person who is neither an authorised person nor (in relation to the regulated activity in question) an exempt person is guilty of an offence if they describe themselves as authorised or exempt.
- Misleading a market or investors by making a misleading or dishonest statement of promise.

The Financial Services Act also makes it an offence to make false or misleading statements. There is also an additional offence of knowingly or recklessly creating a false impression for the purpose of (or with the knowledge that it is likely to lead to) personal gain, or the purpose of causing (or with the knowledge it is likely to lead to) a loss to another person (or exposing that person to risk of loss).

The Financial Services Act also introduces a new offence in respect of misleading statements and impressions in relation to benchmarks. Under section 91 of the Financial Services Act, a person will commit an offence who either:

1. Makes to another person a false or misleading statement if they:
    - make the statement in the course of arrangements for setting of a relevant benchmark;
    - intend that the statement should be used for the purpose of the setting of a relevant benchmark; and
    - know that the statement is false or misleading or is reckless as to whether it is.
2. Does any act or engages in any course of conduct which creates a false or misleading impression as to the price or value of any investment or as to the interest rate appropriate to any transaction if:
    - they intend to create the impression;
    - the impression may affect the setting of a relevant benchmark;
    - they know that the impression is false or misleading or is reckless as to whether it is; or
    - they know that the impression may affect the setting of a relevant benchmark.

This new offence in relation to benchmarks is intended to prevent further manipulation of benchmarks, like the manipulation of LIBOR. This new offence puts into practice the recommendation of the Wheatley Commission.

The FCA will have the lead role in investigating and prosecuting these offences. A person guilty of an offence under the Financial Services Act will be liable to imprisonment for a term up to seven years, or a fine, or both.

12. THE FCA'S RULES REGARDING SENIOR MANAGEMENT ARRANGEMENTS, SYSTEMS AND CONTROLS

The purposes of Senior Management Arrangement, Systems and Controls (SYSC) are:

- To encourage firms' directors and senior managers to take appropriate practical responsibility for their firms' arrangements on matters likely to be of interest to the FCA because they impinge on the FCA's functions under the FSMA.
- To increase certainty by amplifying Principle 3 (of the Principles for Businesses – discussed in section 3 of this chapter), under which a firm must take reasonable care to organise and control its affairs responsibly and effectively, with adequate risk management systems.

- To encourage firms to vest responsibility for effective and responsible organisation in specific directors and senior managers.

- To create a common platform of organisational and systems and controls requirements for firms subject to the Capital Requirements Directive (CRD) and/or MiFID.

The CRD implemented the upgraded Basel Accord in the EU. It affects banks and building societies and certain types of investment firms. It lays down minimum capital requirements that firms have to meet for credit, market and operational risk. It came into force on 1 January 2007.

Common platform

The common platform is a unified set of organisational requirements in chapters 4–10 of SYSC which applies to all firms except insurers, managing agents and the Society of Lloyds. These are high level rules rather than detailed rules and guidance, and are in line with the move towards more principles-based regulation. Chapters 2–3 of SYSC do not apply to common platform firms, but apply to all authorised firms that fall outside the scope of the common platform. Very few firms are now outside the scope of the common platform.

SYSC 4: General organisation of the firm

The provisions of this chapter of SYSC relate to:

- A firm's governance, internal controls and organisation, accounting controls and audit committee. Firms must have a clear organisational structure with well defined and consistent lines of responsibility and effective processes to identify, manage and report risks. They must also have sound accounting procedures.

- A firm's business continuity. A firm must have an adequate business continuity policy to limit losses, preserve data and maintain or resume activities.

- The persons controlling a firm. At least two persons should manage a firm, and these persons must be experienced and of good repute.

- Senior management responsibility. Senior personnel are responsible for ensuring compliance with regulatory obligations and must receive frequent reports on actions taken to address deficiencies.

SYSC 5: Employees, agents and other relevant persons

The provisions of this chapter of SYSC relate to:

- Skills, knowledge and expertise.

- Segregation of duties.

- Awareness of procedures.
- General requirements.

SYSC 6: Compliance, internal audit and financial crime

A firm is required to establish and maintain policies and procedures aimed at ensuring effective compliance with regulations. A firm must also appoint a compliance officer who is responsible for the compliance oversight function. This person is required to report to the governing body of the firm in respect of that responsibility.

A firm should maintain effective and proportionate systems and controls to identify, assess, monitor and manage money laundering risk. Money laundering risk is the risk that a firm may be used to further money laundering. The FCA, when considering whether a firm has breached these rules, will check whether a firm has followed the guidance issued by the Joint Money Laundering Steering Group – see section 7 of this chapter. A firm should ensure that the systems and controls include:

- Appropriate training for its employees in relation to money laundering.
- Appropriate provision of information to its governing body and senior management (including a report, at least annually, from the firm's money laundering reporting officer).
- Appropriate documentation of its risk management policies and risk profile in relation to money laundering.
- Appropriate measures to ensure that money laundering risk is taken into account in its day-to-day operations (e.g. in taking on new customers).
- Appropriate measures to ensure that procedures for identification of new customers do not unreasonably deny access to its services to potential customers.

A firm must appoint a director or senior manager to have overall responsibility for anti-money laundering systems and controls. A firm must also appoint a money laundering reporting officer (who may be the same person) to act as the focal point for activities relating to anti-money laundering.

SYSC 7: Risk control

Firms are required to establish and maintain adequate risk management policies and procedures which identify and set the tolerable level of risk. They must also document the organisation and responsibilities of the risk assessment function.

SYSC 8: Outsourcing

Essentially, these provisions require firms that outsource critical or important operational functions to retain responsibility for discharging their responsibilities under the regulatory system. In particular, a firm's senior managers must not delegate their responsibilities.

SYSC 9: Record keeping

A firm must arrange for orderly records to be kept of its business and internal organisation, including all services and transactions undertaken by it, which must be sufficient to enable the FCA to monitor the firm's compliance with the requirements under the regulatory system, and in particular to ascertain that the firm has complied with all obligations with respect to clients.

A firm must retain all records kept in relation to its MiFID business for a period of at least five years.

SYSC 10: Conflicts of interest

The essential elements of SYSC 10 are:

- Taking all reasonable steps to identify conflicts of interest.
- Maintaining and operating effective organisational and administrative arrangements to prevent conflicts of interest resulting in a material risk of damage to clients' interests.
- Disclosing conflicts where there remains a risk of damage to clients' interests.

A common platform firm must establish, implement and maintain an effective conflicts of interest policy that is set out in writing and is appropriate to the size and organisation of the firm and the nature, scale and complexity of its business.

SYSC 11–17

These chapters of the SYSC set out the risk management and prudential requirements relating to banks and insurance companies, and cover risk management systems for liquidity risk, operational risk, group risk, credit risk, market risk, insurance risk and prudential requirements.

SYSC 18: Whistleblowing

The Public Interest Disclosure Act 1998 (PIDA), as amended, establishes a framework for the protection of employees in cases of whistleblowing. The FCA is a prescribed person to whom disclosures of wrongdoing by firms can be made under PIDA. The FCA encourages firms to consider adopting internal procedures to encourage employees with concerns to blow the whistle internally about matters that are relevant to the FCA. Firms are also warned that if they are found to be acting to the detriment of an employee who has made a protected disclosure, this will call into question the fitness and propriety of the firm or its staff.

Following recommendations in June 2013 by the Parliamentary Commission on Banking Standards, the FCA and PRA have published proposals for formal whistleblowing procedures. The proposals will apply to UK banks, building societies, larger credit unions, PRA-designated investment firms and insurers.

The regulators propose that relevant firms should:

- Have internal whistleblowing arrangements in place and inform their UK-based employees about these arrangements. While the actual arrangements are largely left to the discretion of the firms themselves, the regulators propose that firms should:
  - have written whistleblowing procedures in place;
  - respect whistleblowers' confidentiality;
  - assess and escalate whistleblowers' reports appropriately, including where necessary informing the regulators and/or other law enforcement agencies;
  - track the outcome of the whistleblowing report and the whistleblower themselves; and
  - take all reasonable steps to ensure no-one in the relevant firm's control victimises whistleblowers.
- Inform their UK-based employees that they can blow the whistle to the FCA or the PRA (employees of appointed representatives and tied agents should also be informed of their right to report to the FCA or the PRA).
- Offer protection to all whistleblowers, whatever their relationship with the firm and whatever the topic of their disclosure (this would include contractors, temporary workers and interns).
- Include a provision in new employment contracts and settlement agreements clarifying that nothing in that agreement prevents an employee, or ex-employee, from making a protected disclosure.
- Appoint a 'whistleblowers' champion' – this is a senior individual (a non-executive director who is a senior manager) responsible for:
  - overseeing the effectiveness of the firm's whistleblowing policy;
  - preparing an annual report to the board regarding the operation of the policy; and
  - reporting to the FCA where, in a case before an employment tribunal contested by the firm, the tribunal finds in favour of a whistleblower.

SYSC 19: Remuneration codes

Inappropriate remuneration policies were widely identified as a contributory factor behind the 2008 financial crisis. The FCA introduced remuneration codes to make sure that pay practices do not encourage inappropriate risk taking and that firms do not pay out more than they can afford. The codes apply to around 2,750 firms – including all banks, building societies, large alternative investment fund managers and capital adequacy directive (CAD) investment firms.

The codes apply to senior management, risk takers and staff in control functions, collectively known as 'code staff'. The FCA applies the code taking into account the institution's size, internal organisation and nature and complexity of their activities. The main provisions are:

- At least 40% of a bonus must be deferred over a period of at least three years for all code staff. At least 60% must be deferred for the most senior management or when an individual's bonus is more than £500,000.
- At least 50% of any bonus must be made in shares, share-linked instruments or other equivalent non-cash instruments of the firm (or of the fund for alternative investment fund asset managers). These shares should be subject to an appropriate retention period.
- Firms must not offer guaranteed bonuses of more than one year. Guarantees may only be given in exceptional circumstances to new hires for the first year of service.
- Firms must ensure that their remuneration policy is consistent with and promotes sound and effective risk management.
- Firms must ensure that senior management adopts and periodically reviews the general principles of the remuneration policy and is responsible for overseeing its implementation.
- • Ffirms also need to disclose details of their remuneration policies at least annually.

13. TRUSTEE ACT 2000

The trust deed of a pension fund, charity or other trust fund usually allows for the overall investment policy to be left to the discretion of the trustees, in consultation with investment advisers.

In the case of some older trusts, the trust deed may make no specific statement of investment policy. In the case of these trusts, investment policy used to be laid down in the Trustee Investment Act 1961. This Act restricted trust fund investment to a maximum of 75% of the fund in equities, and did not permit investment in land and property.

The Trustee Investment Act 1961 has been replaced by the Trustee Act 2000, which came into effect in February 2001. The Trustee Act 2000 sweeps away the restrictions imposed by the Trustee Investment Act, and allows a trustee to make any kind of investment, including in land

and property. In exercising the power of investment, a trustee must normally obtain and consider proper advice and have regard to the standard investment criteria. The standard investment criteria are:

- The suitability to the trust of an investment.
- The need to diversify investments insofar as it is appropriate to the circumstances of the trust.

A trustee must also review the investments of the trust, and obtain and consider proper advice about whether the investments should be varied.

The investment provisions of the Trustee Act 2000 do not apply to occupational pension schemes, authorised unit trusts or certain schemes under the Charities Act 1993.

14. PENSION FUNDS

Private occupational pension schemes, approved by HMRC's Pension Schemes Office, have many advantages. For example:

- The employer's contributions will not be taxed as the employee's income and they will be deductible from the employer's taxable profits.
- The employee receives income tax relief on their own contributions.
- The pension fund is exempt from capital gains tax on disposal of investments.
- The pension fund is not subjected to the inheritance tax regime for discretionary trusts involving periodic and exit charges, so no charge will arise on that part of an employee's entitlement that they may take as a capital lump sum.

If they survive until retirement, the employee will either obtain a fixed percentage of their final salary under a defined benefit scheme (e.g. in a 1/60th scheme they will receive a maximum of 1/60th for each year worked, not exceeding 40). With a defined contribution scheme, they will obtain a pension or annuity based on the sum accrued from all the defined contributions made by employer and employee.

A pension fund is normally administered by trustees rather than by the employer. This has the effect of legally separating the scheme's assets from those of the employer, and ensuring that the scheme's benefits may be paid even if the employer goes into liquidation. The general law on trusts introduces various duties of trustees, although these can be modified by the terms of the trust. These duties include the duty to act in the best interests of the beneficiaries without conflicts of interest, and impartially, as between different groups of beneficiaries. These duties are designed to direct the trustees in the exercise of their many discretions, including investment, granting discretionary increases in benefits, winding up, etc.

The effect of these duties could result in the trust assets being managed independently of the employer. Employers have generally used two devices to prevent trust law operating in such a way that they lose control. Firstly, they generally reserve the right to appoint all, or a majority, of the trustees. Secondly, they draft scheme rules so that they have discretion or so that trustees are required to seek the employer's approval prior to the exercise of their discretion. Thus the employer may reserve the right to appoint the trustees' investment advisers or to make investment decisions.

The power of employers over their pension scheme assets was highlighted by the Maxwell affair, where the Mirror Group's pension schemes were rendered insolvent by the fraudulent actions of its controlling shareholder. The government responded to the scandal by appointing the Pension Law Review Committee to report on the whole of the law relating to final salary occupational pension schemes.

The government took up some of the proposals of the Committee, leading to the Pensions Act 1995. In particular, this Act increased the ability of trustees to act independently from the employer. Trustees were given the power (and the duty) to appoint their own actuary, auditor and financial advisers. Trustees were also made responsible, in consultation with the sponsoring company, for producing a statement of investment principles (SIP). The SIP sets out the principles governing how decisions about investments must be made. The SIP must include the scheme's policy on:

- choosing investments;
- the kinds of investments to be held, and the balance between different kinds of investment;
- risk, including how risk is to be measured and managed, and the expected return on investments;
- realising investments;
- the extent the scheme takes account, if at all, of social, environmental or ethical considerations when taking investment decisions; and
- using the rights (including voting rights) attached to investments if the scheme has them.

Before the SIP is drawn up, the trustees must:

- obtain and consider the written advice of a person who is reasonably believed to have the appropriate knowledge and experience of financial matters and investment management; and
- consult with the scheme sponsor.

In this case, 'consultation' means considering the sponsor's views carefully. It does not mean that trustees have to agree with the sponsor or carry out their wishes.

The SIP has to be reviewed every three years or whenever there was a significant change in investment policy. Trustees may appoint investment managers to carry out investment policies, but trustees will be liable for losses resulting from the negligence and criminal acts of such persons, unless the investment manager has been properly appointed and the trustees have taken all reasonable steps to supervise them.

The Pensions Act 2004 introduced a number of developments in relation to occupational pensions, including:

1. The introduction of a new regulatory authority, The Pensions Regulator. Its objectives are:

    - To protect the members of work-based schemes.
    - To reduce the risk of situations arising that could lead to calls for compensation from the Pension Protection Fund (PPF).
    - To promote good administration in the schemes it regulates.

    A work-based pension scheme is any scheme that an employer makes available to employees. This includes all occupational schemes and any stakeholder and personal pension schemes where employees have direct payment arrangements.

2. The introduction of the PPF. Where a sponsoring employer of a defined benefit pension scheme becomes insolvent and the pension scheme is unable to pay its liabilities, the PPF will provide compensation of up to 100% of benefits to existing pensioners and up to 90% of benefits to those who have not yet retired. The PPF is funded by a levy on all defined benefit pension schemes.

3. The introduction of a scheme-specific funding requirement (replacing the minimum funding requirement of the 1995 Act). The scheme funding provisions include requirements for trustees of defined benefit schemes to:

    - Prepare a statement of funding principles specific to the circumstances of each scheme, setting out how the statutory funding objective will be met.
    - Obtain periodic actuarial valuations and actuarial reports.
    - Prepare a schedule of contributions.
    - Put in place a recovery plan where the statutory funding objective is not met.

The statement of funding principles must be reviewed every three years.

The next major development affecting occupational pension schemes came with the Pensions Act 2008, which was implemented in 2012. The Act requires all eligible workers (essentially those between 22 and state retirement age), who were not already in a good quality workplace scheme, to be automatically enrolled into either their employers' pension scheme or a new savings vehicle, which became known as NEST. To encourage participation, employees' pension contributions are supplemented by contributions from employers and tax relief.

Further changes to occupational pensions were introduced in 2015. From 6 April 2015, savings accumulated in a defined contribution pension scheme can be accessed in more flexible ways from age 55. The main options are:

- Lump sum payment – money can be withdrawn directly from the accumulated fund without having to buy an annuity or put the money into drawdown, and 25% of this sum will be tax free. This is called an uncrystallised funds pension lump sum (UFPLS). One or more UFPLS payments can be taken over the retirement period and these can be regular or irregular payments.
- Lifetime annuity – some or all of the accumulated fund can be used to buy an annuity that will be payable until death. This option was previously available and a tax-free lump sum of up to 25% of the fund can still be accessed before the annuity is purchased.
- Flexi-access drawdown – the accumulated fund can be put into a drawdown fund. From 6 April 2015, there are no limits on the amount taken from the drawdown fund each year. A tax-free pension commencement lump sum of up to 25% of a pension pot can also be taken when the fund is put into drawdown. Any drawdown payments are taxed as income.

CHAPTER 3 SECTION 3

THE FINANCIAL CONDUCT AUTHORITY: OBJECTIVES AND HIGH LEVEL STANDARDS

SECTION AIMS

By the end of this section, learners should be able to:

- Explain the role and statutory objectives of the FCA.
- Identify and distinguish between the blocks of the FCA Handbook.
- Identify the FCA's Principles for Businesses (PRIN 2.1.1 and 4) and explain their application and purpose (PRIN 1.1.1 and 2).
- Explain the consequences of breaching the FCA's Principles for Businesses (PRIN 1.1.7 to 9 and DEPP 6.2.14 and 15).
- Explain, in outline, the procedures for authorisation of firms, including knowledge of the threshold conditions and liaison with the PRA where relevant.
- Define an approved person and explain the application and purpose of the Statements of Principle and Code of Practice for Approved Persons (APER).
- Identify the main assessment criteria in the FCA's fit and proper test for approved persons (FIT).
- Explain the application procedure for an approved person (SUP 10A) and how the PRA may also be involved.
- Explain the procedure for an approved person moving within a group and how the PRA may also be involved (SUP 10A).
- Define a controlled function and identify the types of controlled functions defined within the FCA Handbook.
- Explain the regulatory requirements on individual accountability under Banking Reform Act 2013: Senior Managers Regime, Certification Regime, Conduct rules.
- Explain the requirements relating to training and competence (TC 1–3).
- Explain the professionalism requirements that have to be met by retail investment advisers and investment managers (TC 1–3).

1. THE ROLE AND STATUTORY OBJECTIVES OF THE FINANCIAL CONDUCT AUTHORITY

The Financial Services Act 2012 came into effect on 1 April 2013. It created two new regulators, the PRA and the FCA.

The FCA is responsible for regulating conduct in retail and wholesale markets and for the prudential regulation of firms not prudentially regulated by the PRA. Note that the FCA is responsible for the conduct regulation of all financial firms including those regulated by the PRA. The single strategic objective of the FCA is to protect and enhance confidence in the UK financial system. In addition, the FCA has the following operational objectives:

- Securing an appropriate degree of protection for consumers.
- Promoting effective competition in the interests of consumers.
- Protecting and enhancing the integrity of the UK financial system.

2. THE FINANCIAL CONDUCT AUTHORITY HANDBOOK

The FCA is responsible for regulating the conduct of firms that carry out a wide range of business in the retail and wholesale banking, investment, securities and insurance markets. It is also responsible for prudential supervision for most of those firms.

The PRA is responsible for the prudential regulation of deposit taking institutions and insurance companies and systemically important investment firms. Some firms are therefore dual-regulated (FCA and PRA) but most (including investment firms) have the FCA as single regulator.

Previously, the FSA used a single rulebook that regulated the activities of firms. On 1 April 2013, the FSA Handbook was split between the FCA and the PRA to form two Handbooks. Most provisions in the FSA Handbook were incorporated into the PRA's Handbook, the FCA's Handbook, or both, in line with each regulator's set of responsibilities and objectives. Dual-regulated firms need to look to both the PRA and the FCA Handbooks, and FCA-only regulated firms need to look at the FCA Handbook.

The Handbook is separated into several blocks – the blocks relevant for this part of the syllabus are as follows:

Block 1 – High level standards contains the overarching standards expected of authorised persons (firms) and approved persons. The relevant parts are:

i) Principles for businesses (PRIN) sets out the fundamental obligations of all FCA regulated firms under the regulatory system. The FCA's eleven principles are the foundation for the other rules and guidance in the FCA Handbook. Note that not all of the principles are applicable to PRA regulated activity and so the PRA now has eight 'fundamental rules' in place of the principles.

ii) Senior management arrangements, systems and controls (SYSC) focuses on the responsibilities of directors and senior management to ensure the firm has appropriate control, supervision and accountability systems in place, including operational risk systems and controls. SYSC also contains the Remuneration Code and guidance on the whistle blowing requirements in the Public Interest Disclosure Act 1998 (as amended).

iii) Threshold conditions (COND) sets out the minimum statutory conditions which a firm is required to satisfy, and continue to satisfy, in order to be given and to retain authorisation.

iv) Statements of principle and code of practice for approved persons (APER) sets out the standards of behaviour expected from approved persons. The code of practice outlines the behaviour that, in the regulators' opinion, will or will not comply with a statement of principle. This will be affected by the implementation of the senior managers regime in 2016.

v) Fit and proper criteria for approved persons (FIT) sets out the minimum standards for becoming and remaining an approved person. These standards are relevant when a firm submits an application for an employee or other person to become an approved person and for the purposes of assessing the continuing fitness and propriety of approved persons.

vi) Training and competence rules (TC) contains requirements concerning staff competence. TC applies to the initial and ongoing competence of staff and record keeping.

Block 2 sets out the prudential requirements that will affect firms, but is not relevant to the Investment Management Certificate syllabus.

Block 3 – Business standards sets out the requirements that will affect firms on a day-to-day basis. The relevant parts are:

i) Conduct of business rules (COBS) sets out the conduct of business requirements applying to firms carrying out designated investment business.

ii) Code of market conduct (MAR) sets out rules and guidance primarily for the wholesale and professional markets. In particular, it sets out the rules relating to market abuse.

iii) Client assets (CASS) outlines rules and guidance on holding client assets and client money, including requirements for segregation and safe custody of assets, statutory trusts in respect of client money and retrieving information in the event of insolvency.

Block 4 – Regulatory process sets out the operation of the regulators' supervisory and disciplinary functions and contains requirements on firms relating to the supervisory function. The two parts are:

i) Supervision (SUP) deals with supervisory issues and requirements concerning the regulators' relationship with firms, including rules concerning requirement to submit reports to the FCA and its access and that of the firm's external auditor to premises, records and personnel.

ii) Decision procedures and penalties (DEPP) sets out the FCA's decision-making procedures that involve the giving of statutory notices, the FCA's policy in respect of the imposition and amount of penalties, and the conduct of interviews.

Block 5 – Redress deals with the processes for handling complaints and compensation. The relevant parts are:

i) Dispute resolution: complaints (DISP) contains rules and guidance relating to:

- firms' internal handling of complaints about the financial services they provide; and
- the operation of the Financial Ombudsman Service, which aims to ensure that complaints are resolved quickly and with minimum formality.

ii) Compensation scheme (COMP) for compensating consumers either when authorised firms are unable, or likely to be unable, to satisfy claims against them or when those who have assumed responsibility for certain liabilities of authorised firms are unable, or likely to be unable, to satisfy claims against them as the successors. COMP contains rules and guidance governing eligibility under the scheme, the funding of the scheme and its operation.

Block 6 – Specialist sourcebooks contain material relevant to specialist entities with the financial system. The only part relevant to this syllabus is:

i) Collective investment schemes (COLL) provides material for investment companies with variable capital (ICVCs) and authorised unit trusts (AUTs) in relation to:

- the process of authorising them; and
- their constitution and management (including rules and guidance on pricing arrangements, investment powers and on certain information to be provided to investors).

Block 7 – Listing, prospectus and disclosure rules sets out the requirements for issuers listed on, or seeking admission to, the Official List of the UKLA, (TR) rules that apply to a sponsor and a person applying for approval as a sponsor, along with the prospectus (PR) and disclosure document requirements (DTR).

In addition, the FCA publishes a number of regulatory guides, including:

i) Enforcement guide (EG) describes the FCA's approach to using the main enforcement powers given to it under the Financial Services Act 2012.

ii) Perimeter guidance manual (PERG) contains guidance about circumstances in which authorisation is required, or exempt person status is available, including guidance on the activities regulated under the Act and the exclusions that are available.

iii) Financial Crime – a guide for firms which refers to good practice in relation to preventing money laundering, fraud, bribery and corruption.

3. PRINCIPLES FOR BUSINESSES

The principles for businesses are a general statement of the fundamental obligations of firms under the regulatory system. They set out the standards expected from all firms. The principles express the main dimensions of the fit and proper standard set for firms in threshold condition five (Suitability). Being ready, willing and organised to abide by the principles is therefore a critical factor in applications for Part 4A permission. Breaching the principles may call into question whether a Part 4A authorised firm is still fit and proper.

The principles are as follows:

1) Integrity: A firm must conduct its business with integrity.

2) Skill, care and diligence: A firm must conduct its business with due skill, care and diligence.

3) Management and control: A firm must take reasonable care to organise and control its affairs responsibly and effectively, with adequate risk management systems.

4) Financial prudence: A firm must maintain adequate resources.

5) Market practice: A firm must observe proper standards of market conduct.

6) Customers' interests: A firm must pay due regard to the interests of its customers and treat them fairly.

7) Communications with clients: A firm must pay due regard to the information needs of its clients and communicate information to them which is clear, fair and not misleading.

8) Conflicts of interest: A firm must manage conflicts of interest fairly, both between itself and its customers and between a customer and another client (for example, where a firm has a material interest in a transaction, it should either disclose it or disregard it in such a way that it does not disadvantage the customer. An example of a material interest is where a firm recommends a buy order for an investment where the firm holds a long position).

9) Customers: relationship of trust: A firm must take reasonable care to ensure the suitability of its advice and discretionary decisions for any customer who is entitled to rely upon its judgment.

10) A firm must arrange adequate protection for clients' assets when it is responsible for them.

11) A firm must deal with its regulator in an open and co-operative manner, and must disclose to the FCA appropriately anything relating to the firm of which the FCA would reasonably expect notice.

The breach of a principle does not, of itself, enable any person to initiate a court action against an FCA regulated firm, but it will be taken into account by the FCA for purposes of its disciplinary and intervention powers. In determining whether a principle has been breached it is necessary to look to the standard of conduct required by the principle in question. Under each principle, the onus will be on the regulator to show that a firm has been at fault. What constitutes 'fault' varies between different principles. For example under principle 1, the regulator would need to demonstrate a lack of integrity in the conduct of a firm's business. Under principle 2, a firm would be in breach if it was shown to have failed to act with due skill, care and diligence in the conduct of its business. The principles provide a basis on which the FCA may apply to a court for an injunction or restitution order or require a firm to make restitution. However, the principles do not give rise to actions for damages by a private person.

4. APPLYING FOR PERMISSION TO CARRY ON REGULATED ACTIVITIES

As stated, a person wishing to carry on one or more regulated activities needs to be authorised unless they are exempt. A decision tree relating to the question of whether authorisation is required is provided by the FCA, and is reproduced in Figure 3.2 (source: FCA Handbook, Perimeter Guidance (PERG), 2, annex 1).

A UK investment firm will need to apply to the FCA for Part 4A (previously part IV) permission. An applicant for Part 4A permission needs to determine the precise scope of the permission it wishes to apply for in terms of the specified activities and investments involved. The permission granted by the FCA will then specify the activities and investments that the firm is permitted to carry out. The FCA may also specify any limitations in relation to a regulated activity. For example, a limitation may refer to the types of clients a firm is allowed to deal with. The FCA may also impose a requirement in connection with a Part 4A permission. A requirement differs from a limitation, as it is not specific to one particular regulated activity. For example, a firm may be required to submit financial returns more frequently than normal.

Permission is only granted once. If an authorised person wishes to carry on activities in addition to those in their original permission, they will need to apply to the FCA to vary their permission. In order to gain Part 4A permission, an applicant must satisfy the threshold conditions. Threshold conditions (TCs) are effectively the minimum standards for being, and remaining, authorised. The Financial Services and Markets Act 2000 (Threshold Conditions) Order 2013 has changed and re-distributed responsibility for TCs between the FCA and PRA. Some FCA TCs will apply to all firms, including dual-regulated firms. The PRA TCs, however, will apply only to banks, insurance firms and PRA-authorised investment firms.

Note that a dual-regulated firm must apply to the PRA to vary or cancel its Part 4A permission. The PRA may determine an application to vary permission only with the consent of the FCA. An FCA-only regulated firm will have to apply to the FCA to vary or cancel its Part 4A permission except where it seeks to vary its permission to include a PRA-regulated activity, in which case it must apply to the PRA.

FIGURE 3.2: DECISION TREE RELATING TO WHETHER AUTHORISATION IS REQUIRED

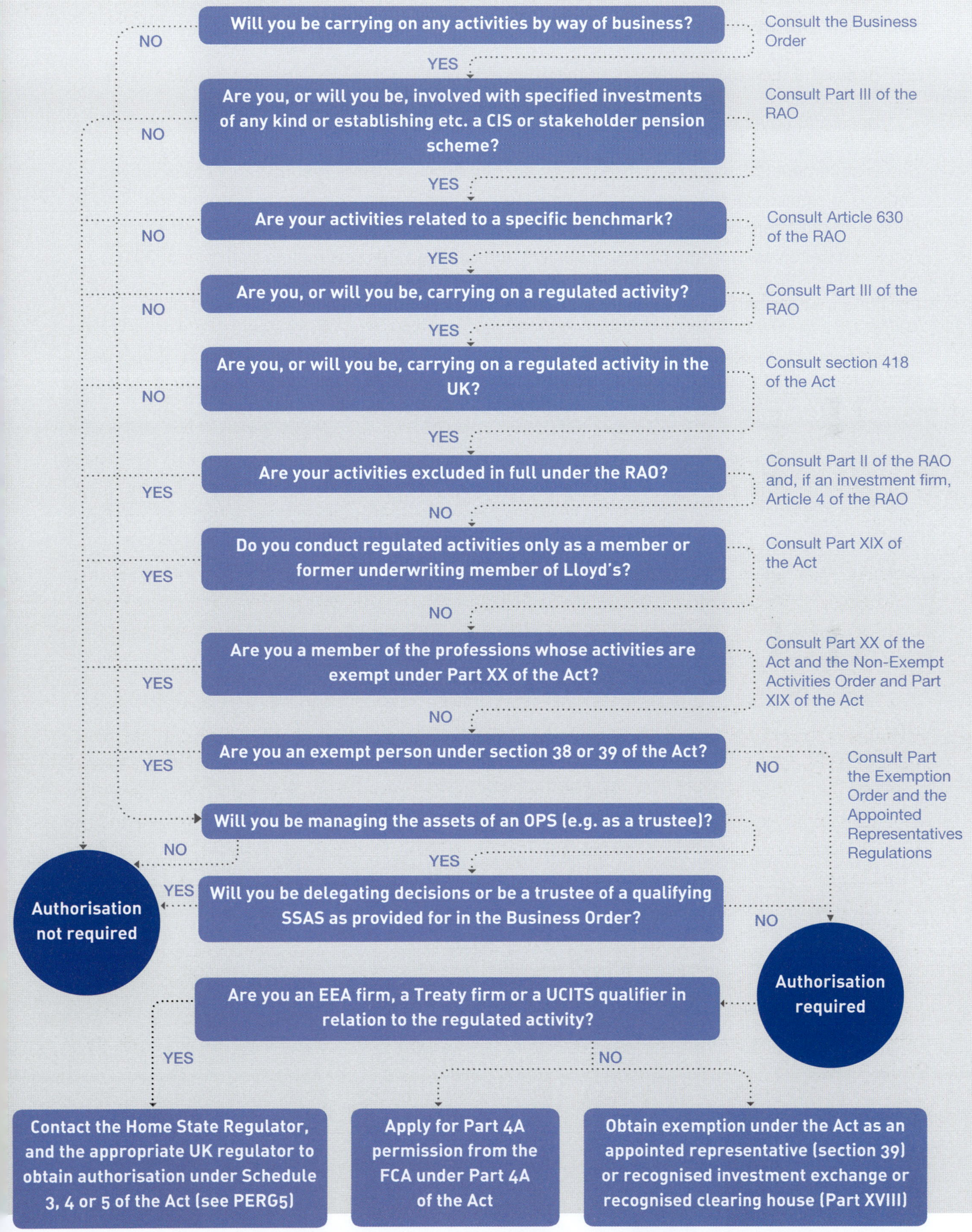

5. APPROVED PERSONS AND CONTROLLED FUNCTIONS

Under the Approved Persons Regime (APER), individuals wishing to perform a controlled function at an authorised UK firm need approval from either the FCA or the PRA. Regulators grant approval to two types of person:

- Those who deal with customers or their property.
- Those that have a significant influence in a financial organisation.

Seven statements of principle, defined by an accompanying code of practice apply to approved persons in significant influence roles but only the first four apply to those in a customer role. Those people granted approval to undertake controlled functions are deemed to be 'approved persons'. APER will be replaced by the Senior Managers and Certified Persons regime from March 2016.

For firms that are only regulated by the FCA there are five categories of controlled functions:

THRESHOLD CONDITION (TC)	DESCRIPTION	APPLICATION OF TC AND REGULATOR RESPONSIBLE	
		FCA FIRMS	DUAL REGULATOR FIRMS
Legal status	If the regulated activity is effecting or carrying out contracts of insurance, the firm must be an incorporated firm (but not a limited liability partnership), a registered friendly society or a member of Lloyd's.	TC does not apply	PRA
Location of offices	A regulated UK firm must have its head office and registered office in the UK or (if not a body corporate) carry on business in the UK.	TC applies	PRA
Effective supervision	Firms will need to ensure that there is no impediment to their effective supervision by virtue of; the nature and complexity of regulated activities undertaken; products offered; and the business organisation.	TC applies	TC applies

Appropriate resources	FCA authorised firms will need to hold resources appropriate to the regulated activities undertaken.	TC applies	TC does not apply
Appropriate non-financial resources	Includes references to the nature and scale of the firm's business, the risks to the continuity of services being provided, the skills and experience of the firm's management, and whether the firm's non-financial resources are sufficient for the firm to comply with requirements imposed by the FCA.	TC does not apply	FCA
Suitability	For FCA regulated firms, the firm's affairs must be conducted in an appropriate manner with regards to the interests of consumers and the integrity of the UK financial system and the need to minimise the extent to which the business carried on by a firm can be used for a purpose connected with financial crime. Also, firms must be generally cooperative in the provision of information to the FCA, and the firm's management must act with probity, in addition to having adequate skills and experience. For PRA firms: contains requirements for firms to comply on a pro-active basis with PRA's requests relating to the provision of information, and that the firm's management act with probity, in addition to having adequate skills and experience.	TC applies	TC applies
Business model	The firm's strategy for doing business must be suitable for its regulated activities.	TC applies	TC applies
Business to be conducted in a prudent manner	Requires firms to have appropriate financial and non-financial resources.	TC does not apply	PRA
Appointment of claims representative	Relates to insurance companies	TC does not apply	TC applies

- Governing functions: chief executive and directors.
- Required functions: apportionment and oversight function, compliance oversight function, money laundering reporting function, etc.
- Systems and control function: the person in a firm responsible for reporting to the governing body in relation to its financial affairs, risk controls and internal systems and controls.
- Significant management function: only relevant to large firms where a significant management function is allocated to a senior manager.
- Customer-dealing functions: the customer functions are giving advice on, dealing and arranging deals in, and managing investments.

All of the functions, except those in the category of customer functions, are classed as significant influence functions. An appointed representative undertaking a controlled function would have to have been granted approved person status.

Two new required functions were introduced in 2013 following the Wheatley review into manipulation of benchmarks such as LIBOR. These functions are CF40 and CF50, which cover submission of benchmarks and administration of benchmarks.

For dual-regulated firms, the significant influence functions are split between the PRA and FCA. This split is designed to minimise the duplication of approvals by the two regulators (although it will not completely eliminate it).

PRA SIGNIFICANT INFLUENCE FUNCTIONS		FCA SIGNIFICANT INFLUENCE FUNCTIONS	
PRA GOVERNING FUNCTIONS		FCA GOVERNING FUNCTIONS	
		CF1	Director
CF2	PRA Non-executive director (PRA)*	CF2	FCA Non-executive director (FCA)*
CF3	Chief executive	CF4	Partner
		CF5	Director of an unincorporated association
		CF6	Small friendly society

PRA REQUIRED FUNCTIONS	FCA REQUIRED FUNCTIONS
CF12 Actuarial	CF8 Apportionment and oversight
CF12A With-profits actuary	CF10 Compliance oversight
CF12B Lloyd's actuary	CF10a Client assets
CF28 Systems and controls	CF11 Money laundering reporting CF40 Benchmark submission CF50 Benchmark administration
	FCA significant management functions
	CF29 Significant management
	FCA customer functions
	CF30 Customer function

Where an individual will carry on both PRA and FCA significant influence functions (SIFs), an application needs only to be made to the PRA, and not to the FCA, under specified circumstances (effectively where two functions overlap).

For example, where the chief executive of a firm (controlled function CF3) is also carrying out the apportionment and oversight function (CF8) they will only need to apply to the PRA. The PRA approval will expand to cover the FCA approval. This arrangement will only apply where the individual is applying for both roles at the same time. Where the person takes on different roles or changes their role they will need to apply to both the PRA and FCA separately.

Where an application is made to the PRA for both a PRA and FCA significant influence function the PRA will need the consent of the FCA before they can grant approval. Either regulator may withdraw approval from a person who is carrying on a SIF in connection with a dual regulated firm, regardless of which regulator granted approval. If withdrawing an approval given by the other regulator, it must consult that regulator first.

The FCA will only grant approved person status if it is satisfied that the individual is fit and proper to undertake the controlled function. In assessing fitness and propriety, the FCA will have regard to a number of factors, including:

- Honesty, integrity and reputation (for example, has the individual been convicted of a criminal offence, has the individual been the subject of any previous disciplinary hearing by the FCA, etc).
- Competence and capability (has the individual satisfied the relevant training and competence requirements).
- Financial soundness (for example, has the person been adjudged bankrupt).

Approval can either be granted or withheld by the regulator. The regulator will not grant conditional approval. The firm must inform the regulator within seven business days if the approved person ceases to perform the controlled function.

The FCA sets out four statements of principle with which all approved persons must comply, and a further three that apply to all approved persons with significant influence functions. These are set out in APER in the FCA Handbook.

These statements of principle are:

1. An approved person must act with integrity in carrying out his controlled function.
2. An approved person must act with due skill, care and diligence in carrying out his controlled function.
3. An approved person must observe proper standards of market conduct in carrying out his controlled function.
4. An approved person must deal with the FCA and with other regulators in an open and co-operative way, and must disclose appropriately any information of which then FCA would reasonably expect notice.
5. An approved person performing a significant influence function must take reasonable steps to ensure that the business of the firm for which he is responsible in his controlled function is organised so that it can be controlled effectively.
6. An approved person carrying out a significant influence function must exercise due skill, care and diligence in managing the business of the firm for which he is responsible in his controlled function.
7. An approved person performing a significant influence function must take reasonable steps to ensure that the business of the firm for which he is responsible in his controlled function complies with the relevant requirements and standards of the regulatory system.

One of the effects of the approved persons regime is that it allows an individual who breaches one or more of the statements of principle, ignoring appropriate arrangements put in place by the firm, to be disciplined without the firm as a whole being disciplined. For example, an individual may mislead a client about the likely performance of an investment by providing inappropriate projections of future investment returns, despite appropriate procedures being put in place by their employer. Each regulator can discipline an approved person who has breached a statement of principle irrespective of whether it has approved the person.

One of the changes to the APER statements of principle introduced by the Financial Services Act 2012 is that they now relate not just to conduct of persons in respect of the controlled functions they perform, but also to any other functions they perform where those functions relate to the firm where they hold their approval carrying on regulated activities.

6. SENIOR MANAGERS AND CERTIFICATION REGIME

From March 2016 the Senior Managers and Certification regime will replace APER. Both the FCA and PRA believe that holding individuals to account is a key component of effective regulation.

The regulators are therefore proposing changes to the way individuals working for UK banks, building societies, credit unions and PRA-designated investment firms are assessed and held accountable for the roles they perform. The new regime will not be applicable to other FCA regulated firms. The changes include:

- A new 'senior managers regime' (SMR) for individuals who are subject to regulatory approval, which will require firms to allocate a range of responsibilities to these individuals and to regularly vet their fitness and propriety. This will focus accountability on a narrower number of senior individuals in a firm than the current APER.

- A certification regime which will require relevant firms to assess the fitness and propriety of certain employees who could pose a risk of significant harm to the firm or any of its customers.

- Conduct rules replacing the statement of principle and approved person code which are applicable to all staff, except a few specific roles such as security, catering and cleaning staff.

The SMR applies to a narrower range of individuals than APER, which it replaces. The scope of the SMR is slightly complicated, as the FCA and PRA have taken different approaches to how important functions and responsibilities are allocated to regulated individuals. There are three main types of responsibility:

- Senior management functions (SMFs), which effectively replace the old significant influence functions, e.g. acting as a chairman or chief financial officer. A person carrying out such a function must be approved by the regulators and subject to the SMR (as was the case with APER).

- Prescribed responsibilities (PRs), which are important functions other than SMFs, each of which must be allocated to one of the existing SMFs 'with which the responsibility is most closely associated' (but not the significant responsibility SMF).

- Key functions, which are important functions other than SMFs and PRs, each of which – if applicable – must be allocated to a significant responsibility SMF.

The regulators have provided exhaustive lists of SMFs, PRs, and key functions.

Senior management functions

SMFs, in certain firms, replace the old APER significant influence functions. SMFs are functions that 'require the person performing it to be responsible for managing one or more aspects of the relevant firm's affairs' which 'involve, or might involve, a risk of serious consequences for the authorised person, or for business or other interests in the UK'. This may include non-executive directors or directors in other group entities that participate in taking decisions for the firm.

The regulators have designated the following functions as SMFs. Both regulators will be able to engage with and take enforcement action against a any senior manager, regardless of which SMF(s) they are approved for.

PRA SMFS		FCA SMFS	
EXECUTIVE	NON-EXECUTIVE	EXECUTIVE	NON-EXECUTIVE
Chief Executive function	Chairman	Executive Director	Non-Executive Director
Chief Finance function	Chair of the Risk Committee	Significant Responsibility Senior Manager	Chair of the Nominations Committee
Chief Risk function	Chair of the Audit Committee	Money Laundering Reporting	
Head of Internal Audit	Chair of the Remuneration Committee	Compliance Oversight	
Head of key business area	Senior Independent Director		
Group Entity Senior Manager			

Prescribed responsibilities

Each of the SMFs is narrowly defined in the rules by reference to its core responsibility. As there are also other important responsibilities at a firm beyond those that fall under the SMFs, the regulators have drawn up a list of PRs and require that each PR is assigned to one of the existing SMFs. The PRA may also require firms to allocate other responsibilities to a specific senior manager.

In order to bring non-board members who are in charge of particular areas of the firm under the SMR, the regulators have created the 'significant responsibility SMF'. The significant responsibility SMF will be responsible for carrying out one or more key functions where these are applicable. To be precise, this SMF will apply to individuals to whom the board has delegated overall responsibility for a key function or identified risk, which does not fall under the definition of another SMF, where they are primarily responsible for reporting to the board about that function or risk. Just as PRs have to be allocated between the different SMFs (other than the significant responsibility SMF), so key functions must be likewise allocated between the significant responsibility SMFs.

Senior managers are subject to approval by the regulators before they may begin carrying out a SMF. The process of applying for approval of a senior manager will remain similar to the current process for applying for approval as a SIF under APER. Individuals may perform more than one SMF, but will require separate approvals for each; they can combine these in a single application, however.

Whether an SMF is an FCA or PRA SMF determines to which regulator the application should be made. Existing arrangements to minimise the need for making applications to both the FCA and PRA will be continued. When applying for an individual to be approved for an SMF, or whenever there is a significant change in a senior manager's responsibilities, a firm will need to submit:

- a statement of responsibility, which is 'a statement setting out the aspects of the affairs of the authorised person concerned which it is intended that the person will be responsible for managing in performing the function',
- a responsibilities map, which sets out how the various responsibilities have been allocated (and to make sure there are no gaps in accountability); and
- other information such as CVs, job descriptions, organisational charts and development plans.

Firms will also be obliged to take reasonable steps to ensure newly-appointed Senior Managers are made aware of all information and risks of regulatory concern.

A regulator will be able to take individual enforcement action against any senior manager, if warranted. There is a new 'presumption of responsibility', whereby, if a firm breaches a regulatory requirement, the senior manager responsible for the area of the breach can be held individually accountable unless they are able to satisfy the regulators that they had taken 'reasonable steps' to stop, prevent, or remedy the breach. In addition, senior managers are subject to a greater number of the new conduct rules than other employees.

Enforcement action, therefore, may now come from three different directions: an individual breach of the conduct rules; being 'knowingly concerned' in a contravention by the firm; or else a contravention of the rules by the area of the firm for which that senior manager is responsible.

Senior managers will also be liable to prosecution for the new criminal offence of taking (or failing to prevent) a decision causing a financial institution to fail, where one is aware of the risks and one's conduct fell 'far below what could reasonably be expected'.

Certification regime

The certification regime (CR) is essentially the level of regulation below the SMR. (The SMR and CR do not overlap: an individual covered by the SMR will not be covered by the CR for work at the same firm.) It applies to a wider range of individuals than APER did, and covers a number of 'significant harm functions' where a person is 'involved in aspects of a firm's affairs (so far as relating to the regulated activity carried on by the firm) that might involve a risk of significant harm to the firm or any of its customers'. Individuals caught by the CR will not be subject to regulatory approval (as SMFs are). Instead, the firm itself will have to certify that they are fit and proper to perform that role, and renew this on an annual basis. The FCA certification regime will apply to:

1) Functions that were previously significant influence functions under APER, but do not fall under SMR.

2) Customer facing roles subject to qualification requirements.

3) Anyone (who is not an SMF) who supervises or manages a certified person.

Where an employee performs multiple CR functions, they must be assessed as fit and proper for each function, although all the different functions may be covered by a single certificate. Neither regulator is proposing to make fundamental changes to the standard of fitness and propriety,

Conduct rules

The FCA and PRA have proposed new conduct rules for banks, building societies, and PRA-authorised investment firms. These will go into a new section of the Handbook: C-CON. The new conduct rules are based on the previous rules for individuals in APER (and also, to a lesser extent, PRIN).

7. TRAINING AND COMPETENCE

There is a requirement that all staff employed in an authorised investment firm are competent. In addition, for those employed for performing certain specified activities that affect retail customers, the firm must ensure:

- The employee has been assessed as competent in that activity.
- The employee is supervised.

Firms should ensure that employees are appropriately supervised at all times. It is expected that the level and intensity of that supervision will be significantly greater in the period before the firm has assessed the employee as competent than afterwards.

A firm should therefore have clear criteria and procedures relating to the specific point at which the employee is assessed as competent, in order to be able to demonstrate when and why a reduced level of supervision may be considered appropriate. At all stages, firms should consider the level of relevant experience of an employee when determining the level of supervision required.

Where a firm permits an employee to give advice on packaged products to retail customers under supervision (having not been assessed as competent), it must ensure that:

- the supervisor has passed an appropriate examination; and
- the employee has an adequate level of knowledge and skill.

Where a firm permits an employee, under supervision, to engage in:

- advising on investments, dealing with or for clients in securities and/or derivatives;
- the activity of a broker fund adviser;
- advising on syndicate participation at Lloyds; and
- the activity of a pension transfer specialist;

The firm must ensure that the employee has passed the appropriate qualification.

Maintaining competence

A firm must review, on a regular and frequent basis, employees' competence and take appropriate action to ensure that they remain competent for their role.

A firm should ensure that maintaining competence for an employee takes into account such matters as:

- Technical knowledge and its application.
- Skills and expertise.
- Changes in the market and to products, legislation and regulation.

8. PROFESSIONALISM REQUIREMENTS FOR RETAIL INVESTMENT ADVISERS

The FSA conducted a review of retail advice in the UK (the retail distribution review – RDR), which resulted in new professionalism requirements for retail investment advisers with the aim of improving trust in the retail investment sector. Advisers must:

- Subscribe to a code of ethics.
- Hold an appropriate qualification, including any qualification gap-fill.

- Carry out at least 35 hours of continuing professional development (CPD) a year.
- Hold a statement of professional standing (SPS) from an accredited body.

These standards will be maintained and enforced by the FCA. Firms will be required to submit data, such as the occurrence of three complaints involving the adviser over any twelve month period, to the FCA about their individual advisers. Accredited bodies will inform the FCA of any advisers who are not meeting the standards required to obtain the SPS.

If existing advisers do not meet these standards, they will not be able to make personal recommendations to retail customers.

Ethical standards

Ethical standards are seen by the FCA as central to achieving its aim of increased professionalism.

The FCA has amended its statements of principle for approved persons (APER) to emphasise personal accountability and how actions affect public perceptions. These statements of principle apply to all approved persons, not just those subject to the RDR. To obtain an SPS, advisers are required to make an annual declaration to their accredited body that they have complied with APER.

Modernised qualifications

The FCA has modernised the qualification requirements to better reflect the actual role of advisers and give them the skills and knowledge to meet the demands of today's investment market. The FCA has listed qualifications that are appropriate for investment advice activities in its Handbook. This list comprises a combination of old qualifications requiring qualification gap-fill, marked (b), and new qualifications that meet the modernised exam standards, marked (a). An adviser must have a qualification marked (a) or (b) in the list of appropriate qualifications.

Keeping knowledge up to date

CPD is seen by the FCA to be as important as modernising qualifications. Advisers will need to complete a minimum of 35 hours of CPD each year for retail investment activities, of which 21 hours should be structured. Structured learning activities include seminars, lectures, conferences, workshops or courses and completing appropriate e-learning.

Accredited bodies

Accredited bodies are responsible for:

- Ensuring that all of the advisers who use their services are subscribing to a code of ethics that is consistent with the statements of principle for approved persons.

- Checking that all of the advisers who use their services hold an appropriate qualification, including verifying 100% of their gap-fill where required.
- Carrying out a random 10% CPD sample check (the body can exceed this requirement if it chooses).
- Recognising CPD activity from a range of providers, including firms' own in-house schemes.

Note that FCA approved person status is the only legal licence to operate as a retail investment adviser in the UK. An accredited body has the role of ensuring that the adviser to retail clients continues to meet the professional standards set out by the FCA.

CHAPTER 3 SECTION 4

REGULATION OF INVESTMENT EXCHANGES

SECTION AIMS

By the end of this section, learners should be able to:

- Explain the role of an investment exchange.
- Explain the need for, and relevance of, investment exchanges to be recognised by the FCA.
- Explain how the Bank of England regulates clearing houses in the UK.
- Identify the recognised investment exchanges and clearing houses in the UK.
- Identify and distinguish the roles of the London Stock Exchange, ICE Futures Europe and ICE Clear Europe.
- Identify the features of trading systems for derivatives.
- Identify the main features of the regulation of derivatives.
- Identify the main features of clearing and settlement for trading on derivatives exchanges, and when trading over-the-counter.
- Explain the arrangements for market transparency and transaction reporting in the main derivative markets.
- Explain the impact of MiFID and International Accounting Standards on the regulation of derivative markets.

The FCA recognises and supervises a number of recognised investment exchanges (RIEs) under the FSMA. Recognition gives an exemption from the need to be authorised to carry on a regulated activity in the UK. To be recognised, RIEs must comply with the recognition requirements laid down in the Financial Services and Markets Act 2000 (Recognition Requirement for Investment Exchanges and Clearing Houses) Regulations 2001. RIEs, in their capacity as market operators, may operate regulated markets and multilateral trading facilities, as respectively defined in the Markets in Financial Instruments Directive (MiFID).

The Financial Services Act 2012 makes the Bank of England responsible for regulating settlement systems and recognised clearing houses (RCHs). The Bank of England is already responsible for the regulation of recognised payments systems under the Banking Act 2009. RCHs and recognised payments systems are collectively referred to as financial market infrastructures (FMIs). Institutions which provide both exchange services and central counterparty clearing services will be regulated by the Bank of England with respect to their activities as an RCH and separately regulated by the FCA.

The FCA has recognised a number of exchanges, including the London Stock Exchange, ICAP Securities and Derivatives Exchange (ISDX), the London Metal Exchange and ICE Futures Europe. The Bank of England has recognised a number of clearing houses including ICE Clear Europe, LME Clear, LCH.Clearnet and CME Clearing Europe. A consequence of this recognised status is that the exchange or clearing house is able to develop its own means of fulfilling its regulatory objectives and obligations, overseen by the FCA or Bank of England as appropriate. A recognised exchange is required to deliver high standards of investor protection and to maintain market integrity. This includes the following:

- Arrangements to ensure performance of transactions.
- Financial resources sufficient for the proper performance of its functions.
- Rules and practices ensuring that business on the exchange is conducted in an orderly manner and affords proper protection to investors.
- Dealings on the exchange should be limited to investments in which there is a proper market, i.e. there should be adequate methods of ensuring price discovery, price transparency and market integrity generally.
- Satisfactory recording of transactions.
- Effective monitoring and enforcement of compliance with rules and clearing arrangements.
- Complaint investigation arrangements.

- Ability and willingness to promote and maintain high standards of integrity and fair dealing, and to co-operate by means such as sharing information with other regulatory bodies (including US regulatory bodies).

- Rules setting out procedures in the event of a default by a member of the exchange.

MiFID introduced various pre- and post-trade transparency requirements on regulated markets and multilateral trading facilities. Pre-trade transparency refers to the obligation to publish (in real time) current orders and quotes (i.e. prices and amounts for selling and buying) relating to securities. For post-trade transparency, the basic requirement is to publish the price, volume and time of the transaction and execution venue. This publication must be as close to real time as possible and no later than three minutes after the transaction took place. It is, however, possible to delay publication for certain transactions that are large compared to normal market size.

The Bank of England focuses its regulation of FMIs (including RCHs) on managing systemic risk, because of their systematic importance. This will include managing the micro-prudential regulation of the risks of the institution, and how problems with one participant can spread to others elsewhere in the system. In regulating FMIs, the Bank of England will expect institutions to meet the principles set out by the European Committee on Payments and Settlement Systems, Technical Committee of the International Organisation of Securities Commissions (known as the CPSS-IOSCO principles) as well as the European Market Infrastructure Regulation (EMIR).

1. THE LONDON STOCK EXCHANGE

The London Stock Exchange is the authority responsible for admitting public companies for listing. Companies can be admitted to the official list if they meet the listing requirements set out by the UK listing authority (UKLA). Companies which do not meet the criteria, but wish to obtain admission to the stock exchange, can apply for admission to the second tier market, AIM. Admission to AIM is subject to lighter requirements than admission to the official list.

The London Stock Exchange is also a recognised investment exchange providing a market in a wide range of securities, including UK and international equities, debt, covered warrants, exchange-traded funds (ETFs), real estate investment trusts (REITs), fixed interest, contracts for difference (CFDs) and depositary receipts.

2. ICE FUTURES EUROPE

ICE Futures Europe (IFE) is a recognised investment exchange where financial futures and options are traded. Trading on IFE takes place using an electronic order matching system. Only IFE members are able to trade and clear contracts. Anyone else wanting a position in an IFE contract must get a member to act on their behalf. A member is responsible for the process of registration, position maintenance (margining) and settlement.

The individuals who execute business on IFE are of two main types: traders and brokers. A trader is acting on their own or on their company's behalf, whereas a broker is acting on somebody else's behalf. Traders who act on their own behalf are known as 'locals'. A trader makes profits from the positions taken in the futures or options contracts, or perhaps in the associated positions taken in the underlying products. A broker makes profit from charging commission on the trading done for others.

3. REGULATION OF DERIVATIVES MARKETS

In the UK, all derivatives exchanges (such as IFE and the London Metal Exchange (LME)) are recognised investment exchanges, and so regulation of the market is largely carried out by the exchange, while the FCA is responsible for regulating the financial soundness and conduct of an exchange member's business. Trading on an exchange or multilateral trading facility (MTF) is subject to the transparency rules set by the exchange. There are currently no requirements for transparency for OTC transactions in derivatives. However, the new requirements for settlement of OTC derivatives include a reporting requirement to a trade depository.

In the US, regulation of derivatives trading is split between the Securities and Exchange Commission (SEC) and the Commodities Futures Trading Commission (CFTC). The main legislation governing derivatives trading in the US are the Commodity Exchange Act 1936 and the Commodity Futures Modernisation Act 2000. Essentially, regulation of securities-based derivatives products was granted to the SEC, which gained sole authority to regulate options on securities, certificates of deposit and stock groups.

The regulation of futures and options on exempted securities (essentially commodities) and broad-based stock indices was left to the CFTC. Regulation of trading of single stock futures and derivatives relating to narrowly based stock indices is the joint responsibility of the SEC and the CFTC. OTC derivatives were not regulated until the passing of the Dodd-Frank Wall Street Reform and Consumer Protection Act in 2010. Title VII of the Dodd-Frank Act divides regulatory authority over swap agreements between the CFTC and SEC. The SEC has regulatory authority over 'security-based swaps', which are defined as swaps based on a single security or loan, or a narrow-based group or index of securities. The CFTC has primary regulatory authority over all other swaps, such as energy and agricultural swaps.

4. CLEARING AND SETTLEMENT ON UK DERIVATIVES MARKETS

In relation to derivatives trading on IFE or the LME, once a trade has been matched it is registered with a clearing house, which becomes the central counterparty to the contract. The clearing house for IFE is ICE Clear Europe and the clearing house for LME is LME Clear. If an IFE member is trading on behalf of a client, then a separate 'back-to-back' contract is established between the member and its client. Thus IFE members act as principals and not agents for their clients. ICE Clear Europe is not counterparty to, and has no involvement with, the member/client relationship.

To hold a position in an IFE/LME future or option, there is an obligation to lodge initial margin at the clearing house. Initial margin is an amount of cash or liquid assets set down by the clearing house that is deemed sufficient to ensure that the customer can satisfy the conditions of the contract should it be required. While initial margins for futures contracts are fixed, initial margins for options can vary according to market conditions. In addition, the positions are revalued on a daily basis and settled to market.

Profits and losses from price changes are paid into a trader's margin account. If a trader's margin level goes below the initial margin requirement, the clearing house will require the account to be topped up to the initial margin level – the additional margin payment is known as 'variation margin'. The clearing house settles margin with the clearing members, who in turn settle with their clients.

A position in an IFE/LME contract undergoes this daily revaluation until delivery or offset. To offset a contract, an equal and opposite position must be entered into, and the clearing house must be notified that it is a closing transaction. At this point, the margin is returned.

5. IMPACT OF MIFID AND INTERNATIONAL ACCOUNTING STANDARDS

MiFID introduced commodity futures into the list of regulated investments. This has brought many of the specialist firms that engage in commodity derivative activity within the scope of MiFID. The remaining firms are oil and energy trading firms that currently qualify for an exemption. These exempted firms are FCA-regulated through specialist rulebooks, which specify the parts of the FCA Handbook of rules apply to them.

The international accounting standard that impacts upon derivatives is IAS 39. Derivatives are contracts such as options, forwards, futures and swaps. They are often entered into at no or very little cost, and therefore prior to IAS 39 were not often recognised in financial statements.

IAS 39 requires derivatives to be measured at fair value, with changes in fair value recognised either in profit or loss or in reserves depending on whether the company uses hedging. Where the derivative is used to offset risk and certain hedging conditions are met, changes in fair value can be recognised separately in reserves (see chapter 10).

Clearing of over-the-counter (OTC) derivatives has now largely moved to central counterparty clearing following the implementation of EMIR (see chapter 3, section 1). This was largely implemented in the UK from 1 April 2013 through the Financial Services and Markets Act 2000 (Over the Counter Derivatives, Central Counterparties and Trade Repositories) Regulations 2013. These regulations impose three new requirements on those who trade OTC derivatives:

1. To clear OTC derivatives, that have been declared subject to the clearing obligation, through a central counterparty (CCP).

2. To put in place certain risk management procedures for OTC derivatives transactions that are not cleared.

3. To report derivatives to a trade repository.

Clearing requirement

A mandatory clearing obligation will apply to contracts between any combination of:

- Financial counterparties which includes banks, insurers, investment firms, fund managers, spread betting firms and pension schemes.
- Non-financial counterparties (NFC) that are above the clearing threshold.

The clearing thresholds are:

- €1bn in gross notional value for OTC credit and equity derivatives (individual thresholds).
- €3bn in gross notional value for interest rate and foreign exchange (individual thresholds).
- €3bn in gross notional value for commodities and others (combined threshold).

Transactions designed to reduce risks to commercial activity or treasury financing activity do not count towards the clearing threshold. Also, when calculating its positions, an NFC must include all contracts entered into by other NFCs within its group.

The European Securities and Markets Authority (ESMA) will decide which classes of OTC derivatives must be cleared. The ESMA will also keep a register that will show, in relation to each class, which CCPs are permitted to clear the derivatives and the date from which the derivatives must be cleared.

The risk management obligation

Both financial and non-financial counterparties that enter into an OTC derivative that is not cleared by a CCP must have appropriate procedures and arrangements to measure, monitor and mitigate the operational and credit risk arising from such contracts.

The reporting requirement

The details of any derivative contract which is concluded, modified or terminated must be reported to a trade repository no later than the following working day. This obligation applies to both financial and non-financial counterparties, and also to all derivatives, regardless of whether they are concluded OTC or are subject to the clearing obligation. A number of trade repositories have been established, including the Depository Trust and Clearing Corporation. ESMA is the regulatory body that recognises trade repositories in Europe.

CHAPTER 3 SECTION 5

FCA BUSINESS STANDARDS

SECTION AIMS

By the end of this section, learners should be able to:

- Explain the purpose of client categorisation.
- Distinguish between a retail client, a professional client and an eligible counterparty (COBS 3.4, 3.5, 3.6).
- Apply the rules relating to treating a client as an elective professional client (COBS 3.5.3).
- Apply the rules relating to treating a client as an elective eligible counterparty (COBS 3.6.4).
- Apply the rules relating to providing clients with a higher level of protection (COBS 3.7).
- Apply the rules relating to client agreements (COBS 8.1).
- Explain the purpose and scope of the financial promotions rules and the exemptions from them (COBS 4.1).
- Explain the fair, clear and not misleading rule (COBS 4.2).
- Explain the rules relating to communications with retail clients (COBS 4.5).
- Explain the rules relating to past, simulated past and future performance (COBS 4.6).
- Explain the rules relating to direct offer promotions (COBS 4.7).
- Explain the rules relating to cold calls and other promotions that are not in writing (COBS 4.8).
- Explain the rules relating to systems and controls in relation to approving and communicating financial promotions (COBS 4.10).
- Explain the record keeping requirements relating to financial promotions (COBS 4.11).
- Explain the rules relating to distance marketing communications (COBS 5.1).
- Explain the rules relating to providing information about the firm and compensation information (COBS 6.1)
- Explain the rules on adviser charging and remuneration (COBS 6.3, 6.4).
- Explain the FCA's approach to temporary product intervention.

- Explain the rules relating to assessing suitability (COBS 9.2).
- Explain the rules relating to assessing appropriateness (COBS 10.2).
- Explain the rules relating to warning a client (COBS 10.3).
- Identify circumstances when assessing appropriateness is not required (COBS 10.4, 10.5, 10.6).
- Identify circumstances when own authority or expertise is limited and there is the need to refer to specialists.
- Distinguish between independent advice and restricted advice (COBS 6.2A).
- Explain the rules relating to best execution (COBS 11.2).
- Explain the rules relating to client order handling (COBS 11.3).
- Explain the rules relating to the use of dealing commission (COBS 11.6).
- Explain the rules on personal account dealing (COBS 11.7).
- Explain the purpose of the principles and rules on conflict of interest, including: identifying, recording and disclosing conflicts of interest and managing them to ensure the fair treatment of clients (PRIN 2.1.1 Principle 8, SYSC 10.1.1–7 and 10.1.8/9 and 10.2).
- Explain the rules relating to investment research produced by a firm and disseminated to clients (COBS 12.2).
- Explain the rules relating to the publication and dissemination of non-independent research (COBS 12.3).
- Explain the disclosure requirements relating to the production and dissemination of research recommendations (COBS 12.4).
- Explain the obligations relating to preparing product information (COBS 13.1 and COLL 4.7).
- Explain the rules relating to the form and content of a key features document and a key investor information document (COBS 13.2, 13.3, 14.2, and COLL 4.7).
- Explain the rules relating to cancellation rights (COBS 15).
- Distinguish between packaged products and retail investment products.
- Apply the rules relating to record keeping for client orders and transactions (COBS 11.5).
- Apply the rules relating to occasional reporting to clients (COBS 16.2).
- Apply the rules relating to periodic reporting to clients (COBS 16.3).

CHAPTER 3 SECTION 5 cont...

FCA BUSINESS STANDARDS

- Explain the rules relating to reporting on the progress of an authorised fund to unitholders (COLL 4.5).
- Explain the concept of fiduciary duty.
- Explain the application and purpose of the rules relating to custody of client assets held in connection with MiFID business (CASS 6.1).
- Explain the rules relating to the protection of clients' assets and having adequate organisational arrangements (CASS 6.2).
- Explain the rules relating to depositing assets with third parties (CASS 6.3).
- Explain the purpose of the rules relating to the use of clients' assets (CASS 6.4).
- Explain the rules relating to records, accounts and reconciliations of clients' assets (CASS 6.5).
- Explain the application and general purpose of the client money rules (CASS 7.10).
- Explain the rules relating to the segregation of client money (CASS 7.13).
- Explain the rules relating to records, accounts and reconciliations of clients' assets (CASS 7.15).
- Explain the rules relating to mandate accounts (CASS 8).

1. ACCEPTING CUSTOMERS FOR BUSINESS

Client categorisation

Before conducting investment business with or for any client, a firm must take reasonable care to establish the client's status. MiFID introduces two main categories of client (retail clients and professional clients, both of which fall within the definition of 'customer'), and a separate and distinct third category of client for a limited range of business (eligible counterparties). Different levels of regulatory protection attach to each category, and hence to clients within each category. The FCA principles, for example, sometimes refer to 'a client' and on other occasions refer to 'customers', in which case the requirement does not extend to eligible counterparties.

This categorisation of clients allows for the tailoring of regulatory requirements according to the knowledge and experience of clients. MiFID provides considerable flexibility to move between categories provided certain criteria are met. Professional clients and retail clients can move between categories either generally, or in relation to one or more particular services or transactions, or one or more types of product or transaction. Also, an eligible counterparty (ECP) can request treatment as a professional or retail client either generally or on a trade-by-trade basis. This movement between categories changes the level of regulatory protection afforded.

- Retail clients are afforded the most regulatory protection.
- Professional clients are considered to be more experienced, knowledgeable and sophisticated and able to assess their own risk, and are afforded fewer regulatory protections.
- ECPs are investment firms, credit institutions, insurance companies, UCITS and their management companies, other regulated financial institutions and, in certain cases, other undertakings. MiFID provides a 'light touch' regulatory regime when investment firms bring about or enter into transactions with ECPs.

A 'per se' professional client is essentially one of the following (unless it is an ECP):

- An entity required to be authorised or regulated to operate in the financial markets, e.g. an investment firm or credit institution.
- In relation to MiFID or equivalent third country business, a large undertaking meeting two of the following size requirements on a company basis:
  - Balance sheet total of €20m.
  - Net turnover of €40m.
  - Own funds of €2m.

- In relation to business that is not MiFID or equivalent third country business, a large undertaking meeting either of the following conditions:
  - A corporate body which has called up share capital of at least £5m.
  - A large undertaking meeting at least two of the following tests:
    (a) a balance sheet total of €12.5m.
    (b) a net turnover of €25m.
    (c) an average number of employees during the year of 250.
- A national or regional government, a public body that issues debt, a central bank, an international or supranational body.
- Another institutional investor whose main activity is to invest in financial instruments (includes entities dedicated to the securitisation of assets or other financing transactions).

A firm may treat a client as an elective professional client if it complies with 1. and 3. below and, where applicable, 2.:

1. The firm undertakes an adequate assessment of the expertise, experience and knowledge of the client that gives reasonable assurance, in light of the nature of the transactions or services envisaged, that the client is capable of making his own investment decisions and of understanding the risks involved (the 'qualitative test').
2. In relation to MiFID or equivalent third country business in the course of that assessment, at least two of the following criteria are satisfied (the 'quantitative test'):
   - The client has carried out transactions, in significant size, on the relevant market at an average frequency of ten per quarter over the previous four quarters.
   - The size of the client's financial instrument portfolio, defined as including cash deposits and financial instruments, exceeds €500,000.
   - The client works or has worked in the financial sector for at least one year in a professional position which requires knowledge of the transactions or services envisaged.
3. The following procedure is followed:
   - The client must state in writing to the firm that it wishes to be treated as a professional client either generally or in respect of a particular service or transaction or type of transaction or product.

- The firm must give the client a clear written warning of the protections and investor compensation rights the client may lose.
- The client must state in writing, in a separate document from the contract, that it is aware of the consequences of losing such protections.

An ECP is a client that is either a per se ECP or is an elective ECP. Article 24 of MiFID permits those investment firms authorised to execute orders on behalf of clients; and/or to deal on their own account; and/or receive and transmit orders to bring about; or enter into transactions with ECPs without complying with certain of the conduct of business obligations in MiFID.

The entities automatically recognised as per se ECP are:

- Investment firms.
- Credit institutions.
- Insurance companies.
- UCITS and their management companies.
- Pension funds and their management companies.
- Other financial institutions authorised and regulated under European Community legislation or the national law of a member state.
- Undertakings exempted from the application of MiFID under Article 2(1)(k) or (l).
- National governments and their corresponding offices, including public bodies that deal with public debt.
- Central banks and supranational institutions.

Note that this 'light touch' ECP regime is limited to specific types of business. These are:

- Executing orders on behalf of clients;
- Dealing on own account; and/or
- Receiving and transmitting orders.

A firm may treat a client as an elective ECP if:

1. The client is an undertaking and:

- is a per se professional client; or
- requests such categorisation and is an elective professional client, but only regarding the services or transactions for which it could be treated as a professional client; and

2. The firm has, in relation to MiFID or equivalent third country business, obtained express confirmation from the prospective counterparty that it agrees to be treated as an eligible counterparty.

Finally, a firm must allow a professional client or an ECP to request re-categorisation as a client that benefits from a higher level of protection. So, for example, a per se professional client may be treated as a retail client, although this does not enable the client to access all aspects of protection – such as the right to complain to the Financial Ombudsman Service.

Client agreements

A firm, before entering into an agreement, or providing any services, relating to designated investment business with a retail client must provide that client with:

- The terms of any such agreement.
- Information about the firm and its services (including information on communication, conflicts of interest and authorised status).

A firm may provide the client with an agreement and the information after the client is bound by the agreement if the agreement was concluded using a means of distance communication.

A firm must keep a record of client agreements for at least whichever is the longer of:

- Five years.
- The duration of the relationship with the client.
- In the case of a pension transfer, opt-out or FSAVC, indefinitely.

2. FINANCIAL PROMOTIONS AND OTHER COMMUNICATIONS WITH CUSTOMERS, INCLUDING INFORMATION ABOUT THE FIRM

A financial promotion is an invitation or inducement to engage in investment activity that is communicated in the course of business.

Section 21 of the Financial Services and Markets Act 2000 imposes a restriction on the communication of financial promotions by unauthorised persons. A person must not, in the course of business, communicate an invitation or inducement to engage in investment activity (a financial promotion) unless:

- the person is an authorised person; or
- the content of the communication is approved by an authorised person.

A financial promotion is not restricted in terms of the media of communication. So the rules on financial promotion apply to printed advertising, radio broadcasts, personal visits, telephone calls, emails, the internet and digital interactive television.

Fair, clear and not misleading communications

Principle 7 for businesses requires firms to ensure that all communication is fair, clear and not misleading. Additionally, Conduct of Business rules for communications, including financial promotions, require clear, fair and not misleading communication and set out a number of requirements for financial promotions. However, the financial promotion rule does not apply to:

- An excluded communication – for example, a 'one-off' promotion that is not a cold call. This exempts correspondence to a specific customer or to one group of customers in the expectation that they would engage in any investment activity jointly.
- Financial promotions communicated only to investment professionals or eligible counterparties. However it should be noted that a communication in relation to designated investment business that is both a communication to a professional client and a financial promotion, will still be subject to the fair, clear and not misleading rule.

In order to achieve compliance with this rule, a firm should ensure that a financial promotion:

- For a product or service that places a client's capital at risk makes this fact clear.
- That quotes a yield figure gives a balanced impression of both the short- and long-term prospects for the investment.
- That promotes an investment or service whose charging structure is complex contains sufficient information, taking into account the needs of the recipients.
- Names the FCA as its regulator.
- That offers packaged products or stakeholder products not produced by the firm gives a fair, clear and not misleading impression of the producer or manager of the underlying investments.

Communication with retail clients

Where a firm communicates with retail clients, except for excluded communications and image advertising, the firm should ensure that the information:

- Includes the name of the firm.
- Is accurate and does not emphasise any potential benefits without also giving a fair and prominent indication of any risks.
- Is sufficient for, and presented in such a way that it is likely to be understood by, the average member of the group it is directed at.
- Does not disguise, diminish or obscure important items, statements or warnings.

Where comparisons are made, these are fair and meaningful and presented in a fair and balanced way. In relation to MiFID or equivalent third country business, the sources or the information used for the comparison must be specified, and key facts and assumptions used to make the comparison must be included.

If any information refers to a particular tax treatment, the firm must ensure that it prominently displays that the tax treatment depends on the individual circumstances of each client and may be subject to change in the future. Where information contains an indication of past performance of a relevant investment or financial index the communication must satisfy the following conditions:

- Past performance cannot be the most prominent feature of the communication.
- The information must include appropriate performance information, which covers at least the immediately preceding five years or the whole period for which the information relates if less than five years. In every case, the performance information must be based on and show complete twelve month periods.
- The reference period and source of information must be clearly stated.
- The information must contain a prominent warning that the figures relate to the past, and that past performance is not a reliable indicator of future results.
- If the indication relies on figures denominated in a currency that is not that of the EEA state the retail client is resident in, the currency must be clearly stated together with a warning that the return may increase or decrease as a result of currency fluctuations.
- If the indication is based on gross performance, the effect of commissions, fees or other charges must be disclosed.

Direct offer financial promotions

A direct offer financial promotion is one that contains:

- an offer by the firm or another person to enter into a controlled agreement with any person who responds to the communication; or

  a) an invitation to any person who responds to the communication to make an offer to the firm or another person to enter into a controlled agreement; and

  b) specifies the manner of response or includes a form by which any response may be made.

In relation to MiFID or equivalent third country business a controlled agreement includes an agreement to carry on an ancillary service.

A firm must ensure that a direct offer financial promotion that is addressed to, or disseminated in such a way that it is likely to be received by, a retail client contains:

a) information referred to in the rules on information disclosure as is relevant to that offer or invitation; and

b) if it does not relate to MiFID or equivalent third country business, additional appropriate information about the relevant business and relevant investments so that the client is reasonably able to understand the nature and risks of the relevant business and relevant investments and consequently to take investment decisions on an informed basis.

This rule does not require the information referred to above to be included in a direct offer financial promotion if, in order to respond to an offer or invitation contained in it, the retail client must refer to another document or documents which contain that information.

Cold calls and other promotions that are not in writing

A cold call is a financial promotion made in the course of a personal visit, telephone conversation or other interactive dialogue, which:

- was not initiated by the recipient of the financial promotion; and
- does not take place in response to an express request from the recipient of the financial promotion; or
- in relation to which it was not clear from all the circumstances when the call, visit or dialogue was initiated or requested, that (during the course of the call, visit or dialogue) communications would be made concerning the kind of investments to which the communications in fact related.

A firm must not make a cold call unless:

- The recipient has an existing client relationship with the firm and the relationship is such that the recipient envisages receiving cold calls; or

- The cold call relates to a generally marketable packaged product that is not:
  - a higher volatility fund;
  - a life policy with a link (or potential link) to a higher volatility fund; or
- The cold call relates to regulated investment business carried on by an authorised firm or exempt person, and involves regulated investments that are readily realisable securities (other than warrants) or generally marketable non-geared packaged products.

Where a firm communicates a non-written financial promotion:

- It should only do so at an appropriate time of day.
- The purpose of the communication, and the firm represented, should be stated at the outset.
- It should clarify whether the client would like to continue or terminate the communication, and should terminate the communication at any time the client requests.
- A contact point should be given, so that any further appointment can be cancelled.

Systems and controls in relation to financial promotions

The rules in SYSC require a firm that communicates with a client in relation to designated investment business, or communicates or approves financial promotions, to put in place adequate systems and controls or policies and procedures. Furthermore, the financial promotion rules contain detailed authorisation and record keeping requirements for financial promotions involving non-mainstream pooled investments.

Before a firm approves a financial promotion for communication by an unauthorised person, it must confirm that the financial promotion complies with the financial promotion rules.

If a firm continues to communicate a financial promotion when the promotion no longer complies with the rules, it will have breached the rules.

Record keeping

A firm must make an adequate record of any financial promotion it communicates or approves. The record must be retained:

- Indefinitely for a pension transfer, opt-out or FSAVC.
- For six years for a life policy, occupational pension scheme, SSAS, personal pension scheme or stakeholder scheme.

- For five years for MiFID or equivalent third country business.
- For three years for other cases.

Distance marketing communications

A firm must provide a consumer with the distance marketing information in good time before the consumer is bound by a distance contract or offer. This information includes:

- Information about the firm.
- Information about the financial service.
- Information about the contract.
- Information about redress.

The information must be presented in a clear and comprehensible manner.

Financial promotions through social media

The FCA published guidance in March 2015 on the use of social media for financial promotions. The underlying principle of the advice is that financial promotions, whether on social media or more traditional media, should be fair, clear and not misleading.

Communications through social media can reach a wide audience very quickly, so firms should take account of that in their decision to promote through social media, and the nature of their promotions. Firms should ensure that their original communication would remain fair, clear and not misleading, even if it reaches a non-intended recipient (for example, through others retweeting on Twitter or sharing on Facebook).

The requirements to be fair and not misleading imply balance in how financial products and services are promoted, so that consumers are made aware of not only the potential benefits but also of any relevant risks. Specific elements of the FCA advice include:

- Promotions for investment products. There is a specific requirement that financial promotions for investment products are identifiable as such. The FCA's view is that – for social media in particular – it is important that, in all cases, it is clear that a promotion is a promotion.
- Stand-alone compliance. Each communication (e.g. a tweet, a Facebook post or page) needs to be considered individually and comply with the relevant rules.
- Risk warnings and other required statements. Firms are reminded that there are requirements to include risk warnings or other statements in promotions for certain products/services. These rules are media-neutral and therefore apply to social media as they would to any other medium.

- Image advertising. The FCA reminds firms that it remains possible to advertise their presence in the market through 'image advertising' in a way which is unlikely to present difficulties with character limits.

Firms must ensure that cross border communications and especially financial promotions comply with local law and in the UK that legal and regulatory requirements besides those of the FCA Handbook are observed, for example the UK Advertising Standards and CAP Code and the Privacy and Electronic Communication Regulations.

Information about the firm

A firm must provide a retail client with the following general information:

- Contact details of the firm.
- In the case of MiFID or equivalent third country business, the languages in which the client may communicate with the firm.
- The methods of communication to be used between the firm and the client.
- A statement of the fact that the firm is authorised and the name of the competent authority that has authorised it.
- In the case of MiFID or equivalent third country business, the contact address of the competent authority that has authorised the firm.
- If the firm is acting through an appointed representative or, where applicable, a tied agent, a statement of this fact specifying the EEA state in which that appointed representative or tied agent is registered.
- The nature, frequency and timing of the reports on the performance of the service to be provided by the firm to the client.
- The conflicts of interest policy of the firm.

A firm that manages investments for a client must establish an appropriate method of evaluation and comparison, such as a meaningful benchmark based on the investment objectives of the client and the types of designated investments included in the client portfolio, so as to enable the client to assess the firm's performance.

If a firm proposes to manage investments for a retail client, the firm must provide the client with the following information as applicable:

- Information on the method and frequency of valuation of the designated investments in the client portfolio.

- Details of any delegation of the discretionary management of all or part of the designated investments or funds in the client portfolio.
- A specification of any benchmark against which the performance of the client portfolio will be compared.
- The types of designated investments that may be included in the client portfolio and
- types of transaction that may be carried out in those designated investments, including any limits.
- The management objectives, the level of risk to be reflected in the manager's exercise of discretion and any specific constraints on that discretion.

Investment adviser charging and remuneration

Since 1 January 2013, a firm making a personal recommendation to a retail client in the UK to invest in a retail investment product can no longer earn commission set by the product provider. Instead, the firm will be paid an adviser charge agreed with the client in advance.

The new rules apply equally to independent and restricted advice, but not to basic advice (advice on stakeholder products using pre-scripted questions), where advisers will still be able to earn commission on sales. Non-advised services, or execution-only sales, where no advice or recommendation is given, will also fall outside the adviser charging regime.

The new definition of retail investment products is deliberately broader than that of packaged product. Advice on stocks and shares or on structured deposits, however, is not covered by the new regime.

Under the new rules, a firm providing personal recommendations on retail investment products and any related services can only be paid by adviser charges and must not solicit or accept any other commission, remuneration or benefit of any kind, regardless of whether it intends to pass it on to the client. Related services include arranging the recommended transaction or carrying out administrative tasks associated with it or managing the relationship between the client and a discretionary investment manager.

Equally, product providers are prohibited from offering or paying commission, remuneration or benefits of any kind to a firm in connection with advice given or any related services. This will not prevent product providers from offering to facilitate the payment of adviser charges from the client's investment or from paying administration or other charges to third parties, such as fund supermarkets, provided certain other rules are complied with.

COBS 6.1B.9 states '…a firm that offers to facilitate, directly or through a third party, the payment of adviser charges, including by means of a platform service must:

1) obtain and validate instructions from a retail client in relation to an adviser charge;

2) offer sufficient flexibility in terms of the adviser charges it facilitates; and

3) not pay out or advance adviser charges to the firm to which the adviser charge is owed over a materially different time period, or on a materially different basis to that in which it recovers the adviser charge from the retail client (including paying any adviser charges to the firm that it cannot recover from the retail client).'

The rules require firms to work out an appropriate charging structure for calculating the adviser charge. This can be in a standard form (a price list), rather than tailor-made for each client. Whether the charging structure is based on a fixed fee, an hourly rate or a percentage of funds invested will be up to the firm, provided it always bears in mind its duty to act in the client's best interests. But the client should only pay ongoing charges if the firm is providing an ongoing, value-added service and this is properly disclosed to the client.

Varying adviser charges 'inappropriately' according to provider or product, or allowing charges to be influenced by what payment facilitation services are on offer would suggest the firm is not complying with the client's best interests rule. This means that firms will not be able to charge more for recommending one product (such as a distributor-influenced fund) instead of another 'substitutable' product (such as a third-party collective investment scheme).

The firm's charging structure must be disclosed to the client in writing 'in good time' before any advice or related services are given, and in 'clear and plain language'. The information can be set out in the services and costs disclosure document or a combined initial disclosure document, and can take the form of a list of services and indicative charges. If the actual charge payable differs materially from the charging structure, this must be disclosed to the client 'as early as practicable'.

The total adviser charge payable to the firm or any of its associates must be agreed with and disclosed to the client 'as early as practicable' in a durable medium or via a website. The cost must be shown in cash terms (or converted into illustrative cash equivalents).

Where payments are to be made over time, the client must be told how much is to be paid and when, and the consequences of cancellation.

Firms are required to keep records of their charging structure, the total adviser charge payable by each client and, where this differs materially from the charging structure, the reasons for the difference.

Adviser charging also applies to product providers advising clients directly on their own products. The product provider must ensure that the level of its adviser charge is 'at least reasonably representative' of the adviser services provided. To be reasonably representative, the adviser charge should not include costs associated with manufacturing and administering the product.

The allocation of costs and profit between the adviser charge and product cost should be such that any cross-subsidisation is insignificant in the long term. Essentially, the amount charged should be at a level that would be 'appropriate' if the advice and related services were being offered by an unconnected firm.

The rules also provide that product providers must take reasonable steps to ensure product costs are not structured so that they mislead or conceal the distinction between product costs and adviser charges. In particular, the FCA wants to end the practice of product providers offering to allocate over 100% of the client's investment, usually without making it clear that higher charges will apply.

Clients can choose to pay the adviser charge up front or have it deducted from their investment. Payment can be made in instalments, but only if the adviser charge is in respect of an ongoing service provided by the firm which has been properly disclosed, or if the retail investment product is one to which the client makes regular contributions.

If payment is to be taken from the investment, the product provider must obtain clear instructions from the client about the amount to be deducted.

The adviser charging regime is backed up by amendments to current rules and guidance on inducements and non-monetary benefits aimed at preventing firms receiving incentives (or 'soft commissions') from product providers. The changes extend existing requirements under the MiFID to retail investment products.

The FCA's approach to temporary product intervention

Product intervention rules are rules made under section 137D of the Financial Services and Markets Act 2000 (FSMA) (as amended by the Financial Services Act 2012) aiming to tackle issues relating to specific products (or types of products), product features or marketing practices relating to specific products.

The rules give the FCA a wide range of powers to intervene. Interventions may range from requiring certain product features to be included, excluded, or changed, requiring amendments to promotional materials, to imposing restrictions on sales or marketing of the product or, in more serious cases, a ban on sales or marketing of a product in relation to all or some types of customer.

Where the product is provided by a business outside of the UK, rules may be made targeting regulated activities by authorised persons in the UK that would lead to a specified agreement being formed (see sections 137D(2)(c) and (d)).

In relation to agreements entered into in breach of product intervention rules, section 137D(7) sets out that the rules may:

i) Provide for a relevant agreement or obligation to be unenforceable against any person or specified person.

ii) Provide for the recovery of any money or other property paid or transferred under a relevant agreement or obligation by any person or specified person.

iii) Provide for the payment of compensation for any loss sustained by any person or specified person as a result of paying or transferring any money or other property under a relevant agreement or obligation.

iv) Provide for the payment of compensation for any loss sustained by any person or specified person as a result of paying.

One of the powers given to the FCA by the Financial Services Act 2012 is the power to make temporary product intervention rules (TPIRs) where the delay involved in complying with the requirements for public consultation would prejudice the interests of consumers.

The FCA has stated it will use TPIRs in cases where a product is in 'serious danger' of being mis-sold. The TPIRs will allow the FCA to take action, including restricting the use of certain product features and requiring that a product not be promoted to some or all types of customers. In the most serious cases, the regulator will be able to use the rules to prevent a product being sold altogether, such as in instances where complex or niche products are being sold to the mass market. The rules will be made before consultation and will last for no longer than twelve months. During this time the FCA will either consult on a permanent remedy or will work to find another way to resolve the problem.

TPIRs sit alongside other regulatory tools, such as general rules (including non-TPIRs), guidance, variations of permission and supervisory and enforcement action. The choice of which approach is used in any particular situation will be made based on the facts of the case.

The regulator has published a non-exhaustive list of scenarios under which the TPIRs could be applied:

- Products that would be acceptable but for the inclusion or exclusion of particular features.

- Products where there is a significant incentive for inappropriate or indiscriminate targeting of consumers.

- Markets where firms restrict their product range or access to their product range in ways designed to increase profitability by restricting consumer choice, reducing competition, or creating barriers to search, switching, or entry.

- Products which may bring about significant detriment as a result of being inappropriately targeted.

- In particularly serious cases, a product may be considered inherently flawed – for example, a product that has such disadvantageous features that the majority of consumers, or specified types of consumer, are unlikely to benefit.

3. IDENTIFYING CLIENT NEEDS (SUITABILITY AND APPROPRIATENESS)

Suitability obligation

Firms providing investment advisory or discretionary portfolio management services are required to assess suitability for all retail clients and for professional clients (including those clients who in relation to the provision of other services would be classified as eligible counterparties).

In order to make an assessment of suitability, a firm needs to obtain the necessary information in relation to the client to assess:

- Their investment objectives.
- Their financial situation.
- Their knowledge and experience.

This is vital for making a recommendation or taking a decision in the course of providing discretionary portfolio management services. Knowledge and experience can be assumed for products, services or transactions in respect of which a client has been classified as professional. It cannot be assumed for retail clients. Similarly, it can be assumed that a per se professional client has the ability to financially bear any related investment risks consistent with his investment objectives if the service provided is investment advice. This cannot be assumed for retail clients or for retail clients that have opted to be professional clients, or when providing discretionary portfolio management services to any type of client.

A firm must provide a suitability report to a retail client if the firm makes a personal recommendation and the client:

- Buys/sells shares/units in a regulated collective investment scheme.
- Buys/sells shares through an investment trust savings scheme.
- Buys/sells/surrenders or cancels rights in, or suspends contributions to, a personal or stakeholder pension scheme.
- Elects to make income withdrawals from a short term annuity.
- Enters into a pension transfer or pension opt-out.
- Enters into any transaction in relation to a life policy.

The suitability report must normally be provided to the client as soon as possible after the transaction is carried out. The report must set out the needs and demands of the client and explain why the transaction is suitable in addition to any possible disadvantages of the transaction. When a retail client is recommended an investment that is not listed above, a firm's policy should address whether the client's best interests rule would require an equivalent explanation of why the recommendation is suitable for the client.

Churning and switching

Churning and switching relates to the deliberate overtrading of client accounts for the purpose of generating commission. Churning relates to investments generally, e.g. a firm may buy/sell shares frequently in a way that is not in the best interests of the client. Switching refers to overtrading within and between packaged products. Of course, churning or switching are difficult to identify unless blatant. Market conditions will play a role in determining whether trading was too frequent or not.

Appropriateness obligation

Firms are also required to test appropriateness where they provide investment services other than investment advice or discretionary portfolio management. This will typically be non-advised services. For this kind of service, as no personal recommendation is provided by the firm, the suitability rules do not apply.

For such services, a firm must ask the client to provide information about their knowledge and experience in the investment field relevant to the specific type of product or service offered or demanded, so as to enable the firm to assess whether the product or service envisaged is appropriate for the client. Firms must either offer only those products that are appropriate or, if the client demands a product that has been assessed as inappropriate, give the client a warning (which can be in standard form) that the product is inappropriate to the client's circumstances.

If a client is provided with a warning but still wishes to proceed, the firm should consider whether this would be in the client's best interests. If the client cannot provide sufficient information to allow the firm to judge appropriateness but the client still wishes to do business with the firm, the firm must warn the client that it is unable to judge appropriateness before doing business.

A professional client can be assumed to possess the knowledge and experience necessary to understand the risks in relation to the products or services in question.

The appropriateness obligation does not apply to a client (of any type) for non-complex financial instruments. A non-complex financial instrument is one that is not a derivative, which can be traded easily, where information on its value is readily available, where it does not involve an obligation that exceeds the cost of acquiring the instrument and where understandable information on the nature of the instrument is publicly available.

Independent and restricted investment advice

Following the RDR, the regulator has decided to further clarify what constitutes independent and restricted investment advice.

Independent advice

If a firm claims to be independent it must:

- Consider a broader range of products (retail investment products).
- Provide unbiased and unrestricted advice based on a comprehensive and fair analysis of the relevant market.
- Inform its clients, before providing advice, that it provides independent advice.

To reflect the range of products that an independent adviser should have knowledge of, the FCA has introduced the term 'retail investment product'. This is wider than packaged products. It also includes structured investment products, all investment trusts, unregulated collective investment schemes (UCIS) and any other investment that offers exposure to underlying financial assets, but in a packaged form, which modifies that exposure compared with a direct holding.

Restricted advice

If a firm gives advice on products from a limited number of providers, or only considers certain types of products, it will need to describe itself as 'restricted'. Firms must disclose in writing and orally, before providing advice, that they provide restricted advice and explain the nature of the restriction.

4. DEALING AND MANAGING

Best execution obligation

Firms must take all reasonable steps to obtain the best possible result for their clients when executing orders.

Firms must establish and implement a best execution policy containing the process by which firms will obtain the best possible result. The policy must be kept up to date.

Firms must take into account price, costs, likelihood of execution and settlement, size, nature or any other consideration that is relevant to the execution of the order when determining what the best possible result is.

Firms must provide clients with information on, and obtain client consent to, their policy. In addition, if firms wish to execute trades outside a regulated market or a multilateral trading facility they must first obtain the express consent of the client.

Firms must be able to demonstrate at the request of a client that they have executed their orders in accordance with the firm's policy.

Notion of reasonableness

When executing a client order, a firm must take into account the following criteria for determining the relative importance of the execution factors:

- The characteristics of the client, including the categorisation of the client as retail or professional.
- The characteristics of the client order.
- The characteristics of financial instruments that are the subject of that order.
- The characteristics of the execution venues to which that order can be directed.

A firm has more latitude as to factors it may take into account in its policy when dealing with professional clients. Priorities will vary from transaction to transaction, market to market and client to client. A large client may consider that fast matching at large volume is important so as to ensure execution at a particular market level. For smaller clients, costs may be a more important factor (which may, in the context of smaller orders, form a larger element of the overall price).

For the purposes of delivering best execution for a retail client where there is more than one competing venue to execute an order for a financial instrument, in order to assess and compare the results for the client that would be achieved by executing the order on each of the execution venues listed in the firm's order execution policy that is capable of executing that order, the firm's own commissions and costs for executing the order on each of the eligible execution venues must be taken into account in that assessment.

Order execution policy

A firm must establish and implement effective arrangements for complying with the obligation to take all reasonable steps to obtain the best possible result for its clients. In particular, the firm must establish and implement an order execution policy to allow it to obtain, for its client orders, the best possible result in accordance with that obligation.

A firm must provide a retail client with the following details on its execution policy in good time prior to the provision of the service:

- An account of the relative importance the firm assigns, in accordance with the execution criteria, to the execution factors, or the process by which the firm determines the relative importance of those factors.

- A list of the execution venues on which the firm places significant reliance in meeting its obligation to take all reasonable steps to obtain on a consistent basis the best possible result for the execution of client orders.
- A clear and prominent warning that any specific instructions from a client may prevent the firm from taking the steps that it has designed and implemented in its execution policy to obtain the best possible result for the execution of those orders in respect of the elements covered by those instructions.

A firm must review its best execution policy annually, as well as its order execution arrangements. This review must also be carried out whenever a material change occurs that affects the firm's ability to continue to obtain the best possible result for the execution of its client orders on a consistent basis using the venues included in its execution policy.

Client order handling

A firm must satisfy the following conditions when carrying out client orders:

- It must ensure that orders executed on behalf of clients are promptly and accurately recorded and allocated.
- It must carry out otherwise comparable orders sequentially and promptly unless the characteristics of the order or prevailing market conditions make this impracticable, or the interests of the client require otherwise.
- It must inform a retail client about any material difficulty relevant to the proper carrying out of orders promptly upon becoming aware of the difficulty.

A firm is not permitted to carry out a client order or a transaction for own account in aggregation with another client order unless the following conditions are met:

- It must be unlikely that the aggregation of orders and transactions will work overall to the disadvantage of any client whose order is to be aggregated.
- It must be disclosed to each client whose order is to be aggregated that the effect of aggregation may work to its disadvantage in relation to a particular order.
- An order allocation policy must be established and effectively implemented, providing in sufficiently precise terms for the fair allocation of aggregated orders and transactions, including how the volume and price of orders determines allocations and the treatment of partial executions.

Use of dealing commission

In summary, an investment manager is prohibited from executing customer orders through a broker for a commission in return for receiving goods or services unless certain conditions are met. The conditions are that the goods and services:

- Are directly related to the execution of trades on behalf of the investment managers' customers, or constitute the provision of substantive research.
- Will reasonably assist the investment manager in the provision of its services to its customers.
- Will not impair compliance with the duty to act in the best interests of its customers.

Key to this regime are the definitions of the executions of trades and the provision of substantive research. Where the goods or services relate to the execution of trades, they must be linked to and provided between the arranging and conclusion of a specific investment transaction (or series of related transactions). So, post-trade analytics cannot be included on a blanket basis in the goods or services that could be acquired with dealing commission. However, the provision of information about how well a broker conducted a particular transaction could be a legitimate service.

Where the goods relate to the provision of research, the FCA emphasises that 'originality' is an essential component of research that can be purchased with dealing commission. So, it is not enough to repackage information that has been presented before, produce information that is widely available or supply data that has not been analysed in some meaningful way. Raw data feeds (i.e. historical price data) where the data has not been analysed or manipulated will not be permitted as investment research.

Substantive research is defined in COBS 11.6.5E as:

a) capable of adding value to the investment or trading decisions by providing new insights that inform the investment manager when making such decisions about its customers' portfolios;

b) whatever form its output takes, represent original thought, in the critical and careful consideration and assessment of new and existing facts, and must not merely repeat or repackage what has been presented before;

c) have intellectual rigour and must not merely state what is commonplace or self-evident; and

d) present the investment manager with meaningful conclusions based on analysis or manipulation of data.

The FCA has produced an indicative list of goods that cannot be acquired with dealing commission:

- Services relating to the valuation or performance measurement of portfolios.
- Computer hardware.
- Connectivity services, such as electronic networks and dedicated telephone lines.
- Seminar fees.
- Corporate access services.
- Subscriptions for publications.
- Travel, accommodation or entertainment costs.
- Order and execution management systems.
- Office administrative computer software, such as word processing or accounting applications.
- Membership fees to professional associations.
- Purchase or rental of standard office equipment or ancillary facilities.
- Employees' salaries.
- Direct money payments.
- Publicly available information.
- Custody services relating to designated investments belonging to, or managed for, customers, other than those services that are incidental to the execution of trades.

Where substantive research is bundled with an ineligible service (e.g. corporate access) the investment manager must disaggregate the services and ensure that only substantive research is paid for using dealing commission.

Investment firms that use dealing commission to purchase relevant goods and services must disclose this to their customers. This disclosure should be made prior to the conducting of relevant investment business and then periodically once a year. The prior disclosure should explain generally why the firm might find it necessary or desirable to use dealing commission to purchase goods or services.

Inducements

Under the conduct of business rules governing MiFID business, firms must act honestly, fairly, professionally and in the best interests of their clients, and provide appropriate information to clients in a comprehensible form.

MiFID provisions on inducements apply to all payments, fees or non-monetary benefits regardless of materiality.

A fee, commission or non-monetary benefit, where paid or provided to or by a third party, must be designated to enhance the quality of the relevant service to the client. The existence, nature and amount of the fee, commission or non-monetary benefit, or the essential details in summary form, must be disclosed to the client by firms within MiFID's scope.

The disclosure must be clear, comprehensive, accurate and understandable before firms provide relevant investment or ancillary services.

Guidance on what constitutes reasonable non-monetary benefits is provided in COBS 2.3.15 and includes:

- Gifts, hospitality and promotional prizes (of a reasonable value).
- Promotional assistance from a product provider – this should not be of a kind or value that would impair the firm's ability to pay due regard to the interest of its clients.
- Generic product literature from a product provider.

Personal account dealing

A firm that conducts designated investment business must establish, implement and maintain adequate arrangements aimed at preventing the following activities in the case of any relevant person who is involved in activities that may give rise to a conflict of interest, or who has access to inside information as defined in the Market Abuse Directive or to other confidential information relating to clients or transactions with or for clients by virtue of an activity carried out by him on behalf of the firm:

1. Entering into a personal transaction which meets at least one of the following criteria:
    - That the person is prohibited from entering into it under the Market Abuse Directive.
    - It involves the misuse or improper disclosure of that confidential information.
    - It conflicts or is likely to conflict with an obligation of the firm to a customer under the regulatory system, or any other obligation of the firm under MiFID.
2. Advising or procuring, other than in the proper course of his employment or contract for services, any other person to enter into a transaction in designated investments which, if a personal transaction of the relevant person, would be covered by (1) or a relevant provision.

3. Disclosing, other than in the normal course of his employment or contract for services, any information or opinion to any other person if the relevant person knows, or reasonably ought to know, that as a result of that disclosure that other person will or would be likely to take either of the following steps:

   - To enter into a transaction in designated investments which, if a personal transaction of the relevant person, would be covered by (1) or a relevant provision.
   - To advise or procure another person to enter into such a transaction.

Each person in the firm must be made aware of the restrictions on personal transactions, and of the measures established by the firm in connection with personal transactions and disclosure. The firm:

- Must be informed promptly of any personal transaction entered into by a relevant person.
- In the case of outsourcing arrangements, must ensure that the service provider to which the activity is outsourced maintains a record of personal transactions entered into by any relevant person and provides that information to the firm promptly on request.

A record must be kept of the personal transaction notified to the firm or identified by it, including any authorisation or prohibition in connection with such a transaction.

These rules do not apply to:

- Personal transactions effected under a discretionary portfolio management service.
- Personal transactions in units or shares in collective undertakings.
- Personal transactions in life policies.

Conflict of interests

SYSC rules require firms to address potential conflicts of interest that may arise between itself (including individual employees) and clients, and also between clients. The firm's duty is to its clients. For the purposes of identifying the types of conflict of interest that arise, or may arise, in the course of providing a service and whose existence may entail a material risk of damage to the interests of a client, a common platform firm and a management company must take into account, as a minimum, whether the firm or a relevant person, or a person directly or indirectly linked by control to the firm:

1. is likely to make a financial gain, or avoid a financial loss, at the expense of the client;
2. has an interest in the outcome of a service provided to the client or of a transaction carried out on behalf of the client, which is distinct from the clients' interest in that outcome;

3. has a financial or other incentive to favour the interest of another client or group of clients over the interests of the client;

4. carries on the same business as the client;

5. receives or will receive from a person other than the client an inducement in relation to a service provided to the client, in the form of monies, goods or services, other than the standard commission or fee for that service.

Firms should take all reasonable steps to:

- Identify conflicts of interest.
- Maintain and operate effective organisational and administrative arrangements to prevent conflicts of interest resulting in a material risk of damage to clients' interests.
- Disclose conflicts where there remains a risk of damage to clients' interests.

A common platform firm must establish, implement and maintain an effective conflicts of interest policy that is set out in writing and is appropriate to the size and organisation of the firm and the nature, scale and complexity of its business.

1. The conflicts of interest policy must include the following:
   - it must identify the specific services and activities carried out by or on behalf of the firm, the circumstances which constitute or may give rise to a conflict of interest entailing a material risk of damage to the interests of one or more clients; and
   - it must specify procedures to be followed and measures to be adopted in order to manage such conflicts.
2. The procedures and measures provided for in paragraph (1)(b) must:
   - be designed to ensure that relevant persons engaged in different business activities involving a conflict of interest of the kind specified in paragraph (1)(a) carry on those activities at a level of independence appropriate to the size and activities of the firm, and to the materiality of the risk of damage to the interests of clients; and
   - include such of the following as are necessary and appropriate for the firm to ensure the requisite degree of independence:
     - effective procedures to prevent or control the exchange of information between relevant persons engaged in activities involving a risk of a conflict of interest where the exchange of that information may harm the interests of one or more clients;

- the separate supervision of relevant persons whose principal functions involve carrying out activities on behalf of, or providing services to clients whose interests may conflict, or who otherwise represent different interests that may conflict, including those of the firm;
- the removal of any direct link between the remuneration of relevant persons principally engaged in one activity and the remuneration of, or revenues generated by, different relevant persons principally engaged in another activity, where a conflict of interest may arise in relation to those activities;
- measures to prevent or limit any person from exercising inappropriate influence over the way in which a relevant person carries out services or activities; and
- measures to prevent or control the simultaneous or sequential involvement of a relevant person in separate services or activities where such involvement may impair the proper management of conflicts of interest.

5. INVESTMENT RESEARCH

'Investment research' means research or other information recommending or suggesting an investment strategy, explicitly or implicitly, concerning one or several financial instruments or the issuers of financial instruments, including any opinion as to the present or future value or price of such instruments, intended for distribution channels or for the public, and in relation to which the following conditions are met:

- It is labelled or described as investment research (or in similar terms), or is otherwise presented as an objective or independent explanation of the matters contained in the recommendation.
- If the recommendation in question were to be made by an investment firm to a client, it would not constitute the provision of a personal recommendation.

Investment research is likely to contain some degree of substantive analysis. It will often be prepared by a person designated by the firm as a financial analyst. Generic material (for example, reports analysing or commenting on general political, economic or market issues, industries, asset classes or broadly based indices) will not be investment research unless it also recommends or suggests an investment strategy and is labelled as investment research. Such non-independent investment research should be clearly labelled as marketing communications.

When producing investment research, a firm should have in place arrangements to ensure that:

- A financial analyst or anyone else having knowledge of the timing or content of investment research is not permitted to deal ahead – also known as 'front running' – (either personally or on behalf of the firm or someone else) of the publication of the research in the financial instruments to which the research relates until the recipients of the research have had a reasonable opportunity to act upon it. The exceptions to this are:

  - A market-maker acting in good faith and in the ordinary course of market-making.
  - In the execution of an unsolicited client order.

- The firm, the financial analysts or any other relevant person involved in the production of investment research do not accept inducements from those with a material interest in the subject matter of the research.

A financial analyst's remuneration should not be linked to a specific transaction or to recommendations contained in the research. Firms should ensure that financial analysts who publish investment research are not directly supervised by, and do not report directly to, investment banking or sales and trading personnel.

It is inappropriate for firms to use a financial analyst in a marketing capacity if this would create a lack of independence in their investment research or possibly give rise to a conflict with the interests of the persons to whom their investment research is disseminated.

A firm which disseminates investment research produced by another person to the public or to clients is exempt from complying with the requirements on investment research if the following criteria are met:

- The person that produces the investment research is not a member of the group to which the firm belongs.
- The firm does not substantially alter the recommendations within the investment research.
- The firm does not present the investment research as having been produced by it.
- The firm verifies that the producer of the investment research is subject to the investment research requirements in relation to the production of that investment research, or has established a policy setting such requirements.

A firm must, in a research recommendation produced by it:

- Disclose clearly and prominently the identity of the person responsible for its production, and in particular:
  - The name and job title of the individual who prepared the research recommendation; and
  - The name of the firm; and

- Where the firm is an investment firm or a credit institution, disclose the identity of the competent authority of the firm.

These requirements may be met for non-written research recommendations by referring to a place where the disclosures can be directly and easily accessed by the public, such as an appropriate internet site of the firm.

A firm must take reasonable care to ensure that:

- Facts in a research recommendation are clearly distinguished from interpretations, estimates, opinions and other types of non-factual information.
- Its sources for a research recommendation are reliable, or if there is any doubt as to whether a source is reliable, that this is clearly indicated.
- All projections, forecasts and price targets in a research recommendation are clearly labelled as such and the material assumptions made in producing or using them are indicated.
- The substance of its research recommendations can be substantiated as reasonable, upon request by the FCA. A firm must make and retain sufficient records to disclose the basis of this substantiation.

These requirements do not apply in the case of non-written research recommendations, to the extent that they would be disproportionate.

6. PRODUCT DISCLOSURE – PACKAGED PRODUCTS

'Packaged products' refer to investment products designed generally for retail clients and consist of:

- A life policy.
- An interest in an investment trust savings scheme.
- A unit in a regulated collective investment scheme.
- A stakeholder pension scheme.
- A personal pension scheme.

Where a firm provides advice on packaged products, it must disclose whether it expects its scope to be:

- The whole of the market or market sector.
- Limited to several product providers.
- Limited to a single product provider.

The scope of a firm's advice relates to the number of product providers whose products it sells. The range of the firm's advice relates to which products from those providers it sells. A firm must keep records of the scopes and ranges it uses, and keep those records for at least five years.

Where a firm claims to be independent with a scope across the whole market or across a sector, the firm's selection of products must be sufficiently large to satisfy the client's best interests. The FCA does not specify how to identify what sufficiently large is, but states that a firm can use 'panels' of product providers to cover the whole of the market. A firm must review these panels regularly.

Where a firm makes a recommendation to a private customer to buy a packaged product, the firm must provide the key features of the product in written form. A key features document must:

- Be produced and presented to at least the same quality and standard as the sales or marketing material used to promote the relevant product.
- Display the firm's brand at least as prominently as any other.
- Include the 'key facts' logo in a prominent position at the top of the document.
- Include the following statement in a prominent position:

  "The Financial Conduct Authority is the independent financial services regulator. It requires us, [provider name], to give you this important information to help you to decide whether our [product name] is right for you. You should read this document carefully so that you understand what you are buying, and then keep it safe for future reference."

A key features document must:

1. Include enough information about the nature and complexity of the product, how it works, any limitations or minimum standards that apply and the material benefits and risks of buying or investing.
2. Explain:
   - The arrangements for handling complaints about the product.
   - That compensation might be available from the Financial Services Compensation Scheme if the firm cannot meet its liabilities in respect of the product (if applicable).
   - That a right to cancel or withdraw exists, or does not exist, and (if it does exist) its duration and the conditions for exercising it.
   - For a child trust fund (CTF), that stakeholder CTFs, cash-deposit CTFs and share CTFs are available, and which type the firm is offering. Note that the government stopped issuing CTF vouchers from January 2011.

- For a personal pension scheme, clearly and prominently, that stakeholder pension schemes are generally available and might meet the client's needs as well as the scheme on offer.

One of the key provisions of the UCITS IV Directive is the introduction of the key investor information document (KIID). This document replaces the simplified prospectus introduced by the UCITS III Directive, which had a number of shortcomings.

As the KIID is aimed at retail investors, the language must be written in a concise manner in non-technical language and presented in a way that is likely to be understood by retail investors. It must be fair, clear and not misleading, and should consist only of the kind of information that potential investors need to make an informed investment decision. The document must provide information on the following essential elements in respect of the UCITS scheme:

1. Identification of the scheme;
2. A short description of its investment objectives and investment policy;
3. Past performance presentation or, where relevant, performance scenarios;
4. Costs and associated charges; and
5. A risk/reward profile of the investment, including appropriate guidance and warnings in relation to the risks associated with investments in the scheme.

The essential elements of the KIID must be kept up to date. The KIID can be updated as frequently as a UCITS wishes; however, it must be updated prior to or following any material change; prior to a proposed change to the fund rules, instrument of incorporation or prospectus; or at least annually, and within 35 business days of each calendar year end, to reflect the updated past performance information.

A retail client has a right to cancel a packaged product within 14 days, except for life policies and pension (including personal and stakeholder pension) schemes where the cancellation period is 30 days. Cancellation rights apply to transactions that have been advised or that are subject to the distance selling rules.

The firm must make adequate records concerning the exercise of a right to cancel or withdraw, and must retain them:

- Indefinitely in relation to a pension transfer, pension opt-out or FSAVC.
- For at least five years in relation to a life policy, pension contract, personal pension scheme or stakeholder pension scheme.
- For at least three years in any other case.

Retail investment products

The FCA has introduced a new category of retail investment product. It includes what elsewhere in the FCA Handbook are termed 'packaged products': life policies, a unit in a collective investment scheme, stakeholder and personal pension schemes and an interest in an investment trust savings scheme.

It also includes a security in an investment trust and a structured capital-at-risk product, as well as a 'catch all' provision: 'any other designated investment which offers exposure to underlying financial assets, in a packaged form which modifies that exposure when compared with a direct holding in the financial asset'. This could include an exchange traded fund (ETF).

An adviser that classifies itself as offering independent investment advice would need to have knowledge of retail investment products rather than just the narrower range of packaged products. The new rules on adviser charging also apply to retail investment products.

7. RECORD KEEPING AND REPORTING INFORMATION

Investment firms are required to keep various records to comply with FCA rules. Some examples of the record keeping requirements are:

- Firms must keep records of client categorisations, with supporting information. This requirement applies to retail clients, professional clients and eligible counterparties. The records must be kept for five years from the end of the business relationship for MiFID or equivalent third country business and for life and pension contracts and three years for other regulated business.
- Suitability records in relation to MiFID business and life policies and pensions must also be kept for five years from the date of the advice. Again, for other business the transaction record keeping requirement is for three years except for pension transfers or opt-outs where records should be kept indefinitely.
- Investment firms must keep detailed records for five years of every order received from a client and for portfolio management services of every dealing decision. This requirement applies to retail clients, professional clients and eligible counterparties. Records of client categorisation before any pension transfers or opt-outs must be kept indefinitely.

Occasional reporting

If a firm has carried out an order in the course of its designated investment business on behalf of a client (except where the firm is managing investments), it must:

- Promptly provide the client, in a durable medium, with the essential information concerning the execution of the order.
- In the case of a retail client, send the client a notice in a durable medium confirming the execution of the order and such of the trade confirmation information as is applicable:

  - As soon as possible, and no later than the first business day following that execution; or
  - If the confirmation is received by the firm from a third party, no later than the first business day following receipt of the confirmation from the third party.
  - Supply a client, on request, with information about the status of his or her order.

'Essential information' includes:

- For transactions in a derivative:
  - The maturity, delivery or expiry date of the derivative.
  - In the case of an option, a reference to the last exercise date, whether it can be exercised before maturity and the strike price.
  - If the transaction closes out an open futures position, all essential details required in respect of each contract comprised in the open position and each contract by which it was closed out, and the profit or loss to the client arising out of closing out that position (a difference account).
- For the exercise of an option:
  - The date of exercise, and either the time of exercise or that the client will be notified of that time on request.
  - Whether the exercise creates a sale or purchase in the underlying asset.
  - The strike price of the option (for a currency option, the rate of exchange will be the same as the strike price) and, if applicable, the total consideration from or to the client.

Periodic reporting

Where a firm manages investments on behalf of a client:

- In the case of a retail client, it must provide a periodic statement once every six months, except in the following cases:
  - If the retail client so requests, the periodic statement must be provided every three months.
  - If the retail client elects to receive information about executed transactions on a transaction-by-transaction basis, and there are no transactions in derivatives or other securities giving the right to acquire or sell a transferable security or giving rise to a cash settlement determined by reference to transferable securities, currencies, interest rates or yields, commodities or other indices or measures, the periodic statement must be provided at least once every twelve months.

- If the agreement between a firm and a retail client for the managing of investments authorises a leveraged portfolio, the periodic statement must be provided at least once a month.
- A firm must inform a retail client that he has the right to request the provision of a periodic statement every three months. If a firm:
  - Manages investments for a retail client; or
  - Operates a retail client account that includes an uncovered open position in a contingent liability transaction, it must report to the retail client any losses exceeding any pre-determined threshold, agreed between it and the retail client.
- The firm must report:
  - No later than the end of the business day in which the threshold is exceeded; or
  - If the threshold is exceeded on a non-business day, the close of the next business day.

A firm must make, and retain, a copy of any occasional or periodic statement:

- For MiFID or equivalent third country business, for a period of at least five years from the date of despatch; or
- For business that is not MiFID or equivalent third country business, for a period of at least three years from the date of despatch.

Reporting information about authorised funds to unitholders

In order to provide the unitholders with regular and relevant information about the progress of the authorised fund, the authorised fund manager must:

1. Prepare a short report and a long report half-yearly and annually;
2. Send the short report to all unitholders; and
3. Make the long report available to unitholders on request.

These reports must be prepared every annual accounting period and half-yearly accounting period.

The short report for an authorised fund or, for a scheme which is an umbrella, its sub-fund, must contain for the relevant period:

- The name of the scheme or sub-fund;
- Its stated investment objectives and the policy and strategy pursued for achieving those objectives;

- A brief assessment of its risk profile;
- In the case of a UCITS scheme, the figure for the synthetic risk and reward indicator disclosed in its most up-to-date key investor information document and any subsequent changes to that figure during that period;
- The name and address of the authorised fund manager;
- A review of the scheme or sub-fund's investment activities and investment performance during the period;
- A performance record so as to enable a unitholder to put into context the results of the investment activities of the scheme during the period;
- Sufficient information to enable unitholders to form a view on where the portfolio is invested at the end of the period and the extent to which that has changed over the period;
- Any other significant information which would reasonably enable unitholders to make an informed judgement on the activities of the scheme or sub-fund during the period and the results of those activities at the end of the period; and
- A statement that the latest long report is available on request.

The long report essentially contains the accounts and reports prepared by the fund manager, the depository and the auditor.

An authorised fund manager must also draw up a short document in English containing key investor information for investors. Key investor information must include appropriate information about the essential characteristics of the UCITS scheme which is to be provided to investors so that they are reasonably able to understand the nature and risks of the investment product that is being offered to them and, therefore, to take investment decisions on an informed basis.

8. CLIENTS' ASSETS AND CLIENT MONEY RULES

Fiduciary duty

Fiduciary duty means an obligation to act in the best interest of another party. For instance, a company director has a fiduciary duty to the shareholders, a trustee has a fiduciary duty to the trust's beneficiaries, and an investment manager has a fiduciary duty to their clients.

A fiduciary obligation exists whenever one person, the client, places special trust and confidence in another person and relies upon that person, the fiduciary, to exercise his discretion or expertise in acting for the client. The fiduciary knowingly accepts that trust and confidence, and thereafter undertakes to act on behalf of the client by exercising their, the fiduciary's, own discretion and expertise.

The existence of a business relationship between two persons does not mean that either owes a fiduciary obligation to the other. If one person engages or employs another and thereafter directs, supervises or approves their actions, the person so employed is not a fiduciary. Rather, it is only when one party proposes, and the other accepts, a special trust and confidence involving the exercise of professional expertise and discretion that a fiduciary relationship comes into being.

When one person undertakes to act for another in a fiduciary relationship, the law forbids the fiduciary from acting in any manner adverse or contrary to the interests of the client, or from acting for his own benefit in relation to the subject matter. The client is entitled to the best efforts of the fiduciary on his behalf, and the fiduciary must exercise all of the skill, care and diligence at their disposal when acting on behalf of the client.

The FCA Principle for Business 10 states 'a firm must arrange adequate protection for clients' assets when it is responsible for them'. In this context, client assets include both client money and other custody assets, including safe custody investments. The FCA rules therefore cover a firm's responsibility for custody assets (CASS 6) and for client money (CASS 7). A firm is required to determine, and notify the FCA, once a year what type of CASS classification the firm falls into. The CASS classification then determines the CASS rules that apply to the firm. The classifications are:

FIRM TYPE	HIGHEST AMOUNT OF CLIENT MONEY HELD OVER LAST YEAR OR PROJECTED TO HOLD OVER NEXT YEAR)	HIGHEST AMOUNT OF SAFE CUSTODY ASSETS HELD OVER LAST YEAR (OR PROJECTED TO HOLD OVER NEXT YEAR)
CASS large firm	>£1bn	>£100bn
CASS medium firm	>£1m and <£1bn	>£10m and <£100bn
CASS small firm	<£1m	<£10m

A CASS medium or large firm must allocate to a director or senior manager the CASS operational oversight function (CF10a). A CASS small firm must allocate responsibility for compliance with CASS rules to a director or senior manager.

Custody of clients' assets

The Client Assets custody rules (CASS 6) require a firm to arrange adequate protection for assets for which it is responsible for all of its clients. The custody rules are designed primarily to restrict the co-mingling of client and firm assets (especially in the case of insolvency) and minimise the risk of a client's assets being used without their consent or against their wishes.

The firm must effect appropriate registration or recording of legal title of a client's assets in the name of the client or an appropriate nominee company. Only where the investment is subject to law or market practice outside the UK is it appropriate to record the legal title in the name of a custodian or the firm.

Depositing assets with third parties

- A firm may deposit safe custody assets held by it on behalf of its clients into an account opened with a third party, but only if it exercises all due skill, care and diligence in the selection, appointment and periodic review of the third party and of the arrangements for the holding and safekeeping of those safe custody assets.
- A firm must take the necessary steps to ensure that any client's safe custody assets deposited with a third party are identifiable separately from the financial instruments belonging to the firm and from the financial instruments belonging to that third party.
- When a firm makes the selection, appointment and conducts the periodic review, it must take into account:
  - The expertise and market reputation of the third party; and
  - Any legal requirements or market practices related to the holding of those financial instruments that could adversely affect clients' rights.
- A firm must make a record of the grounds upon which it satisfies itself as to the appropriateness of its selection of a third party (and periodically review this), must keep this record until five years after the firm ceases to use the third party to hold financial instruments belonging to clients.
- A firm must have entered into a written agreement with any person with whom it deposits clients' safe custody assets under or with whom it arranges safeguarding and administration of assets which are clients' safe custody assets. This agreement must, at minimum:
  1) set out the binding terms of the arrangement between the firm and the third party;
  2) be in force for the duration of that arrangement; and
  3) clearly set out the custody service(s) that the third party is contracted to provide.

Use of clients' assets

A firm must not enter into arrangements for securities-financing transactions (such as stock lending or repurchase agreements), unless:

- the client has given prior consent to the use of the financial instruments on specified terms; and
- the use of that client's financial instruments is restricted to the specified terms to which the client consents.

Reconciliation of clients' assets

All firms must perform internal custody record checks as regularly as necessary, but at least monthly, to ensure that their records of safe custody assets correspond with their obligations to clients for holding safe custody assets. Internal custody record checks must be carried out by one of two methods.

Internal custody reconciliation method

A comparison on a particular date between two separately maintained records (which need not be independent of one another). This ensures that the firm's records of its safe custody assets correspond with its obligations to clients to hold safe custody assets.

Internal system evaluation method

A process to evaluate:

- The completeness and accuracy of the firm's internal records and accounts of custody assets held for clients. This includes whether sufficient information is being recorded by the firm to enable it to identify a client-specific safe custody asset record, and readily determine the total of all custody assets held for clients.

- Whether the firm's systems and controls correctly identify and resolve all ddiscrepancies in its internal records and accounts of custody assets it holds for its clients.

All firms that physically hold custody assets must undertake a physical asset reconciliation as often as necessary, but at least every six months. This comprises a comparison between a firm's internal records and a count of the actual physical safe custody assets it holds for its clients. This must be performed by one of two methods:

- Total count method – the count of all physical custody assets held by the firm on a particular date.

- Rolling stock method – the count of all physical custody assets held by the firm being undertaken in more than one stage, with each stage referring to a count of a line of stock or group of stock lines.

Firms will be permitted to use either of the physical count methods without first obtaining a written report on the adequacy of the proposed method from an independent auditor. However, a review of the method used will be a requirement of the annual auditor's client assets report.

Reconciliation of externally held assets

Where a firm deposits client's custody assets with third parties it must carry out external custody reconciliations. The requirements for external reconciliations are:

- The reconciliations must be performed as regularly as necessary, but at least monthly.
- Reconciliations must be carried out between the firm's internal records and those provided by the relevant third party – being the entity with whom the firm deposits custody assets; or with whom it registers custody assets.
- The third party's records for the purpose of carrying out the external custody reconciliation may comprise any appropriate information (including statements or other confirmations).
- Where firms hold physical custody records such as paper share certificates, they are not required to undertake external custody reconciliations in respect of the relevant assets. However, firms would be expected to carry out periodic 'spot checks' on whether title to an appropriate sample of custody assets they hold is registered in accordance with the CASS rules.

Where a reconciliation has highlighted a shortfall in the safe custody assets held by the firm caused by a discrepancy, the firm must resolve the discrepancy immediately. If it is unable to do so, it must ensure client protection by segregating an equivalent amount of the firm's own assets/client money, so that this is held in such a way that it will be realised for clients' benefit if the firm fails.

If another party is responsible for the shortfall (or it is caused by timing differences between the firm's and a third party's accounting systems), the firm does not have to make good the deficit but may do so. Firms should take steps to resolve any such shortfalls as soon as possible. In certain circumstances firms may also need to consider whether to inform affected clients of the shortfall (for instance if the firm is informed by a third party of the loss of a custody asset).

Client money rules

The client money rules apply to a firm that receives or holds money from, or on behalf of, a client in the course of MiFID or designated investment business. The purpose of these rules is to protect investors' money in the event of insolvency of the investment firm. This is achieved by requiring the firm to keep clients' money separate from its own.

Where a client transfers full ownership of money to a firm for the purpose of securing or otherwise covering present or future, actual or contingent or prospective obligations, such money should no longer be regarded as client money.

A firm, on receiving any client money, must promptly place this money into one or more accounts opened with any of the following:

- A central bank.
- A BCD credit institution (a bank with a registered office in an EEA state and subject to the Banking Consolidate Directive).

- A bank authorised in a third country.
- A qualifying money market fund.

These accounts are known as 'client bank accounts'. A firm must normally take the necessary steps to ensure that client money deposited in a client bank account is held in an account or accounts identified separately from any accounts used to hold money belonging to the firm.

The firm should take care in selecting the institution used to hold client money, should review its selection periodically and should keep records of the reasons for its selection for five years after ceasing to use the institution to hold client money. Unless the firm uses the alternative approach, all client money must be received directly into a client bank account, and may not be received via the firm's own accounts. Firms should ensure that clients and any third parties make transfers of any money that will be client money directly into the firm's client bank accounts.

A firm that does not adopt the normal approach must first send a written confirmation to the FCA from the firm's auditor that the firm has in place systems and controls which are adequate to enable it to operate another approach effectively (this approach is termed the 'alternative approach').

The alternative approach would be appropriate for a firm that operates in a multi-product, multi-currency environment for which adopting the normal approach would be unduly burdensome and would not achieve the client protection objective. Under the alternative approach, client money is received into and paid out of a firm's own bank accounts; consequently the firm should have systems and controls that are capable of monitoring the client money flows so that the firm can comply with its obligations to perform reconciliations of records and accounts.

A firm must establish and document its reasons for using the alternative approach when applying it to any business line. A firm is required to review at least annually the appropriateness of its reasons for continuing to operate the alternative approach for each business line. If, having conducted a review, a firm considers that it is no longer appropriate to use the alternative method, it must cease using this method within six months. Smaller firms may be able to justify using the alternative approach; however, the FCA would not generally expect this.

A firm may open a client bank account in the form of a general client bank account, a designated client bank account or a designated client fund account. With a designated client bank account, the account should include the word 'designated' in its title and, in the event of the failure of that bank, the account is not pooled with any other type of account unless the firm fails. The money in a client bank account should be held in accounts identified separately from any accounts used to hold money from the firm.

Firms may transfer their own funds into a client money bank account and keep it there in order to prevent a shortfall occurring – such fundsamounts becoming client money and being referred to as 'prudent over-segregation'. Firms must have a written policy to set out why they consider the use of prudent over-segregation ais a reasonable means of addressing each risk and the method that the firm used to calculate the amount segregated to address each risk. Firms must maintain a 'prudent segregation record' relating to segregation payments made into a client bank account and amounts withdrawn when no longer necessary under the relevant rules.

A firm should keep accurate records to enable it to distinguish client assets and money from those of other clients and from those of the firm. These records should be held for five years.

Reconciliation of client money

A firm should carry out internal reconciliations of records and accounts of the entitlement of each client for whom the firm holds client money with the records and accounts of the client money the firm holds in client bank accounts and client transaction accounts. Internal reconciliations should normally be carried out each business day. A firm should also conduct external reconciliations between its internal accounts and records and those of any third parties by whom client money is held.

For internal client money reconciliation a firm may use standard methods or non-standard methods. Standard methods of internal client money reconciliation, set out in the client money rules, require a firm to calculate its client money requirement:

- Individual client balance (available to all firms). Here a firm calculates its client money requirements by reference to how much the firm should be holding in total for each of its individual clients with a positive balance in respect of non-margined transactions, margined transactions and certain other matters.

- Net negative add-back (only available to CASS 7 asset management firms and CASS loan-based crowd-funding firms, and only when the firm does not engage in any margined transactions for clients). This requires a firm to calculate its client money requirement by reference to the balances in each client bank account, adding any individual client's net position in a specific client bank account that is negative and certain other matters.

Non-standard methods of internal client money reconciliation do not meet the requirements placed on firms undertaking one of the standard methods of internal client money reconciliation.

Every firm must maintain its records in a way that allows the firm at any time to be able to promptly determine the total amount of client money it should be holding for each client. 'Promptly' means no later than two business days. Some firms will have up to two business days to accurately determine the total amount of client money that should be held for each client.

This rule will not require a firm to determine the total amount of client money it is holding for each client on an ongoing basis, rather it will only require that the firm ensure it has the ability to do so within the requisite timeframe. Not all breaches need to be notified to FCA specifically,; although the FCA expects all breaches to be reported in a firm's annual client assets report. Materiality is to be decided on a case-by-case basis.

If a firm has deposited custody assets with a third party under the custody rules and money arises in connection with those assets (e.g. a dividend is received), the firm should treat that money as client money unless otherwise agreed. The firm must ensure that the third party either deposits the money in a client bank account of the firm or records it in a client transaction account for the benefit of its clients.

Where the third party custodian is also a bank, the firm may arrange for the client money to be held in a client bank account (from the perspective of the firm rather than the third party custodian), at the third party custodian itself. Where the third party custodian is not a bank, the firm may arrange for the third party custodian to deposit the money in a client bank account (at a third party bank) or in a client transaction account.

Mandated accounts

A mandate is any means that give a firm the ability to control a client's assets or liabilities, which meet the following conditions:

1. they are obtained by the firm from the client, and with the client's consent;
2. they are retained by the firm;
3. they put the firm in a position where it is able to give any or all of the types of instructions described in (a) to (d):
   - (a) instructions to another person in relation to the client's money that is credited to an account maintained by that other person for the client;
   - (b) instructions to another person in relation to any money to which the client has an entitlement, where that other person is responsible to the client for that entitlement;
   - (c) instructions to another person in relation to an asset of the client, where that other person is responsible to the client for holding that asset;
   - (d) instructions to another person such that the client incurs a debt or other liability to that other person or any other person (other than the firm); and
4. their circumstances are such that the client's further involvement would not be necessary for the firm's instructions described in 3(a) to 3(d) to be given effect.

A mandate can take any written form and need not state that it is a mandate. For example it could take the form of a standalone document containing certain information or conferring a certain authority on the firm, a specific provision within a document or agreement that also relates to other matters or a combination of provisions within a number of documents.

The instructions referred to in point 3 above are all instructions given by a firm to another person who also has a relationship with the firm's client. For example, the other person may be the client's bank, intermediary, custodian or credit card provider. This means, for example, that any means by which a firm can control a client's money or assets for which it is itself responsible to the client (rather than any other person) would not amount to a mandate.

A mandate in relation to the type of instructions referred to in 3(a) could include a direct debit instruction over a client's bank account in favour of the firm.

CHAPTER 3 SECTION 6

FCA SUPERVISION AND REDRESS

SECTION AIMS

By the end of this section, learners should be able to:

- Explain the FCA's risk based approach to supervision and the enforcement and disciplinary powers of the FCA.
- Explain the FCA rules relating to handling of complaints (DISP 1.3).
- Explain the role of the Financial Ombudsman Service (DISP Introduction and DISP 2).
- Apply the rules relating to determination by the Financial Ombudsman Service (DISP 3).
- Distinguish between compulsory and voluntary jurisdiction (DISP Introduction).
- Explain the procedure and time limits for the resolution of complaints (DISP 1.4, 1.5, 1.6).
- Apply the rules relating to record keeping and reporting concerning complaints (DISP 1.9, 1.10).
- Explain the purpose of the Financial Services Compensation Scheme (FSCS) (COMP 1.1.7)
- Identify the circumstances under which the FSCS will pay compensation (COMP 1.3.3, 3.2.1, 4.2.1, 4.2.2).
- Identify the limits on the compensation payable by the FSCS (COMP 10.2.1, 10.2.2, 10.2.3)

1. SUPERVISION AND ENFORCEMENT POWERS OF THE FCA

The FCA's overall approach to supervision of firms is one of judgment-based supervision. This implies the FCA will be making supervisory judgments about a firm's business model and culture and whether this poses unacceptable risks to consumers. At the heart of this assessment will be the treating customers fairly (TCF) initiative set out in chapter 5, section 1.

The FCA will put the firms it supervises into one of four conduct supervision categories: C1, C2, C3 or C4.

C1: Banking and insurance groups with a large number of retail customers and universal/ investment banks with very large client assets and trading operations.

C2: Firms across all sectors with a substantial number of retail customers and/or large wholesale firms.

C3: Firms across all sectors with retail customers and/or a significant wholesale presence.

C4: Smaller firms, including almost all intermediaries.

The FCA will focus its supervisory attention on those firms and industry sectors that could cause, or are causing, consumers harm or threaten market integrity. This means that some firms in some sectors might experience a very high level of supervisory contact while others may experience substantially less. It is envisaged that C4 categorised firms will be assessed only every four years.

The FCA's supervision model will be based on three pillars:

- Firm systematic framework (FSF): preventative work through structured conduct assessment of firms.
- Event-driven work: dealing with problems that are emerging or have happened, and securing customer redress or other remedial work where necessary. This will cover issues that occur outside the firm assessment cycle.
- Issues and products: intensive campaigns on sectors of the market or products within a sector that are putting or may put consumers at risk.

The purpose of the FSF is to assess a firm's conduct risk with the aim of identifying whether the interests of customers and market integrity are central to how the firm is run. The common features of the framework will include business model and strategy analysis and an assessment of how the firm embeds fair treatment of customers and ensures market integrity. This latter assessment will have four modules comprising governance and culture, product design, sales or transaction processes and post-sales/services and transaction handling.

The assessment of the four modules will take place through interviews between FCA supervisors and the firm to look at processes in relevant areas – detailed testing will not be used unless it is the only way to assess a particular risk.

The FCA has the power to require the production of information, to require reports to be written and to conduct investigations. To facilitate this, the FCA has the power to gain access to premises. In addition, the firm must make its records and personnel available (SUP 2.3.3).

Where a firm has breached rules, the FCA has the power to issue a private warning to the firm, or for more serious breaches the FCA may issue a public statement about the breach or impose a financial penalty. For very serious matters, the FCA may issue a warning notice before the enforcement action has reached a final decision, the principal purpose of this power is to promote the early transparency of enforcement proceedings.

Where the FCA has serious concerns about the circumstances of an authorised firm or about the way its business has been conducted, the FCA can vary or cancel that firm's Part 4A permission.

Where a party has concerns over a decision made by the FCA, it may appeal to the Tax and Chancery Chamber of the Upper Tribunal. This is a body independent of the FCA with procedural rules set by the Lord Chancellor.

The Financial Services Act 2012 gave the FCA the power to ban products that it believes provide an unacceptable risk to consumers. Before banning a product, the FCA must first consult with the market. Where there is a need for prompt intervention, the FCA may temporarily ban a product for twelve months without consultation.

The Act also gives the FCA the power to ban misleading financial promotions. The use of this power is determined by the specific financial promotion and not used against the firm as a whole. It can be used on its own or before the FCA takes enforcement action against a firm. The FCA will take three steps when using this power:

- The FCA will 'give a direction' to an authorised firm to remove its own financial promotion or one it approves on behalf of an unauthorised firm, setting out its reasons for banning it.

- Firms can make representations to the FCA if they think it is making the wrong decision. The FCA will decide whether to confirm, amend or revoke its direction. If it is confirmed, the FCA will publish it, along with a copy of the promotion and the reasons behind its decision.

Following the third step, firms will be able to refer the matter to the Upper Tribunal if the FCA decides not to revoke the direction.

The FCA also has the power to prosecute a number of offences through the criminal courts. These include:

- Carrying on a regulated activity without authorisation or exemption.
- Making false claims to be authorised or exempt.
- Communicating an invitation to engage in investment activity in breach of the restrictions on financial promotion.
- Failing to co-operate with or giving false information to an FCA-appointed investigator.
- Misleading the FCA.
- Insider dealing (under Part V of the Criminal Justice Act 1993).
- Breaches of the money laundering regulations.

2. COMPLAINTS AND THE FINANCIAL OMBUDSMAN SERVICE

The FCA has established a system for the consideration of complaints against a firm by customers who feel aggrieved and entitled to seek redress. The system involves:

- Consideration of the complaint by the firm itself.
- If the customer is not satisfied and is eligible to use the Financial Ombudsman Service (FOS) independent investigation of the complaint, involving both a mediation stage and a possible subsequent determination stage, by a financial ombudsman.

A firm must have in place and operate appropriate and effective procedures for handling complaints. These procedures need to be written down, and all staff need to be made aware of them. A firm must publish its own internal complaints handling procedures.

A firm receiving a complaint must, by the end of eight weeks after its receipt of the complaint, send the complainant:

- A final response; or
- A written response which:
  - Explains why it is not in a position to make a final response and indicates when it expects to be able to provide one.
  - Informs the complainant that he may now refer the complaint to the FOS.
  - Encloses a copy of the standard explanatory leaflet.

A firm must retain records of complaints for at least five years for MiFID business and three years for other types of business. Most firms must also provide the FCA with a twice-yearly report on (among other things) the number of complaints, completions of complaints within four weeks, eight weeks and over eight weeks from receipt, and the number of complaints accepted as valid by the firm.

The FOS has two jurisdictions:

- Compulsory jurisdiction automatically covers firms regulated by the FCA for certain types of complaints.
- Voluntary jurisdiction covers firms for certain types of complaints not covered automatically by law under compulsory jurisdiction. Firms sign up to join the voluntary jurisdiction by contractual agreement with the FOS.

The FOS operates a scheme to facilitate the settlement of disputes between a customer and a firm where a complaint has not been resolved to the satisfaction of the complainant. The scheme can be used by a customer where a complaint has not been settled within two months. However, the complaint must be referred to the FOS within six years of the event complained of, or within three years of the customer knowing of the problem and currently within six months of the firm's final response.

The FOS may dismiss a complaint without considering its merits if, for example:

- It is satisfied that the complainant has not suffered financial loss, material inconvenience or material distress.
- It considers the complaint to be frivolous or vexatious.
- It considers that the firm has already made a reasonable offer of compensation.

When the Ombudsman investigates a complaint, the firm must co-operate with the FOS. When the FOS considers that there is a reasonable prospect of resolving the complaint by mediation, they will attempt to negotiate such a settlement between the parties. If there is no prospect for a mediated settlement, then they will investigate the complaint.

During this investigation, both parties are given the opportunity to make representations. A provisional assessment of the complaint is then made. If either party disagrees with this, the FOS will present a written statement of the determination and the reasons for this. If the complainant accepts the determination, it is binding on the firm but if the complainant rejects the determination, the firm is not bound by it. The maximum money award the FOS can make is £150,000. For awards over this the firm is invited to pay the excess, but is not compelled to do so.

The Financial Services Act 2012 introduced a requirement on the FOS to publish determinations and firms are expected to use these when assessing the merits of a complaint and calculating compensation for redress of similar circumstances.

3. FINANCIAL SERVICES COMPENSATION SCHEME

The Financial Services Compensation Scheme (FSCS) deals with claims against authorised firms that are insolvent or are no longer trading. Where a firm is still trading, redress must be sought through the FOS. Only certain kinds of claim are eligible for compensation. In relation to investment business, these are known as protected investment business and are defined as:

- Designated investment business carried on by the relevant person with the claimant or as agent on his or her behalf.
- The activities of the manager or trustee of an AUT, provided that the claim is made by a unit holder.
- The activities of the authorised corporate director (ACD) or depositary of an ICVC (e.g. an OEIC), provided that the claim is made by a shareholder.

A claim must be brought to the FSCS within a set time (normally within six years of the date on which the event giving rise to the claim occurred). The maximum payout for a claim against an investment firm (i.e. in relation to protected investment business) is £50,000. Separate FSCS arrangements exist to protect deposit accounts at UK authorised banks and policy holders of UK authorised insurers.

CHAPTER 3 SECTION 7

FINANCIAL CRIME

SECTION AIMS

By the end of this section, learners should be able to:

- Explain the various sources of money laundering and counter-terrorism regulation and legislation (FCA rules, Money Laundering Regulations, Proceeds of Crime Act 2002).
- Explain the role of the Joint Money Laundering Steering Group (JMLSG).
- Explain the main features of the guidance provided by the JMLSG.
- Explain the three stages involved in the money laundering process.
- Explain the four offence categories under UK money laundering legislation.
- Explain the meaning of 'inside information' covered by Criminal Justice Act (CJA) 1993.
- Explain the offence of insider dealing covered by the CJA 1993.
- Identify the penalties for being found guilty of insider dealing.
- Explain the FCA's powers to prosecute insider dealing.
- Describe the behaviours defined as market abuse (MAR 1.3–1.9).
- Explain the enforcement powers of the FCA relating to market abuse (MAR 1.1.4, 1.1.5 and 1.1.6).
- Explain the main features of the Bribery Act 2010.

1. MONEY LAUNDERING AND TERRORIST FINANCING

Money laundering is the process by which criminals disguise the source of their proceeds of crime. Its secondary objectives include providing a safe haven for those proceeds and providing a financial return on those proceeds by using legitimate business.

The Proceeds of Crime Act 2002 (POCA) replaced all previous anti-money laundering legislation. It extended the offence of money laundering to the proceeds of any crime and not just serious crime, drug trafficking and terrorist offences. Specific obligations to combat terrorist financing were set out in the Terrorism Act 2000.

POCA imposes an objective burden of proof for suspicion. Under previous legislation, it was only a criminal offence to fail to report suspicion of money laundering. Under POCA, it is a criminal offence to fail to be suspicious of behaviour that would ordinarily give rise to such suspicion. In other words, an offence is committed where the person ought to have suspected that another person was laundering the proceeds of crime. Members of staff within a financial firm are provided with a defence against not reporting knowledge or suspicion of money laundering if their employer did not provide them with the training required under the regulations.

The laundering process is accomplished in three stages, which may comprise many transactions that could alert an investment business that criminal activity is being undertaken:

- Placement: the physical injection into the financial system of cash proceeds obtained from criminal activity.
- Layering: the separation of criminal proceeds from their source by creating complex layers of financial transactions designed to disguise the audit trail.
- Integration: the provision of apparent legitimacy to criminally derived wealth. Integration schemes place the laundered proceeds back into the economy in such a way that they appear to be legitimate investment funds.

As cash settlement of investment transactions is extremely unusual in the UK, it is more likely that the placement stage will involve banks and building societies. However, bearer securities delivered other than through an established clearing system should merit special attention. Investment businesses are more likely to find that they are used in the second and third stages of money laundering.

2. THE MONEY LAUNDERING REGULATIONS 2007

The Money Laundering Regulations 2007 implement the Third EU Money Laundering Directive and came into effect in December 2007. They impose on firms a risk-based approach to combat money laundering. This breaks down into four key questions:

1. What are the firm's money laundering and terrorist financing risks? This requires consideration of the following:
   - What risks arise as a result of the jurisdictions in which the firm does business?
   - What risks arise as a result of the products and services the firm offers?
   - What risks arise because of the type of customers that the firm does business with? E.g. what jurisdictions with weak anti-money laundering rules are those customers from, what type of activity is required, are they high net worth individuals or potential recipients of bribes, etc?
2. What steps could be taken to reduce those risks?
3. What policies and procedures therefore need to be adopted in light of those risks?
4. What procedures are 'appropriate'?

There is an obligation on firms to pursue customer due diligence (CDD), essentially verifying the identity of the customer and determining the basis for the client relationship. Under the 2007 regulations, firms must:

- Identify the customer and verify the customer's identity on the basis of documents, data or information obtained from a reliable and independent source.
- Identify the beneficial owner and take adequate measures on a risk-sensitive basis to verify their identity, so that the firm is satisfied that it knows who the beneficial owner is.
- Obtain information on the purpose and intended nature of the business relationship.
- Keep the documents, etc, obtained for the purpose of applying CDD up-to-date.
- Conduct ongoing monitoring of the business relationship.

The requirement in the regulations is that firms – upon identifying a beneficial owner who is not the customer – take adequate measures, on a risk-sensitive basis, to verify their identity so that the relevant person is satisfied that they know who the beneficial owner is.

Firms are also required to undertake enhanced or simplified CDD in certain circumstances. The simplified due diligence (SDD) regulation provides that certain CDD measures do not need to be applied to specified types of customers and products. For example:

- Credit or financial institutions subject to the Third Money Laundering Directive.
- Supervised credit or financial institutions in states with comparable anti-money laundering controls.

- Listed companies on regulated markets with specified disclosure obligations.
- The beneficiaries of solicitor's accounts.
- Certain defined public authorities.
- Certain insurance products and pension schemes.
- Certain other types of defined products, such as child trust funds.

Enhanced due diligence (EDD) applies in four circumstances:

- Where business is conducted on a non-face-to-face basis.
- In respect of correspondent banking relationships.
- Where a situation by its nature can present a higher risk of money laundering or terrorist financing.
- Where the customer is a politically-exposed person (PEP).

With PEPs, a firm is obliged to have in place procedures to ascertain whether an individual is a PEP. The 2007 regulations provide that a firm has to have in place:

- A requirement that all PEP relationships must be approved by senior management.
- Adequate measures to establish source of funds and source of wealth.
- Enhanced ongoing monitoring procedures.

A PEP is defined as a person who discharges, outside the UK, prominent public functions (which are defined in the regulations), an immediate family member of such a person and known close associates. The 2007 regulations also place emphasis on ongoing monitoring of relationships with customers.

The FCA rules require firms to appoint a money laundering reporting officer (MLRO). The MLRO is responsible for the oversight of the firm's anti-money laundering activities and is the key person in the firm's implementation of anti-money laundering strategies and policies.

The 2007 money laundering regulations require investment businesses to establish and maintain specific policies, procedures and training programmes to prevent their business being used for the purposes of money laundering. In brief, these regulations are designed to achieve two purposes:

- To enable suspicious customers and transactions to be recognised and reported to the authorities (the National Crime Agency (NCA)).

- To ensure that if a customer comes under investigation, the firm can provide its part of the audit trail.

The FCA no longer provides detailed rules on combating money laundering, but instead has a set of high level principles and informal guidance relating to money laundering contained in SYSC. To supplement that guidance, the Handbook also includes examples of good practice in its Regulatory Guide: 'Financial Crime: a guide for firms' (updated in April 2015).

The FCA also places emphasis on the guidance provided by the Joint Money Laundering Steering Group (JMLSG), which is approved by HM Treasury. It states that the FCA, when considering whether a breach of its rules on systems and controls against money laundering has occurred, will have regard to whether a firm has followed relevant provisions in the guidance for the UK financial sector issued by the JMLSG.

The JMLSG is made up of the leading UK trade associations in the financial services industry. Its aim is to promote good practice in countering money laundering, and to give practical assistance in interpreting the UK money laundering regulations.

The main requirements are:

- Internal controls, policies and procedures. Firms are required to ensure that policies, procedures and controls are introduced to deter criminals from using their facilities for money laundering. All firms should establish a central point of contact with the law enforcement agencies (i.e. a MLRO or Nominated Officer).

- Identification procedures. Firms are required to obtain satisfactory evidence of the identity of those with whom they do business in a timely manner.

- Record keeping. Records must be retained for at least five years after the completion of the business. Firms should retain records concerning inter alia, customer identification, transactions, suspicion reports and training and competence monitoring. This enables the firm to provide a clear audit trail.

- Recognition and reporting of suspicious transactions. A suspicious transaction is one which is inconsistent with an investor's known legitimate business or personal activities. Thus, the first key to recognition is to have sufficient knowledge of the investor's business to recognise that a transaction, or a series of transactions, is unusual. There is an obligation on all staff to report suspicious transactions to the MLRO/Nominated Officer. The MLRO is also required to report to the NCA where they have received an internal report and have knowledge, suspicion or reasonable grounds to suspect money laundering.

- Training. In order for procedures and recommendations above to be effective, it is important that staff are made aware of their obligations and are trained to provide a prompt report of any suspicious transactions.

Offences under the law are:

- Assistance: any person assisting money laundering is punishable on conviction by a maximum of 14 years' imprisonment, or a fine, or both.
- Tipping-off: where a person informs anyone connected with an investigation into money laundering that such an investigation is occurring. Under section 333A of POCA, where the offence is committed by someone in the regulated sector (broadly, the financial services sector), the punishment on conviction is a maximum of two years' imprisonment, or a fine, or both.
- Failure to report: where a person fails to report knowledge or suspicion of money laundering, the punishment on conviction is a maximum of five years' imprisonment, or a fine, or both. It should be noted that the Serious Crime Act 2015 introduced protection from civil liability for those making a report in good faith.
- Failure to comply: failure to comply with the requirements of the regulations, (e.g. failure to implement satisfactory identification procedures) constitutes an offence punishable by a maximum of two years' imprisonment, or a fine, or both.

3. INSIDER DEALING

The legislation covering insider dealing is the Criminal Justice Act 1993, Part V (CJA), which came into force in April 1994. This Act gave effect to an EU directive on insider dealing. The overall objective of insider dealing laws is to protect corporate confidences and to prevent insiders privy to such confidences from benefiting from an unfair advantage when they deal in the market. There are three principal insider dealing offences:

- Dealing while in possession of inside information.
- Encouraging another to deal, knowing, or reasonably believing, that dealing will occur. Dealing, in this context includes any communication that refers to a security that a person may hold and encourages them not to sell.
- Disclosing information to another other than in the proper performance of one's duties.

The investments covered by the CJA include shares, debentures, options, warrants and public sector debt instruments. The dealings in such securities that are covered by the CJA are those on any investment exchange, as well as off-market deals facilitated by professional intermediaries (professional intermediaries include UK and overseas market makers and brokers, but not usually accountants and solicitors). Thus transactions like arranging underwritings and firm placings are covered by the legislation.

The CJA defines information as price-sensitive information of a specific and precise nature. If such information were to be made public, it would be likely to have a significant effect on the price. The CJA provides the following main defences to insider dealing:

- An individual passed on information in the proper performance of their duties but did not expect the recipient to deal.
- The deal was not done to make a profit or avoid a loss.
- A new issue was stabilised under the strict terms of the FCA's stabilisation rules.
- A market maker had inside information in the course of their business but acted bona fide for that business.
- The person dealing only had the information that certain securities were to be or had been issued, acquired or disposed of, and it was therefore reasonable to deal.

For example, this defence would cover predator companies purchasing shares in target companies before announcing a bid, or institutional shareholders not announcing their intentions of buying or selling a large volume of securities before doing so. A person acting in such a capacity on a recognised investment exchange is not prevented from dealing while in possession of unpublished price-sensitive information if such information was obtained in the normal course of their business.

An individual found guilty of insider dealing shall be liable:

- On summary conviction (in a magistrates' court), to a fine not exceeding the statutory maximum or imprisonment for a term not exceeding six months, or both.
- On conviction or indictment (in a crown court), to a fine or imprisonment for a term not exceeding seven years, or both.

4. MARKET ABUSE

On 1 July 2005, the Financial Services and Markets Act 2000 (Market Abuse) Regulation 2005 came into force in order to implement the EC directive on insider dealing and market manipulation (market abuse). The directive also introduced a new requirement for firms to report transactions giving rise to suspicions of market abuse.

A person who engages in conduct amounting to market abuse may find that it is also in breach of the provisions of the criminal law which runs in parallel to the FSMA market abuse regime.

Sections 401 and 402 of the FSMA give the FCA power to prosecute a number of offences under FSMA and other legislation. The offences for which the FCA can take criminal action are broad. Some of the most important are:

- Offences relating to breaches of the FCA listing rules, including that of offering new securities to the public in the UK before publishing a prospectus, if required by listing rules.
- Making misleading statements and market manipulation.
- Misleading the FCA.
- Insider dealing under Part V of the Criminal Justice Act 1993.
- Breaches of prescribed regulations relating to money laundering.

In the majority of cases, the FCA is likely to commence an investigation based on breaches of the civil market abuse regime.

For market abuse to occur, the behaviour must relate to a 'qualifying investment' traded on a 'prescribed market'. A prescribed market is essentially a recognised investment exchange located in the UK and all other regulated markets in the EEA. A qualifying investment is essentially a security, right or interest traded on a prescribed market.

The types of behaviour that can constitute market abuse are listed below, together with an example of the behaviour taken from the FCA Code of Market Conduct:

Insider dealing: where an insider deals, or attempts to deal, in a qualifying investment or related investment on the basis of inside information (this sits alongside the criminal offence of insider dealing).

An example of insider dealing is where A, a director at X PLC, has lunch with a friend, B. A tells B that their own company has received a takeover offer that is at a premium to the current share price at which it is trading. B enters into a spread bet priced by reference to the share price of X PLC, based on their expectation that the price of X PLC will increase once the takeover offer is announced.

Improper disclosure: where an insider discloses inside information to another, other than in the proper course of the exercise of their employment, profession or duties.

An example of encouraging another to engage in market abuse (improper disclosure): X, an analyst employed by an investment bank, telephones the finance director at B PLC and presses for details of the profit and loss account from the latest unpublished management accounts of B PLC.

Manipulating transactions: this includes practices that give a false or misleading impression of the price or demand of a qualifying investment.

An example of manipulating transactions type behaviour is where a trader simultaneously buys and sells the same investment (that is, trades with themselves) to give the appearance of a legitimate transfer of title or risk (or both) at a price outside the normal trading range for the investment.

The price of the qualifying investment is relevant to the calculation of the settlement value of an option. They do this while holding a position in the option. Their purpose is to position the price of the investment at a false, misleading, abnormal or artificial level, making a profit or avoiding a loss from the option.

Manipulating devices: effecting transactions or orders to trade which employ fictitious devices or other forms of deception.

An example of behaviour that amounts to manipulating devices is that of taking a short position in an investment and then disseminating misleading negative information about the investment, with a view to driving down its price.

Dissemination: the dissemination of information which gives a false or misleading impression as to a qualifying investment by a person who knew, or could reasonably be expected to know, that the information was false or misleading.

An example of this type of behaviour is where a person posts information on an internet forum or social networking site which contains false or misleading statements about the takeover of a company whose shares are qualifying investments, and the person knows that the information is false or misleading.

Misleading behaviour and distortion: behaviour that gives a false or misleading impression of either the supply of, or demand for, an investment; or behaviour that otherwise distorts the market in an investment.

An example of this behaviour is the movement of physical commodity stocks, which might create a misleading impression as to the supply of, demand for, or price or value of a commodity or the deliverable into a commodity futures contract.

The FCA can ask the courts to impose a fine for insider dealing or make a statement to the effect that a person has engaged in market abuse and issue a 'sanction' in the form of a financial penalty. Market abuse is therefore a civil offence, and does not replace or modify any existing criminal legislation.

5. UK BRIBERY ACT 2010

The Bribery Act 2010 came into force on 1 July 2011. The Act repeals and replaces the old laws on bribery with a new comprehensive anti-bribery code.

There are four offences:

1. Paying bribes. It is an offence to offer, promise or give a financial or other advantage with the intention of inducing a person to perform a 'relevant function or activity' 'improperly' or to reward that person for doing so.
2. Receiving bribes. It is an offence to receive, request or agree to receive a financial or other advantage intending that a 'relevant function or activity' should be performed 'improperly' as a result.
3. The bribery of foreign public officials.
4. Failure of commercial organisations to prevent bribery.

'Relevant function or activity' includes any function of a public nature and any activity connected with a business. The person performing that activity must be expected to perform it in good faith or impartially or be in a position of trust. 'Improper performance' will be judged by whether it breaches the expectation of what a reasonable person in the UK would expect in relation to the performance of the type of function or activity concerned. However, the function or activity need have no connection to the UK.

The last offence is probably the most important change from the previous legislation, as it places the onus on a company to have in place anti-bribery procedures. The most controversial offence is this new offence, which can be committed only by commercial organisations (companies and partnerships). It will be committed where:

- a person associated with a relevant commercial organisation (which includes not only employees, but agents and external third parties) bribes another person (i.e. commits one of the offences numbered one or three) intending to obtain or retain a business advantage; and
- the organisation cannot show that it had adequate procedures in place to prevent bribes being paid.

Under the previous law (and under the new general offences numbered one and two), a company was likely to be guilty of a bribery offence only if very senior management were involved. Under this new corporate criminal offence, the company may be guilty even if nobody in the company knew of the bribery.

The company's defence is limited to showing that it had 'adequate procedures' to prevent bribery. That effectively creates a burden on corporates to ensure that their anti-corruption procedures are sufficiently robust to stop any employees, agents or other third parties acting on the corporates' behalf from committing bribery.

The government has published illustrative guidance on what amounts to 'adequate procedures'. This requires procedures to be tailored to the individual circumstances of each business based on an assessment of where the risks lie. Ultimately, it will be left to the courts to assess whether a corporate has adequate procedures in place, and it will be for the corporate body to prove that it has.

Penalties

The Act raised the maximum jail term for bribery by an individual from seven years to ten years. A company convicted of failing to prevent bribery could receive an unlimited fine.

CHAPTER 03 KEY FACTS

3.1

1. European Union directives are issued under section 58 of the European Treaty and have to be complied with by all member states. The aim of a directive is the harmonisation of laws across member states.

2. A directive prescribes a particular result to be achieved by a particular date. It is left to member states to implement the directive into national law.

3. There are two methods of implementing a directive:

   - By primary legislation;
   - By delegated legislation under section 2 of the European Communities Act (1972).

   Method (ii) is now more commonly used in the UK, and allows regulations issued as a statutory instrument to alter a statute in so far as it is necessary to implement a directive.

4. MiFID enables an investment firm established in one member state to operate throughout the European Economic Area without separate authorisation by the member states in which it does business.

5. The UCITS Directives give automatic recognition in the UK to other collective investment schemes constituted in an EU member state other than the UK.

3.2

6. There are three regulatory bodies:

   - The Financial Conduct Authority (FCA) – responsible for regulating the conduct of business (although will also prudentially regulate all but the largest financial firms).
   - The Prudential Regulation Authority (PRA) – responsible for the prudential regulation of banks, insurance companies and systemically important investment firms.
   - The Financial Policy Committee (FPC) – responsible for macro-prudential (systemic) regulation of the financial system.

7. The FCA has three operational objectives:

   - The consumer protection objective.

- The integrity objective.
- The competition objective.

8. The Competition and Markets Authority (CMA) largely acts as an independent competition authority. The Secretary of State at the Department for Business, Innovation and Skills will only intervene in exceptional cases where there are public interest issues.
9. The CMA must investigate all mergers where the merged company will control greater than 25% of the UK market, or where UK turnover of the target firm exceeds £70m.
10. The Panel on Takeovers and Mergers is responsible for enforcing the City Code on Takeovers and Mergers.
11. Any bidder acquiring more than 30% of the voting rights of a company is required to make a cash offer to other shareholders.
12. Where a company acquires 90% of another company, it can force the remaining shareholders to sell their shares.
13. The Information Commissioner is the person responsible for regulating compliance with the Data Protection Act 1998.
14. Anyone who undertakes investment business in the UK has to be an authorised person, passported under an EU directive or an exempted person.
15. The investment activities that require regulation are set out in the Regulated Activities Order.
16. Specified investments are set out in the Regulated Activities Order and include investments other than physical objects. Deposits and general insurance contracts are also regulated.
17. Some investment persons are classed as exempted and hence do not require authorisation. Appointed representatives are an example of an exempted person.
18. The main purpose of SYSC is to encourage firms' directors and senior managers to take appropriate practical responsibility for their firms' arrangements on matters of interest to the FCA.
19. For common platform firms (firms subject to one or both of MiFID and the CRD), chapters 4–10 of SYSC apply.

20. The Pensions Act 2004 requires trustees to appoint their own actuary, auditor, legal and financial advisers.

21. Trustees are responsible, in consultation with the sponsoring employer, to produce a statement of investment principles (SIP). This sets out in writing the trustees' attitude to various issues, including:

    - The scheme-specific funding requirement.
    - The nature of investments held by the fund.
    - The risk of the fund.

    The SIP is to be reviewed every three years.

22. Where the trust instrument allows, trustees may appoint an investment manager to carry out investment policies. Where the trust instrument does not allow this, the trustees must select investments themselves, although they must seek investment advice.

23. The Pensions Act 2004 also introduced the scheme-specific funding requirement, which requires all occupational defined benefit schemes to be periodically valued by an actuary.

24. The Pensions Regulator investigates occupational pension schemes in response to infringement of statutory rules.

3.3

1. There is a Handbook to cover all aspects of FCA regulation. The Conduct of Business rules apply to all firms conducting designated investment business.

2. The eleven Principles for Businesses set out the standards expected of all authorised persons.

3. The breach of a principle does not, of itself, enable any person to initiate a court action against an FCA regulated firm, but it will be taken into account by the FCA for purposes of its disciplinary and intervention powers

4. A UK firm undertaking investment business must apply to the FCA for Part 4A permission. The permission granted will specify the scope of the activities and investments that the firm is authorised to undertake. Limitations or requirements may also be imposed by the FCA.

5. In order to gain Part 4A permission, an applicant must satisfy the threshold conditions.

6. Before an individual in an investment firm can undertake a controlled function, he/she must first be approved by the FCA.

7. The following five categories of functions are classified as controlled functions:

   - Governing functions.
   - Required functions.
   - Systems and control functions.
   - Significant management functions.
   - Customer functions.

8. There are seven statements of principle with which approved persons in a significant influence function must comply.

9. The approved status regime allows the FCA to discipline an individual without the firm being disciplined.

10. Where an individual has attained threshold competence, they can operate without close supervision.

11. The professionalism requirements for retail investment advisers require advisers to:

    - Subscribe to a code of ethics.
    - Hold an appropriate qualification.
    - Carry out at least 35 hours continuous professional development a year.
    - Hold a statement of professional standing from an accredited body.

3.4

1. The FCA recognises and supervises a number of exchanges; it requires high standards of investor protection and investor integrity. MiFID introduced requirements regarding pre- and post-trade transparency.

2. The LSE admits companies if they satisfy the criteria of the UKLA. The prospectus directive allows capital raising in any EU country. Listing on AIM requires different and less onerous size and other requirements than on the main market.

3. Derivatives exchanges in the UK are regulated by the FCA, while in the US it is the SEC and CFTC. In the UK, clearing takes place through LCH.Clearnet.

4. MiFID brought commodity futures into the list of regulated investments and introduced new rules for pre- and post-trade transparency.

5. IAS39 requires derivatives to be measured at fair value for accounting purposes.

3.5

1. A client is classed as a retail client, a professional client or an eligible counterparty.

2. A professional client would be an investment company, a local or public authority or a large company.

3. An expert retail client can be classed as a professional client if:

   - The client has sufficient experience/understanding (and, for MiFID business, passes a quantitative test relating to size of portfolio, etc).

   - The client is given written warning of the protections lost.

   - The client has given written consent.

4. An authorised firm will be classified as an eligible counterparty for specific types of business.

5. Any large undertaking can be classified as an elective eligible counterparty providing consent is obtained.

6. A retail client should be provided with a client agreement before any business is undertaken.

7. Any inducement paid to an investment firm must be designed to enhance the quality of the firm's services.

8. The Financial Promotion Rules set the standard for determining whether a promotion is fair and reasonable. They apply mainly to promotions aimed at retail clients.

9. Exceptions to the financial promotion rules apply to:

   - One-off promotions.

   - Generic advertising.

- Financial promotions aimed at investment professionals and eligible counterparties.

10. An unsolicited call to obtain investment business is prohibited except where calling on:

    - Investment professionals.
    - Retail clients where the client agreement permits this.

11. Direct offer promotions are promotions aimed at retail clients containing an offer, or an invitation to respond by making an offer, to enter into an investment agreement.

12. From 1 January 2013 a firm giving investment advice to a retail client in the UK to invest in a retail investment product no longer earns commission set by the product provider.

13. A firm providing advice or discretionary portfolio management services to retail or professional clients must assess the suitability of such products/services for the client.

14. A firm providing investment services other than advice or discretionary portfolio management is required to assess the appropriateness of services/products for clients.

15. A firm offering independent advice must have knowledge of the full range of retail investment products.

16. Firms must establish a best execution policy and keep this up to date.

17. Firms should be able to demonstrate that they have executed client orders in accordance with the firm's policy.

18. A firm should provide a retail client with its order execution policy prior to provision of its services.

19. A firm should review annually (or where there is a change) its best execution and order execution policies.

20. Firms are not permitted to execute orders through a broker for commission in return for receiving goods and services, unless the goods and services constitute research or will assist the firm in the provision of its services.

21. A firm must make its employees aware of the FCA restrictions on personal account dealing and must keep a record of any personal transactions.

22. Firms are required to address potential conflicts of interest between itself (including individual employees) and clients and between clients. To achieve this firms should take

all reasonable steps to:

- Identify conflicts of interest.
- Maintain and operating effective organisational and administrative arrangements to prevent conflicts of interest resulting in a material risk of damage to clients' interests.
- Disclose conflicts where there remains a risk of damage to clients' interests.

A common platform firm must establish, implement and maintain an effective conflicts of interest policy that is set out in writing.

23. Investment research means research containing analysis and recommending an investment strategy.
24. Investment analysts or firms providing investment research are not permitted to deal ahead of publication to clients for whom the research is intended.
25. Packaged products are investment products designed for retail clients, and include life policies, personal pensions and authorised unit trusts.
26. Where a firm recommends a packaged product to a retail customer, it must provide key features of the product in written form.
27. One of the key provisions of the UCITS IV Directive (implemented in 2011) is the introduction of the key investor information document (KIID). This provides key facts about a UCITS scheme to retail investors.
28. A firm must normally keep records of advice given to customers and any cancellations for at least five years for life policies, pension contracts or stakeholder pensions, and three years for other packaged products.
29. Retail investment products is wider than the category of packaged products, including investments that offer exposure to an underlying financial asset, in a packaged form.
30. Fiduciary duty means to act in the best interest of another party.
31. A firm which has safekeeping of a client's investments must register the investments in the name of the customer or another prescribed manner and always keep them segregated from the firm's investments.

32. A firm must comply with the client money rules and keep clients' money separate from its own in a client bank account or other authorised fund.

33. A firm must maintain accurate records of money and assets at all times, and reconcile as often as necessary.

34. A mandate is any means that give a firm the ability to control a client's assets or liabilities.

3.6

1. The FCA has the power to require a firm to produce information. It can issue a private warning or a public statement about breaches of rules. It can also impose fines on firms for breaches of rules, and in extreme cases can cancel a firm's permission.

2. A firm has right to appeal to the Tax and Chancery Chamber of the Upper Tribunal in relation to any decision made by the FCA.

3. The Financial Services Act 2012 gives the FCA the power to ban products that it believes provide an unacceptable risk to consumers.

4. The Financial Services Act 2012 also gives the FCA the power to ban misleading financial promotions.

5. A firm must ensure its complaints procedures are set out in writing and that this document is made available to each person engaged in the firm's business.

6. An eligible complainant has a right to complain to the Financial Ombudsman Service if the complaint is not settled by the firm within eight weeks.

7. The maximum award the Financial Ombudsman can make is £150,000.

8. The Financial Services Compensation Scheme (FSCS) deals with claims against authorised firms that are insolvent or no longer trading.

9. The maximum payout from the FSCS for protected investment business is £50,000.

3.7

1. Money laundering is the process by which criminals hide the source of their proceeds of crime. It is an offence for an investment business not to have in place procedures for preventing and investigating money laundering or terrorist financing transactions.

2. POCA provides the legislative framework for money laundering offences.

3. All investment firms should appoint a money laundering reporting officer.

4. Firms are required to obtain evidence of identity of those they do business with and report suspicious transactions.

5. The FCA places emphasis on the guidance provided by the Joint Money Laundering Steering Group in determining whether a firm has breached the rules on money laundering.

6. The Criminal Justice Act 1993 makes insider dealing a criminal offence.

7. The three principle offences of insider dealing are:

   - Dealing while in possession of inside information.
   - Encouraging another to deal on the basis of inside information.
   - Disclosing inside information to another (other than in the proper performance of one's duty).

8. Inside information is defined as price-sensitive information of a specific and precise nature.

9. The FCA Code on Market Conduct gives guidance on what constitutes market abuse.

10. Market abuse is a civil offence. The FCA can impose a financial penalty or make a statement to the effect that a person has engaged in market abuse.

11. For market abuse to occur, the behaviour must relate to a qualifying investment traded on a prescribed market.

12. There are certain types of behaviour which constitute a safe harbour in relation to market abuse. These include behaviour in accordance with the price stabilisation rules.

13. The Bribery Act 2010 introduces four offences:

    - Paying bribes (active bribery (offer, promise, pay)).
    - Receiving bribes (passive bribery (receive, request, agree to receive)).
    - Bribing foreign public officials.
    - Failure of a commercial organisation to prevent bribery.

CHAPTER 03 SELF-ASSESSMENT QUESTIONS

1. **The Financial Policy Committee (FPC) is responsible for which of the following?**

(a) *Monetary policy.*

(b) *Prudential regulation of banks.*

(c) *Conduct regulation of financial firms.*

(d) *Macro-prudential policy.*

2. **Which one of the following investments is not a regulated investment under the Regulated Activities Order?**

(a) *Land.*

(b) *Traded options.*

(c) *Commodity futures.*

(d) *Gilt-edged securities.*

3. **The Competitions and Markets Authority has a duty to investigate all mergers where the target company has a UK turnover exceeding:**

(a) *£30m.*

(b) *£50m.*

(c) *£70m.*

(d) *£100m.*

4. **A company seeking to take over a target company needs to acquire what percentage of the target company's shares before it can force the minority shareholders in the target company to sell their shares?**

(a) *50%.*

(b) *70%.*

(c) *75%.*

(d) *90%.*

5. **The Scorlotti trust fund is governed by the Trustee Act 2000. Which of the following types of investments is the fund permitted to invest in?**

(i) UK growth unit trust units.

(ii) Commercial property.

(iii) Gilt-edged securities.

(a) *(i) and (ii) only.*

(b) *(i) and (iii) only.*

(c) *(ii) and (iii) only.*

(d) *(i), (ii) and (iii).*

6. **The FCA Principles for Businesses apply to:**

(a) *Appointed representatives only.*

(b) *Banks only.*

(c) *Investment firms only.*

(d) *All FCA authorised persons.*

7. **A large undertaking with assets valued at £20m and with own funds of £5m approaches a firm for investment advice. Under which one of the following categories would this client normally be classed?**

(a) *A retail client.*

(b) *A professional client.*

(c) *An eligible counterparty.*

(d) *An exempted person.*

8. **When a financial promotion aimed at retail clients uses comparisons with other products, the comparisons should be:**

(i) Meaningful.

(ii) Balanced.

(iii) Sourced.

(a) *(i) only.*

(b) *(i) and (ii) only.*

(c) *(i) and (iii) only.*

(d) *(i), (ii) and (iii).*

9. The requirement to assess suitability of a client is for which type of investment services?

(i) Investment advice.

(ii) Discretionary portfolio management.

(iii) Derivatives business.

(a) *(i) only.*

(b) *(i) and (ii) only.*

(c) *(ii) and (iii) only.*

(d) *(i), (ii) and (iii).*

10. Which one of the following is not classed as a packaged product?

(a) *Personal pension.*

(b) *Life policy.*

(c) *Gilt-edged security.*

(d) *Units in an authorised unit trust.*

11. Under which circumstances is a firm that is holding client money able to hold this money in the firm's own bank account?

(a) *Where it holds the money for a period of less than two weeks.*

(b) *Where it can demonstrate it earns a better rate of interest.*

(c) *Where the account is held with one of the UK clearing banks.*

(d) *Where the firm can demonstrate compliance with the alternative approach.*

12. Which of the following services, provided free to an investment firm by a broker, would be deemed as acceptable acquisitions using dealing commission?

(i) Investment research.

(ii) Computer hardware.

(iii) Salaries of certain employees of the investment firm.

(a) *(i) only.*

(b) *(i) and (ii) only.*

(c) *(ii), and (iii) only.*

(d) *(i), (ii) and (iii).*

13. Under which one of the following circumstances is a firm not required to provide immediate confirmation to a customer?

(a) *A one-off transaction in an authorised unit trust.*

(b) *A one-off transaction in a share.*

(c) *A one-off transaction in a share relating to a discretionary management agreement.*

(d) *A one-off transaction in a gilt-edged security.*

14. If an investment firm receives a complaint from a customer and is unable to settle it to the satisfaction of the customer, after what period of time can the customer take up the matter with the financial ombudsman?

(a) *Two weeks.*

(b) *Four weeks.*

(c) *Six weeks.*

(d) *Eight weeks.*

15. **Which of the following types of dealings are covered by the insider dealing provisions of the Criminal Justice Act 1993?**

(i) Dealings in IFE traded options.

(ii) Underwriting of a share issue by a professional intermediary.

(iii) A placing of new shares by a professional intermediary.

(a) *(i) only.*

(b) *(i) and (ii) only.*

(c) *(ii) and (iii) only.*

(d) *(i), (ii) and (iii).*

16. **If an employee of an investment firm notices a suspicious transaction undertaken by a client, they should report this to:**

(a) *The firm's compliance officer.*

(b) *The firm's money laundering reporting officer.*

(c) *The Bank of England.*

(d) *The Financial Conduct Authority.*

17. **What best describes a European Union (EU) directive?**

(a) *A reprimand to a state that is breaking an EU law.*

(b) *A directive that an EU state can choose to implement into national law.*

(c) *A directive that all EU member states have to implement into national law.*

(d) *A note of guidance issued to EU states on an aspect of EU law.*

ANSWERS

1. *(d) The Financial Policy Committee is responsible for implementing macro-prudential policy. The Prudential Regulation Authority is responsible for prudential regulation of banks. The Financial Conduct Authority is responsible for regulating the conduct of financial firms and the Bank of England is responsible for monetary policy.*
2. *(a) Physical investments such as land are not regulated investments.*
3. *(c) The CMA has a duty to investigate where the target company has a UK turnover of £70m.*
4. *(d) Once an acquiring company has acquired 90% or more of a target company's shares it can force the remaining shareholders to sell.*
5. *(d) The Trustee Act 2000 is relatively permissive and allows a fund governed by it to invest in most asset classes, including land and property.*
6. *(d) The FCA Principles for Businesses apply to all FCA regulated firms and set out the fundamental principles under which all FCA regulated firms are expected to operate.*
7. *(b) A large undertaking meeting two of the following size requirements on a company basis:*

   – Balance sheet total of €20m;

   – Net turnover of €40m;

   – Own funds of €2m.

   would be classed as per se professional client. The client in this question satisfies the first and third requirements.
8. *(d) For promotions aimed at retail clients all three characteristics are important.*
9. *(b) Investment advice and discretionary portfolio management require an assessment of suitability. Derivatives business would normally be classed as complex business and, if the transactions are entrusted by the client on a non-advised basis, would require a test of appropriateness.*
10. *(c) A gilt-edged security is an original security and therefore cannot be a packaged product.*

11. *(d) A firm is not permitted to hold client money in one its own accounts unless it can demonstrate compliance with the alternative approach.*

12. *(a) An investment manager is prohibited from executing customer orders through a broker for dealing commission in return for receiving goods or services unless the goods or services are (i) related to the execution of trades on behalf of the investment managers' customers, or constitute the provision of research, or (ii) will reasonably assist the investment manager in the provision of its services to its customers. Only (i) in the question satisfies these conditions.*

13. *(c) One-off transactions as part of a discretionary management agreement do not have to be immediately confirmed to the client.*

14. *(d) A firm has eight weeks to respond to a complaint before the complainant can take the matter to the Financial Ombudsman.*

15. *(d) All of the categories are covered by insider dealing regulations.*

16. *(b) Employees of an investment firm should first report any suspicions of money laundering to the firm's designated money laundering reporting officer.*

17. *(c) All EU directives have to be implemented into national law.*

LINK TO CFA LEVEL 1

The material in this chapter is mainly UK-focused and is therefore not covered in CFA Level 1.

CHAPTER 4

LEGAL CONCEPTS

The relationship between an adviser and their client is shaped by a number of legal concepts. In carrying out their role, the adviser must understand their own legal status as well as that of their firm and their client. This chapter describes the nature of power of attorney, which can give the adviser the legal power to make decisions on their client's behalf.

A crucial consideration is the agency relationship, where a financial services entity acts on behalf of their clients. Laws of contract and ownership must also be fully understood to appreciate the significance of the agency relationship.

The unique legal nature of the various types of trust that may be used by individuals in family and personal financial planning and by larger entities, such as unit trusts, is also discussed. Key financial planning rules associated with wills and intestacy rules together with individual bankruptcy company insolvency rules make up the remainder of the chapter.

CHAPTER 4

LEGAL CONCEPTS

CHAPTER AIMS

By the end of this chapter, learners should be able to:

- Explain legal persons and power of attorney.
- Explain basic law of contract and agency.
- Explain the types of ownership of property.
- Explain insolvency and bankruptcy.
- Explain wills and intestacy.
- Describe the main types of trusts and their uses.

1. LEGAL PERSONS AND POWER OF ATTORNEY

A legal person has rights, protections, privileges, responsibilities and liabilities under law, just as natural persons do. Legal personality allows one or more natural persons to act as a single entity (a composite person) for legal purposes.

In many jurisdictions, legal personality allows such a composite to be considered under law separately from its individual members or shareholders. They may sue and be sued, enter into contracts, incur debt and have ownership over property. Entities with legal personality may also be subject to certain legal obligations, such as the payment of tax. Legal personality may shield an entity's participants, such as shareholders, from personal liability.

Common examples of legal persons include companies, sovereign states and co-operatives.

A power of attorney is a legal document that allows a person to give another person or persons the power to make decisions about their financial affairs and/or their health and personal welfare. It can take two forms: either an enduring power of attorney (EPA) or a lasting power of attorney (LPA).

The LPA was created in 2007 under the Mental Capacity Act 2005 and replaces the previous EPA, although EPAs created before 2007 remain valid. There are two types of LPA:

- A property and affairs LPA gives a person the ability to make decisions about somebody else's financial affairs.
- A personal welfare LPA gives a person the ability to make decisions relating to somebody else's personal healthcare and welfare, including decisions to give or refuse consent to treatment on their behalf.

Unlike its predecessor, the LPA must be registered with the Office of the Public Guardian to be effective. An EPA established before 1 October 2007 does not need to be altered.

2. THE BASIC LAW OF CONTRACT

A contract is essentially an agreement creating and defining the obligations between two or more parties.

The elements of a contract and the offer

For any contract to be considered legally binding, the elements of offer and acceptance must exist. The origin of a contract or agreement will begin with an offer and after the offer is accepted unconditionally, the contract is then formed. But there are other contract elements that are required by law, and if these are not present the courts may decide there is no contract.

Acceptance

Following an offer, there must be a willingness from the accepting party to enter into the contract. In order to make the contract complete, there must also be specific terms and conditions set out and accepted. Once the terms and conditions have been offered and accepted, and no further negotiations are intended, the contract can said to be complete or full.

Consideration

A contract may not be deemed to be enforceable by law if there was no consideration. This means that there must be mutual consideration on either side; one person promises to provide a service and the other pays in return.

Intention

When parties make an agreement with no intention of the agreement becoming legally binding, it will not be judged to be a contract under the eyes of the law. In some cases, such as commercial contracts, there is an assumption that the contract is intended to be legally binding. If one of the parties wants to bring the matter to court and argue that there was never any intention of a binding contract, they will need to have some form of clear written evidence.

Terms and conditions

If a contract dispute is brought to the law courts, strong emphasis will be placed on the terms and conditions of the contract – a contract cannot be said to be complete if the terms and conditions are not fully laid out. These conditions must not be vague or ambiguous. A contract will not usually be seen as legally binding if the terms and conditions are unclear. However, every case is different, and a judge may try to clarify the terms and conditions of the disputed contract.

Types of contract

In most cases, it makes sense to take the precaution of formalising all agreements with a written contract. But a contract may still be upheld if it is made orally. There are certain circumstances where contracts must be made in writing, such as the sale of property or tenancy agreements. If no written contract or statement exists, and the contract dispute has reached the courts, then the judge may look at how services, promises and exchanges were carried out practically in order to make a decision.

Contract discharge

A contract can come to an end in one of four ways: breach, performance, agreement and frustration. Discharge by performance means that all the obligations of the contract have been accomplished by both parties. Agreement of discharge can mean that both parties agree to end the contract or one party releases the other party from the agreement. Frustration means that events have occurred that made the completion of the contract impossible, and the obligations of the contract could not be met.

Breaching a contract

A breach of contract can occur if one party does not fulfil one or more of the specified terms and conditions. It can also occur if the work carried out is defective or if one party makes the other aware that they will not be carrying out the agreed work. The law can then be brought to judge on this contract dispute and can award the innocent party damages. Financial damages may only be awarded if the innocent party can prove financial loss. Court costs and solicitors' fees should be weighed up against the likelihood of any damages being awarded before proceeding with court cases.

3. OWNERSHIP OF PROPERTY

There are two types of property ownership under English law: legal ownership and beneficial ownership.

Legal ownership: The people named on the title documents are the legal owners. For example, the legal owners are the people listed as the 'registered proprietors' in the proprietorship register at the Land Registry or on share registers, etc. However, legal ownership is not significant as the use and title to the property lies with the beneficial owner.

Beneficial ownership: Beneficial owners have the right to live in or use a property where they may not be the legal owner. They also have the right to share in the proceeds of any sale. Beneficial owners have the power to control a sale of land or buildings. Other forms of property may have legal and beneficial ownership in different persons. For example, client money is money held in an account in the name of a firm but which is identified as being held in trust for its beneficial owner, or assets such as shares may be registered in a nominee name of a custodian who is not the beneficial owner.

Most people own their property as both legal and beneficial owners. In general, property can be held:

- in the absolute ownership of an individual;
- by two or more co-owners as tenants in common, where each person holds a share and is free to dispose of that share; or
- by two or more co-owners as joint tenants. A joint tenant can only dispose of their interest during their lifetime by giving notice to the other joint tenant and converting it into a tenancy in common. On the death of a joint tenant, their share passes to the other joint tenant(s).

A common practice for a couple is to change the ownership of the property to tenants in common. Each person then owns their share of the property. The individual person can then make changes to their will and bequeath their half of the property to their family on death. Provided the person has made provisions in their will to allow for market rent to be paid, there should be no liability to pre-owned assets tax (POAT).

4. INSOLVENCY AND BANKRUPTCY

Insolvency is generally defined as a financial state in which a company can no longer pay its bills and other obligations on time. It occurs when liabilities or debts exceed assets and cash flow. When a company becomes insolvent, it must take immediate action to generate cash and settle or renegotiate current debts. Companies which cannot successfully recover from insolvency often face bankruptcy proceedings, receivership or liquidation of all assets.

Insolvency is commonly confused with bankruptcy, and the two concepts are not dissimilar. Both insolvency and bankruptcy deal with liabilities exceeding assets, but insolvency is a state of being and bankruptcy is a matter of law. Companies can be insolvent but not legally bankrupt. Insolvency can lead to bankruptcy, but the condition may also be temporary and fixable without legal protection from creditors.

Anyone can apply to the court to become bankrupt, including individuals, sole traders and members of a partnership. There are different bankruptcy procedures for companies and partnerships. A person's creditors can usually petition the court to use a bankruptcy order if the person owes more than £5,000.

Once a bankruptcy order has been made against a person, the official receiver administers the bankrupt person's financial affairs. In the case of a bankrupt person with significant assets, the official receiver will appoint an insolvency practitioner as a trustee. Essentially, the duty of the trustee is to sell all the person's permitted assets (primarily those of high value) and use the money to pay as much as possible to the person's creditors.

5. WILLS AND INTESTACY

A will is a written document that sets out how a deceased person's estate is to be distributed. Certain conditions have to be met for a will to be valid:

- It must be in writing.
- It must be signed and witnessed.
- The person must be over 18 when it is made.
- The person must have the mental capacity to make the will and understand the effect it will have.
- The person must not have made it as a result of pressure from someone else.

Probate is the process to establish ownership of deceased person's estate before the assets are distributed. Probate is normally the responsibility of the executors of a will.

A person who dies without having written a will, or who has an invalid will, dies intestate. In these circumstances, the estate must be distributed according to the laws of intestacy, which set out a statutory set of rules that leave a person's estate to their next of kin in a fixed order.

6. THE MAIN TYPES OF TRUSTS AND THEIR USES

A trust is an arrangement under which a person (the settlor) transfers property to another person (the trustee), who then manages the trust property on behalf of certain specified persons (the beneficiaries). A trust can be created during the lifetime of the settlor, by writing a trust deed, or on the death of the settler by a will or by the intestacy statutory provisions.

There are four main types of trust.

A bare trust

The assets in the trust (the 'trust fund') belong to the beneficiary but are managed by the trustees of the fund. The income and any capital gains are treated as the beneficiary's for tax purposes. This type of trust is typically used when a proposed beneficiary is a child or incapable of dealing with money, through a disability or illness.

An interest in possession trust

These trusts are also known as life interest trusts as the beneficiary normally 'enjoys' the benefits of the assets held in the trust until their death. The assets in the trust are invested and one party, A, has the right to the income (or occupation of property if this power is given in the trust deed). Party A has an 'interest in possession'. After a specified event (usually the death of A), A's interest in possession ceases. After the death of A, the assets of the trust or reversionary interest will be held for the benefit of the second class of beneficiary, known as the remainderman.

This type of trust is commonly used in wills to provide for a spouse or partner, while protecting the assets for the ultimate beneficiaries from claims on the survivor's estate (e.g. from a new spouse/partner or from creditors once the spouse has died).

A charitable trust

This type of trust is set up for the purpose of charitable deeds. Charitable deeds are defined as the relief of poverty, advancement of religion, the advancement of education or purposes beneficial to the community.

A discretionary trust

The assets in the trust are held for the benefit of one or more beneficiaries. The trustees have discretion about how much to give to which beneficiaries and when. There are a number of ways to do this:

- For the benefit of the settlor's children and future grandchildren, with each becoming entitled to their share of the fund at a specified age. This is the most common will trust for children and grandchildren, with discretion over payment of income until each child becomes entitled to their share in the estate at a given age.

- Naming various beneficiaries (which may include the settlor's widow(er)) who are to benefit at the trustees' discretion according to need. This type of trust is useful when there is a need to defer the decision about who gets what when. The decision could then be made by the trustees depending upon the circumstances or needs of the beneficiaries at any given time, bearing in mind the tax consequences.

One unique feature of a discretionary trust is the amount of freedom given to the trustees. The assets placed in trust become the property, in title at least, of the trust itself, and the trustees assume responsibility for the management of these assets. In other trust types, the ways in which trustees can act with regard to the assets is very strictly defined, but with a discretionary trust, the trustees must use their discretion to decide which (if any) of the intended beneficiaries should receive income or capital from the trust. They also have the power to decide how much the beneficiaries will receive and when.

Discretionary trusts are particularly useful for ensuring that inheritance tax (IHT) liabilities are mitigated as far as is possible. IHT is discussed in more detail in chapter 6. An efficient method of mitigating IHT is to establish a discretionary trust in the will of the first individual. Under this arrangement, the assets that would otherwise have been transferred to the surviving spouse are instead placed in trust. The spouse is made a beneficiary (or perhaps the sole beneficiary), and trustees are appointed. The beneficiary does not have absolute entitlement to the assets; they cannot demand income or capital as they please. As a result, the assets placed in trust are not treated as part of that individual's estate for tax purposes.

The settlor should leave a 'letter of wishes' attached to their will. This document contains guidance for the trustees regarding the way in which assets should be disbursed to the beneficiaries. The over-arching theme of a letter of wishes will normally be that the beneficiary should be sufficiently provided for until their death. As such, the surviving spouse will have access to the deceased individual's assets, but their heirs will avoid a potentially significant IHT liability.

Finally, in relation to managing the investments within a trust, trustees need to follow the provisions of the Trustee Act 2000 (covered in chapter 3), unless the trust deed specifically overrides it.

CHAPTER 04 KEY FACTS

4.1

1. A legal person, such as a company, may sue and be sued, enter into contracts, incur debt and have ownership over property.
2. A power of attorney is a legal document that allows a person to give another person (or persons) the power to take decisions with regard to their financial affairs and/or their health and personal welfare.
3. A contract is essentially an agreement creating and defining the obligations between two or more parties.
4. The essential elements of a contract are offer and acceptance, consideration and intention.
5. There are two types of property ownership under English law: legal ownership and beneficial or equitable ownership.
6. Real property can be held solely by an individual or by two or more co-owners, either as tenants in common or joint tenants.
7. Both insolvency and bankruptcy deal with liabilities exceeding assets, but insolvency is a state of being and bankruptcy is a matter of law.
8. Once a person has had a bankruptcy order made against them in the courts, the official receiver (or a trustee appointed by the official receiver) administers the bankrupt person's financial affairs.
9. A will is a written document that sets out how a deceased person's estate is to be distributed.
10. Probate is the process to establish ownership of an estate before a deceased person's assets are distributed.
11. A person who dies without having written a will, or who has an invalid will, dies intestate.
12. A trust is an arrangement under which a person, the settlor, transfers property to another person(s), the trustee(s), who then manages the trust property on behalf of certain specified persons, the beneficiaries.
13. Trustees need to follow the provisions of the Trustee Act 2000 when making investment decisions, unless the trust deed specifically overrides it.

CHAPTER 04 SELF-ASSESSMENT QUESTIONS

1. Probate can be described as:

(a) *The process to establish the ownership of an estate before assets are distributed.*

(b) *The situation where a person dies without having written a will or has an invalid will.*

(c) *A legal ruling in a bankruptcy court.*

(d) *A legal document that gives a person the right to take control of another person's financial affairs.*

2. The Mental Capacity Act 2005 created which of the following?

(a) *The enduring power of attorney.*

(b) *The lasting power of attorney.*

(c) *The beneficial power of attorney.*

(d) *The official power of attorney.*

3. Which type of trust is typically used when a proposed beneficiary is a child?

(a) *A discretionary trust.*

(b) *A charitable trust.*

(c) *An interest in possession trust.*

(d) *A bare trust.*

4. Which party manages the payment of capital and income from the assets of a discretionary trust?

(a) *The executor.*

(b) *The trustees.*

(c) *The settlor.*

(d) *The named beneficiaries.*

ANSWERS

1. *(a) Probate is the process that occurs after someone has died, to establish how the assets of the deceased's estate are to be distributed.*
2. *(b) Lasting power of attorney was created by the Mental Capacity Act 2005 replacing the previously used enduring power of attorney.*
3. *(d) With a bare trust the assets in the trust (the 'trust fund') belong to the beneficiary but are managed by the trustees of the fund. This makes them more suitable when the beneficiary is a child who is not able to manage the assets.*
4. *(b) The trustees normally manage payments from a discretionary trust.*

LINK TO CFA LEVEL 1

Much of the material in this chapter has a UK focus and is therefore not directly covered in CFA Level 1.

CHAPTER 5

CLIENT ADVICE

The process of advising clients requires that a client's objectives, circumstances and attitudes to various factors (including risk) are fully understood before giving any advice or recommendations. Clients differ greatly in their nature, and this topic describes a number of types of investor and discusses the variety of their needs. Retail clients, in particular, are important due to their potential lack of investment experience and knowledge.

The need for a logical information gathering process, which frequently begins by establishing and quantifying the client's financial objectives, is discussed here. Understanding a client's objectives often takes place within a fact-find process.

A questionnaire or structured discussion is often used during a fact-find to ascertain a client's current financial circumstances, financial requirements and attitude. Determining a person's attitude to risk can be particularly difficult, and the chapter discusses various types of investment risk together with a number of methods which can be used to determine a client's attitude to risk.

The communication and interpretation skills required by a financial adviser to successfully understand a client's needs and capability to understand the investment choices available to them are also discussed.

Having gathered investor information and established the investment objectives, an adviser must go on to make suitable recommendations. It is generally considered appropriate to decide upon a suitable asset allocation before moving on to select individual investments, where considerations about the nature of particular fund providers are as important as the nature of the fund investments themselves.

To monitor investments, suitable benchmarks must be identified. Monitoring investment performance, together with reviewing client needs and objectives, is an ongoing process.

CHAPTER 5 SECTION 1

TYPES AND CHARACTERISTICS OF INVESTORS

SECTION AIMS

By the end of this section, learners should be able to:

- Describe and compare different types of investors.
- Explain the obligations of a firm towards retail clients.
- Explain the main needs of retail clients and how they are prioritised.

1. TYPES OF INVESTORS

Generally, investors can be categorised into two types: individual (or retail) or institutional, such as a pension fund. Institutions employ professional fund managers to manage funds on a large scale, and these fund managers spend a lot of time and money on searching and analysing information. Individual investors, however, have limited time and resources.

There is no defined standard to categorise individual investors; each investment firm uses its own categories and values within those categories. For example, one firm may use three categories (retail, high net worth and ultra-high net worth) and another may use four categories (retail, affluent, high net worth and very high net worth).

The Financial Conduct Authority (FCA) categorises retail investors according to their wealth and experience in order to restrict promotions of, and investments in, more risky types of investment. A high net worth investor is defined as a person with an annual income of £100,000 or more, or net investable assets of £250,000 or more.

A certified sophisticated investor is a person who has a certificate in the required form confirming that they have been assessed by a firm as being sufficiently knowledgeable to understand the risk of a particular investment. They have also signed a prescribed statement including an acceptance that the particular investment may result in significant risk of loss.

In addition, a retail investor can state they are a self-certified sophisticated investor if they can state at least one of the following:

- I am a member of a network or syndicate of business angels and have so far been so for at least the last six months prior to the signature date.
- I have made more than one investment in an unlisted company in the two years prior to the signature date.
- I am working, or have worked in the two years prior to the signature date, in a professional capacity in the private equity sector, or in the provision of finance for small and medium-sized enterprises (SMEs).
- I am currently, or have been in the two years prior to the signature date, a director of a company with an annual turnover of at least £1m.

Non-mainstream pooled investments (NMPI), which include unregulated collective investment schemes (UCIS) as well as special purpose vehicles that invest in anything other than shares or bonds, are not marketed to retail investors. Promotion of NMPIs is restricted to high net worth and sophisticated investors, or investment professionals.

There are many different types of institutional investors with varying investment requirements and constraints. Some institutions manage their investments internally and employ investment professionals. Others outsource the investment of the portfolio to one or more external investment firms. The decision to manage investments internally or externally is generally determined by the size of the institution, with larger institutions more likely to have the resources required for internal management. Examples of institutional investors include pension funds, insurance companies, mutual funds (including unit trusts and open-ended investment companies (OEICs)), hedge funds, charitable trusts (such as the Wellcome Trust) and sovereign wealth funds (such as the Abu Dhabi Investment Authority and the Government Pension Fund of Norway).

2. OBLIGATIONS OF A FIRM TOWARDS ITS RETAIL CLIENTS

The obligations of a firm towards its customers are essentially set out in the FCA's Principles for Businesses (PRIN) – see chapter 3, section 3. In particular, Principle 6 ('A firm must pay due regard to the interests of its customers and treat them fairly') is central to an investment firm's dealings with its customers.

There are, of course, other principles in PRIN that have a direct bearing on treating customers fairly. The FCA has said the treating customers fairly (TCF) initiative is important to its work in ensuring a fair deal for consumers. The FCA has further stated 'we expect customers' interests to be at the heart of how firms do business. Customers can expect to get financial services and products that meet their needs from firms that they can trust.'

TCF aims to deliver six improved outcomes for retail clients.

Outcome 1

Consumers can be confident that they are dealing with firms where the fair treatment of customers is central to the corporate culture.

The FCA has identified the key cultural drivers to be:

- leadership;
- strategy;
- decision making;
- controls;
- recruitment, training and competence; and
- reward.

The FCA considers TCF to be a cultural issue. This means that it has to be delivered from the top of an organisation, and therefore the firm's senior management needs to provide leadership and integrate TCF into all levels of operation. The FCA expects firms to integrate TCF culture into their recruitment policies, ensuring that staff taken on have the same TCF values as the firm. Firms should also take care that their remuneration policies – in particular, where bonuses are offered based on meeting targets – do not lead to unfair outcomes for customers.

Outcome 2

Products and services marketed and sold in the retail market are designed to meet the needs of identified consumer groups and are targeted accordingly. Products and services should be designed to suit the market they are aimed at. They should also be marketed carefully to reduce the potential risk of mis-selling.

Outcome 3

Consumers are provided with clear information and are kept appropriately informed before, during and after the point of sale.

One of the main aims of the FCA in retail financial markets is to ensure that consumers are provided with clear and easily understood information about products and services – this is captured in Principle 7 of PRIN ('A firm must pay due regard to the information needs of its clients, and communicate information to them, which is clear, fair, and not misleading').

Communication with clients includes financial promotions, key features documents for financial products, investment research and disclosure documents. The detailed rules on these types of communication are covered in chapter 3.

The financial capability of retail customers is an important consideration in the design of communications. The FCA's 2014 Risk Outlook remarked that 'research has shown that financial capability, the ability to understand information on financial products and services, is generally weak among consumers.' For example, results from a survey on financial capability, reported by the FCA, noted that "the impact of inflation is clearly not understood by a large proportion of the population. When asked to identify whether inflation at 5% would have eroded the purchasing power of money in an account paying 3% interest, a third of people got this wrong. Startlingly, this rose to 44% of those aged under 35."

Outcome 4

Where consumers receive advice, the advice is suitable and takes account of their circumstances.

Firms should obtain adequate 'know your customer' information before giving recommendations, including on affordability and customer needs and objectives. Those providing investment

advisory or discretionary portfolio management services are also required to assess suitability for all retail clients and for professional clients. A suitability report should be provided in relation to advice on certain transactions. Firms should ensure that these reports are succinct but highlight the key information the customer needs, explain why they are making a particular recommendation, give a balanced view of the product and highlight the risks associated with it.

Outcome 5

Consumers are provided with products that perform as firms have led them to expect, and the associated service is both of an acceptable standard and as they have been led to expect.

Firms should communicate clearly with consumers about the characteristics of products they are selling them. An example of mis-selling in relation to investment products was structured capital-at-risk products (SCARPs). These are products that typically offer consumers a high rate of return over a fixed investment period, commonly three to five years. The return of the initial capital invested at the end of the fixed period is determined by a formula based on the performance of an equity index, a combination of indices or a 'basket' of selected stocks. This exposes the customer to a range of outcomes in relation to the return of their initial capital sum.

In addition, the amount of initial capital repaid may be 'geared', e.g. consumers may lose 2% of their capital for every 1% fall in the market past a certain level. If the index/indices perform/s within certain thresholds, full repayment of the capital invested occurs (in addition to the income or growth on the capital). However, if the performance is outside these thresholds, consumers could lose a substantial part (or even all) of the capital they invested. In many cases, the regulator found that firms had recommended these products to customers where the risks were not adequately explained (or were not in line with the risk profile of the customer established by the fact-find) and the (high) returns were given undue emphasis.

Outcome 6

Consumers do not face unreasonable post-sale barriers imposed by firms to change product, switch provider, submit a claim or make a complaint.

The main part of this outcome relevant to investment advice is the complaint element. To meet this outcome, firms need to make customers aware of their complaints handling procedures in communications. The FCA requirements on complaints handling and compensation claims are explained in chapter 3, section 6.

3. INVESTORS' NEEDS

Each investor, individual or institutional, will have different investment objectives related to their circumstances, attitudes and constraints. There are three main factors that are important determinants of each investor's needs and objectives.

Time horizon

An investor saving to meet school fees for children is likely to have an investment horizon of a few years, whereas someone early in their working life who is saving for retirement will have a much longer investment horizon. In general the longer the investment horizon, the less need there is for liquidity in the investment and the more risk can be taken.

Return requirement

The return required on the investment can be calculated based on the desired outcome at the end of the investment horizon. For example, if an investor wishes to accumulate £500,000 by retirement, then an adviser may determine the return required on the investments to be, say, 7% after tax. If the return looks unachievable, the adviser may ask the client to reconsider their investment objectives.

There is clearly a link between return and time horizon. The longer the time horizon, the lower the return will need to be to meet the investment goal. Similarly, the more risk the investor is willing to tolerate, the higher the return the investor is likely to achieve.

Risk tolerance

Willingness to take risk is related to the investor's psychology, which may be assessed using questionnaires completed by the investor. Also, the longer the investment horizon is, the more risk the investor is likely to be willing to take on.

Other specific needs that investors may have include liquidity, tax considerations, regulatory requirements, religious or ethical restrictions and other unique circumstances. For individual investors, liquidity requirements will increase as the end of the investment horizon gets closer (e.g. retirement approaches). Certain individuals may also need to keep part of their investments in liquid form so they can be drawn on quickly.

Tax is also likely to be an issue for individual investors and advisers will recommend tax efficient investments. Tax is covered in more detail in chapter 6. Some investors may have strong religious or ethical beliefs that restrict the kind of investments they can include in their portfolio. For example, some people may not want to invest in the shares of firms that produce cigarettes or armaments. It should also be noted that investors' circumstances and needs are likely to change over time, so it is important to re-evaluate their needs on a regular basis.

CHAPTER 5 SECTION 2

THE CLIENT'S FINANCIAL OBJECTIVES

SECTION AIMS

By the end of this section, learners should be able to:

- Explain the importance of establishing and quantifying a client's objectives.
- Explain the need to prioritise objectives to accommodate a client's affordability.

The first step in the investment advice or financial planning process is to establish, in financial terms, what the investor is seeking to achieve.

1. ESTABLISHING AND QUANTIFYING A CLIENT'S OBJECTIVES

Ideally, a client's objectives should be specified in financial terms and clearly state how much is needed and when.

For example, an investor may say that they want to save for their retirement. Any proposed solution should take account of both the term to retirement and how much pension income they would like. An investor aged 25 wanting to retire at age 65 has a 40-year term in which to save, which should allow greater flexibility to achieve than, say, a 45-year-old investor wanting to retire at age 60 with only a 15-year term. Just how much lump sum capital is needed to provide a pension will surprise most people. A male aged 60 wanting a pension of £25,000 a year, which will increase in line with inflation, would need a capital lump sum of approximately £630,000. If he were prepared to defer retirement to age 65, the lump sum required would be £525,000, thus giving him both more time to save and a lower target to reach.

Another objective may be to provide some form of financial protection for dependants in the event of death or illness. The timescale of the need for protection could last for the whole of the life assured's expected lifespan, or it may relate to a shorter term, such as while children are financially dependent on the life assured. The amount of cover needed will depend on the amount of replacement capital or income needed by the family unit.

2. PRIORITISING OBJECTIVES

Budgetary constraints may mean that it is not possible to meet all of a client's objectives, in which case the financial planning process will need to agree a priority for those deemed most critical. Affordability (often termed as 'capacity for loss' by the FCA) is a real constraint that means that a client literally cannot achieve all of their financial goals. Many clients need assistance in understanding the financial implications of prioritising their objectives and agreeing either revised financial targets or amended timescales.

3. ESTABLISHING AFFORDABILITY

Affordability can be established by preparing a cash flow statement showing all of the family unit's income and expenditure. A surplus would indicate funds available for potential savings plans, to fund protection policies or to repay mortgage debt. A deficit, in which expenditure exceeds income, is of itself a major cause for concern and may prompt a completely different approach to prioritising the client's objectives.

CHAPTER 5 SECTION 3

THE CLIENT'S CURRENT CIRCUMSTANCES

SECTION AIMS

By the end of this section, learners should be able to:

- Explain the importance of the fact-find process in establishing a client's current financial circumstances and requirements.
- Identify the factors shaping a client's circumstances.

In addition to establishing a client's goals, the financial planning process should also build up a comprehensive picture of their current situation. The client's current position may affect their objectives, so the process is often iterative.

1. COLLECTING HARD FACTS

A lot of background information is needed in order to understand a client's current position. A fact-find is often used as part of this process.

A fact-find will cover personal information, such as full name, date of birth, state of health, marital status, residence and domicile status, National Insurance number, address, employment details and family details. These are all examples of 'hard facts'.

A fact-find will also cover financial information such as details of income, including savings income as well as earned income or pensions. An expenditure analysis is a useful aid in both determining affordability and establishing the level of income needed for any insurance policies. Other financial information will include details of the client's investments, pensions and liabilities, such as mortgages and credit card balances.

2. LETTERS OF AUTHORITY

A fact-find often requires details that the client cannot answer from their own memory or records. For example, clients may be asked for details of the exact funds within their individual savings account (ISA) investments. This information will help in terms of understanding their existing asset allocation, the current potential yield from these existing holdings and the client's attitude to risk.

Another area of enquiry may involve pensions. Any form of retirement planning will require a detailed analysis of the client's existing pension arrangements to determine their likely pension if they were to take no further action. The financial plan would then provide options to address any shortfall against their target. A thorough understanding of the client's current pension arrangements is a critical part of the advice process.

Another objective may be the repayment or rebroking of a mortgage, in which case the terms of any existing mortgage must be fully understood. Is the current rate competitive and are there early surrender penalties?

In all of these cases, many clients will not have the necessary details within their own files, and the adviser will therefore have to collect information from relevant third parties. The adviser will need a 'letter of authority' from the client which authorises the third party to release information regarding the client to the adviser. Enquiries made to third parties can take several weeks to resolve, depending on the level of detail required.

3. COLLECTING SOFT FACTS

In addition to hard facts, the fact-find process should involve the adviser asking question and listening to the client to form a better understanding of exactly what the client is trying to achieve.

This information can only be collected face-to-face, and by the adviser asking the client open questions and listening carefully to the replies. Questions may include, 'How do you feel about your current spread of investments?' The client's reply will help the adviser gauge the level of the client's current understanding and determine their attitude to risk. The information gained in this way is essentially opinion and is referred to as 'soft facts'.

The following table, published by the FCA, identifies some examples of good and poor practice in fact-finds:

TOPIC	GOOD PRACTICE	POOR PRACTICE
Customers' goals, objectives and priorities explored fully	The adviser takes account of the customer's future goals and aspirations including plans for the future, e.g. having children, paying for further education etc. They then assess the customer's current circumstances including income, expenditure, protection, retirement plans, savings, investment, etc. and compare this against what the customer feels they will require over a period of time, e.g. what they want to do in retirement and therefore how much pension income they would require to do this.	No or incomplete fact-find documents. Inadequate records of customers' objectives. Failure to fully consider the implication of customers' tax position.
Information updated at subsequent review meetings	Know your customer (KYC) obtained is extensive and updated on an annual or bi-annual basis. This includes updating wills, attitude to risk, dependants/beneficiaries, portfolio valuations, state pension benefits, projected cash flow analysis, personal and health details, detailed personal tax computations, details of client's other professional advisers.	Information held on file had not been updated for seven years, yet advice was given on the strength of the original details.
Attitude to risk	The firm recognises that when advising couples and/or people with a number of needs they could have a different attitude to risk for each.	Fact-finds contained contradictory information relating to the customer's attitude to risk.
Existing arrangements	A firm discussed and recorded all existing plans the customer has in place and builds these into its subsequent recommendations wherever appropriate.	A failure to record or update information on existing policies, plans and investments resulted in a customer being recommended two ISAs in the same tax year.

Source: FCA factsheet for small firms

CHAPTER 5 SECTION 4

THE CLIENT'S ATTITUDE TO RISK

SECTION AIMS

By the end of this section, learners should be able to:

- Analyse the main types of investment risk as they affect investors.
- Explain the role of diversification in mitigating risk.
- Analyse the impact of timescale on a client's attitude to risk.
- Explain the key methods of determining a client's attitude to risk.

Financial planning involves establishing the client's financial objectives, determining their current position and then analysing different options that might help them to achieve their objectives. In evaluating the different options, full account must be taken of the client's attitude to risk.

1. DIFFERENT TYPES OF INVESTMENT RISK

Most retail investors have a one-dimensional understanding of investment risk – quite simply, they focus only on the risk that their investment may be worth less in future than it is today. This is known as capital risk. In terms of asset classes, this interpretation of investment risk would mean that cash would be the only option for a low risk investor.

What many retail investors fail to understand is that by taking such a cautious attitude to capital risk, they are significantly increasing their exposure to inflation risk, interest rate risk and shortfall risk.

- Inflation risk is the risk that the future purchasing power of both the capital base and its income will be eroded by inflation. In early 2008, the bank base rate was 5% at a time when the retail prices index (RPI) was running at 4.3%. If a basic rate taxpayer had cash deposits earning 5% gross, the net of tax interest would be only 4%, which means that the rate of monetary interest was less than inflation.

- Interest rate risk relates to the fact that the bank base rate is likely to change over time and ultimately feed through to the rates of interest paid on deposit accounts. The interest rate is set by the Monetary Policy Committee (MPC) of the Bank of England. Normally, the rate will be increased during times of inflation, but this is not always the case. The 2008 financial crisis saw the MPC reduce the base rate during a period of rising inflation.

- Shortfall risk is the risk that the investment return will literally fall short of the amount required for the investor to achieve their objectives. The response to such a shortfall could be to reduce the target, increase the amount saved or extend the period of saving. Historically, over the medium to long term, cash has significantly underperformed both fixed interest and equities. Cash therefore has the highest level of shortfall risk over the medium to long term.

2. DIVERSIFICATION TO SUIT THE CLIENT'S OBJECTIVES

Ideally, a client will be given a thorough explanation of the different facets of investment risk. No one asset class is low risk in all regards. Cash has a low capital risk, but has a higher risk, among others. Equities, by contrast, have a higher capital risk but relatively low inflation, interest rate and shortfall risk over the medium to long term.

Diversification of a portfolio between different asset classes is central to investment management. A diversified portfolio at aggregate level can reduce various aspects of risk. However, the asset allocation must be appropriate to the client's objectives and attitude to risk.

3. TIMESCALE OF THE INVESTMENT

A client's attitude to risk will be affected by the timescale of the investment. For example, a client wanting to save for retirement in 30 years' time may be prepared to take a capital risk in order to reduce the shortfall risk and will thus invest heavily in equities. The same client may have a much more cautious attitude if the capital is needed in, say, three years for school fees, and therefore this part of their portfolio should probably remain in cash-type investments with little capital risk.

This reinforces the need to quantify the client's objectives in terms of both how much is needed and when. Different objectives with different timescales may mean that the investor has more than one attitude to risk, which in turn will affect the asset allocation of their investment capital.

4. DETERMINING A CLIENT'S ATTITUDE TO RISK

There are two ways of determining a client's attitude to risk: by examining their existing investments and by asking specific questions.

Reviewing existing investments with a client will give the adviser an indication of the level of the client's understanding of investments and help to understand their attitude to risk. For example, a client may be comfortable with a volatile past performance of equity-based investments, or may be reluctant to risk further loss of capital in the event of market falls.

An analysis of existing investments is a useful indicator of attitude to risk, but cannot be relied on in isolation. A client may not understand the implications of direct shareholdings or over-concentration in just one asset class.

The adviser must spend time with the client to establish exactly what the client means by investment risk and, if appropriate, to let the client know about interest rate, inflation and shortfall risk. The client's attitude to risk has a major role in agreeing an appropriate asset allocation for each financial objective. Asset allocation is the major factor in investment performance, so this is a critical stage in the financial planning process.

CHAPTER 5 SECTION 5

ADVICE AND RECOMMENDATIONS

SECTION AIMS

By the end of this section, learners should be able to:

- Explain why asset allocation always comes before investment or product selection.
- Explain the key roles of charges and the financial stability of the provider as criteria within the fund selection process, and the use of past performance.
- Explain the importance of stability, independence and standing of trustees, fund custodians and auditors in the fund selection process.
- Identify benchmarks and other performance measures.
- Explain the importance of reviews within the financial planning process.

The financial planning process should ideally adopt the following sequence:

1. Identify and quantify the client's financial objectives.
2. Collect data to establish the client's current circumstances.
3. Analyse different options to meet any identified shortcomings.
4. Prepare a report and arrange a meeting with the client.
5. Implement the plan.
6. Review regularly, in the light of changed client circumstances, changed objectives and/or changed market conditions.

1. REPORTING BACK TO THE CLIENT WITH RECOMMENDATIONS

There are many different ways in which a client can be presented with recommendations. For more straightforward cases, it may be possible to arrange a meeting at which the client is immediately presented with various investment- or product-specific recommendations. For more complex cases, this stage may involve an initial strategic report that simply outlines the different options. This report would then form the basis for a client meeting, at which the adviser and client review the different options and agree a course of action at a strategic level. Specific product recommendations would be the subject of a later meeting.

A firm must provide a suitability report to a retail client if the firm makes a personal recommendation and the client:

- buys/sells shares/units in a regulated collective investment scheme;
- buys/sells shares through an investment trust savings scheme;
- surrenders or cancels rights in, or suspends contributions to, a personal or stakeholder pension scheme;
- elects to make income withdrawals from a short-term annuity;
- enters into a pension transfer or pension opt-out; and
- enters into any transaction in relation to a life policy.

Suitability reports are covered in more detail in chapter 3.

2. ASSET ALLOCATION IS STRATEGIC

Asset allocation is the mix of underlying asset classes held within an investment portfolio. The main asset classes are cash, fixed interest securities, property and equities. Each asset class behaves differently with very different risk profiles.

A number of academic studies have shown that asset allocation is the single most important factor in determining the returns of an investment portfolio. The implication is that other factors such as fund selection or market timing are less important when compared to being in the right asset class (or mix of asset classes).

Of course, stock or fund selection can sometimes make a difference to the performance of portfolios. Some fund managers do add value, but it is virtually impossible to know which fund managers will add value on a consistent basis. A number of academic studies have shown that picking a 'winner' this year does not imply that this fund manager will be perform as well in subsequent years.

'Determinants of Portfolio Performance' (Brinson, Hood and Beebower, *The Financial Analysts Journal*, July/August 1986: 39–44) examined the investment performance of 91 institutional pension funds between 1974 and 1983. The conclusion of this study, which was confirmed in a follow-up study in 1991 (Brinson, Singer and Beebower, 'Determinants of Portfolio Performance II: An Update', *The Financial Analysts Journal*, May/June 1991: 40–48), was that asset allocation is responsible for over 90% of the variation in the return of an investment portfolio each quarter.

Other academic studies have questioned this figure of 90%, but the consensus view is that asset allocation is the primary determinant of performance. See chapter 17 for further discussion of performance measurement.

Specific investment recommendations can only be made within the context of an agreed asset allocation that is appropriate to the client's objectives and attitude to risk. If individual shares, fixed-interest stock or other investments are purchased, the skills of the investment department would then be commissioned to recommend a specific portfolio.

If collective products are being used, asset allocation will guide the adviser towards specific fund sectors from which individual funds can be selected.

3. FUND SELECTION PROCESS

If appropriate, fund selection is the last step in the process. The range of funds available to an adviser depends on whether they are tied to a specific provider or are independent and therefore free to choose from the 'whole of the market'. However wide or narrow the choice, the following factors should be taken into account as part of the fund selection process.

Past performance

This is arguably an indicator of the skill of the fund manager, particularly when compared to the sector average. However, the current risk warning in the FCA Handbook is 'Past performance is not a reliable indicator of future performance', and therefore the appropriate risk warnings need to be given to the client.

Charges

There are normally two main types – initial charges and annual management charges (AMCs). Initial charges are applied at point of sale or as exit charges if the funds are withdrawn during, say, the first five years. AMCs run throughout the life of the investment. Initial charges are more obvious to the client, but the AMC will be much greater over the longer term. An AMC of 1.75% a year will significantly suppress the returns of an actively managed fund compared to, say, an AMC of 0.30% a year from a passively managed fund. The higher the charges, the bigger the hurdle for the fund to outperform its peers.

Financial stability of the provider

This is most relevant to with-profits based investments as managed by life assurance companies. The rate of bonus passed on to investors is not directly related to the performance of the underlying managed fund. The objective of with-profits funds is to deliver a smoothed return by means of bonuses rather than returns directly linked to the markets, which may be volatile. This means putting funds into reserves during periods of strongly positive investment returns and drawing on reserves during periods when the rate of bonus is above that actually achieved on the underlying managed fund. If a life office continued to pay bonuses in excess of actual returns, it would deplete its reserves, and this could jeopardise the sustainability of future bonuses.

Stability, independence and standing of trustees, fund custodians and auditors

The collapse of the brokerage firm Bernard L. Madoff Investment Securities (BMIS) in December 2008 provided an important illustration of the requirement to undertake due diligence in the fund selection process. Madoff effectively operated a Ponzi scheme, whereby existing investors were paid from new money coming in. Investors had to invest in an approved feeder fund, which in turn opened up a brokerage account with BMIS. The feeder fund had to delegate to BMIS the full trading authority of their portfolios.

A typical hedge fund uses a network of service providers, which can include an investment manager to manage the assets, a broker to execute trades, a fund administrator to calculate the net asset value (NAV) and custodian(s)/prime broker(s) to custody the assets. These service providers should normally be independent of each other. With BMIS, all the functions were performed internally with no independent oversight. This should have provided warning signals to investors, as it allows for performance manipulation and misappropriation of assets.

The auditors of BMIS were a small accountancy firm that was virtually unknown within the investment management industry. Investors should have questioned the choice of such a small auditor with little track record for such a large fund. Additional investigations would have revealed that the accounting firm had declared in writing in its annual returns to the American Institute of Certified Public Accountants that it had not conducted any audit since 1993.

4. BENCHMARKS AND REVIEWS

Clients will of course be interested in how their investment is performing. Performance can be measured in terms of an absolute return but is more meaningful when compared to a benchmark. This could be the performance of another similar investment or fund manager. However, it is not meaningful to compare one fund manager to another when one is a small cap manager and the other is a broad index manager. In this case, it is best to avoid manager comparisons and to use a neutral, unbiased benchmark that comprises similar investment types. Market indices are the common benchmark used, and these (and other performance measurement issues) are discussed in chapter 17.

Reviews are a vital part of the financial planning process. The frequency of reviews should be at least annually, but some advisers may agree to more regular reviews with certain clients. A regular review system is essential if the client's portfolio is to be kept on track with the client's objectives and changing investment perspectives.

A review is an opportunity to:

- Check for any changes to the client's circumstances, risk preferences and objectives. With long-term objectives, most plans need to be modified over time.
- Monitor investment performance, ideally against a benchmark. Is the portfolio matching or outperforming the relevant market, and (if not) should some of the investments or funds be changed?
- Rebalance the portfolio in line with the agreed asset allocation. Revisions to holdings may be required because of portfolio drift, i.e. the tendency for a portfolio to move away from the initial recommended allocation due to different assets providing different returns. Rebalancing may involve taking gains from asset classes that have grown significantly and reinvesting in asset classes where the portfolio is underweight. Account needs to be taken of both potential tax liabilities on any disposals, and the charges involved.

CHAPTER 5 SECTION 6

SKILLS REQUIRED WHEN ADVISING CLIENTS

SECTION AIMS

By the end of this section, learners should be able to:

- Describe the need for advisers to communicate clearly, assessing and adapting to the differing levels of knowledge and understanding of their clients.
- Identify and apply suitable investment solutions to suit different needs of retail clients.

1. CASE STUDY: DARREN

The fact-find

Darren is 60 years old and has just retired. He has received a tax-free cash lump sum of £90,000 from his occupational pension scheme. Seeking advice on the best way to invest this, Darren decided to visit his local financial adviser for advice.

The adviser conducted a fact-find with Darren but without his wife, Carol, present. Early on in the fact-find, the adviser established that Darren has a repayment mortgage of £60,000 with ten years to maturity. The adviser was able to confirm that the mortgage payments appeared affordable over the next five years.

As Darren indicated that he was interested in advice on what to do with his tax-free cash, the adviser mainly concentrated on this area and went on to discuss Darren's existing savings and investments. The adviser asked how much Darren currently holds on deposit and how he had accumulated the money. Darren explained that the money in his ISA was the result of deposits made during the previous four years, although he had not yet contributed for this tax year. He also has money in an instant access account. The adviser asked whether Darren has any plans for this money and over what term. Apart from going on holiday with Carol, Darren stated that he has no immediate plans. The adviser therefore concluded that Darren has adequate cash reserves for emergencies and that the money from the tax-free cash is surplus to his immediate requirements.

The adviser went on to discuss Darren's existing investments. Darren already has some investments in manufacturing sector shares, valued at approximately £30,000. These are not held through an ISA, but are held in his name.

The adviser explained risk and reward in very general terms, stating simply that 'greater risks need to be taken for greater returns'. Darren stated that he wanted the best return on his investment to generate income to supplement his pension. Darren recognises that he would have to accept a minimal risk to his capital to achieve his desired return. The adviser and Darren agreed that a cautious approach to investment would be appropriate. Finally, the adviser established that Darren is a higher rate taxpayer, but that Carol is a basic rate taxpayer, has a small pension of her own and has no investments. She also has not used her ISA allowance for this year.

Recommendations

Based on the information regarding Darren's tax position obtained during the fact-find process, the adviser recommended that he invest £24,000 into an ISA. The investments would take the form of an OEIC, which has a cautious risk profile. The adviser also recommended that, to shelter further money from tax, Darren should transfer £24,000 to Carol for her to invest with her ISA allowance.

When the adviser explained his recommendations to Darren, they referred back to Darren's attitude to risk, and stated that the funds recommended for him were in line with his approach to investing and should provide the growth required without the risk to his capital. However, to allow for the importance of diversification they recommended higher risk funds for Carol's ISA. The remaining capital was placed into an investment bond in Darren's sole name. The risk profile of the bond was not explained.

The adviser sent a suitability report to Darren immediately after their conversation. This was written in plain language and set out the facts ascertained during the fact-find and the reasons for the recommendations. In particular, Darren's risk profile was stated to be cautious. However, under the description of the recommended funds, some had too much exposure to risk and, as such, has the potential to fall in value. The adviser explained that this was required for Darren to achieve a better return.

The adviser re-confirmed in the report the reason for recommending an ISA in Carol's name and the importance of diversification. The report confirmed that the adviser had restricted their advice to that of investing Darren's tax-free cash. It also mentioned other potential need areas and suggested that Darren might like to meet the adviser again in the near future to discuss these.

Comments on the fact-find

Did the fact-find process capture all pertinent customer details? These include:

- The customer's current and future circumstances and objectives, e.g. current and expected income and expenditure levels.
- All relevant details regarding current financial status, e.g. mortgage arrangements and access to emergency funds.
- Other money the customer may be entitled to, e.g. state and occupational benefits.
- The risk attitude of the customer.

Issues to consider:

1. Although Darren indicated that he wanted advice on investing his tax-free lump sum, it may have been helpful to find out about his other objectives, such as provision for dependants on death.
2. The adviser failed to find out enough information about the mortgage – e.g. was it possible to repay early, are there penalties for early repayment? The adviser simply investigated whether the mortgage payments were affordable over the next five years. It may have

been possible to repay the mortgage early, and this could have formed part of the recommendations. The adviser ascertained whether Darren had sufficient emergency funds – this is good practice.

3. The adviser ascertained the risk profile of Darren.

4. If the adviser is going to recommend that Carol undertakes any investment, then she should have been interviewed with a view to determining her objectives and attitude to risk.

Comments on the recommendations

- Do the adviser's recommendations match the information (about circumstances, objectives, attitude to risk, etc.) obtained during the fact-find?

- Did the adviser explain clearly and fully how any recommendation is suitable for the customer?

Issues to consider:

1. The recommended investments did not always match Darren's risk profile. In addition, Carol was not interviewed and her attitude to risk was not determined, so the recommended investments for Carol may be unsuitable.

2. The adviser did not explain why the investment bond was a suitable investment for Darren.

3. The investments recommended may have been consistent with the customer's circumstances and objectives as determined during the fact-find, but the fact-find was probably not wide enough to determine the best recommendations.

4. The adviser did not identify that switching some or all of Darren's existing investments in manufacturing shares to Carol may have reduced tax on dividends, as she is a basic rate taxpayer.

5. The suitability report was sent promptly and was written clearly. However, the explanation of why the investments in funds which are higher risk than Darren's stated attitude to risk was not properly justified.

6. The recommendation to use the ISA allowances for both Darren and Carol for the current year is a sensible recommendation.

7. The adviser was correct to establish that the advice was limited to one need – to invest the tax-free cash – but should have explained in the suitability report the potential limitations and risks of not receiving full advice.

2. CASE STUDY: JUAN

The fact-find

Juan is 45 years old, married, employed and a basic rate taxpayer. He has just received a sum of £300,000 from an inheritance. He would like advice on how to invest this. In the last six months, he had a full financial review and, as a result, has put in place life insurance and is contributing what he feels is a sufficient amount to his personal pension.

His main objective is to provide capital growth to enable him to purchase a second home in Majorca in the next two to three years. His current investments are gilts held in his name, valued at approximately £40,000 (not held through an ISA). He has very few cash holdings, but his expected income is sufficient to cover his expected outgoings over the next few years. He regards himself as cautious when it comes to investments.

Recommendations

The adviser recommended that Juan should invest his available lump sum into a venture capital trust (VCT). This was recommended as providing capital growth and having tax advantages. The adviser stated that the risk of loss on VCT investments was relatively low and so was consistent with Juan's attitude to risk. He suggested that the tax relief from investing in a VCT could be invested in a building society deposit, thus giving some cash for emergency uses.

The adviser did not send a suitability report, as the recommended investment was not a packaged product.

Comments on the fact-find and recommendations

The fact-find was reasonably thorough, although it did not investigate the circumstances of Juan's partner.

The recommendation is clearly inappropriate for a number of reasons:

- A VCT investment is high risk and therefore not consistent with Juan's stated attitude to risk. The adviser did not give Juan any explanation of the capital risk or liquidity risk associated with a VCT investment.
- There was also no explanation given of the withdrawal of tax relief if the VCT investment is cancelled within five years. This period is longer than the stated investment period established by the fact-find.
- There is no mention that the maximum investment in a VCT in one tax year that qualifies for tax relief is £200,000. This is less than the amount Juan wishes to invest.

In short, the adviser has recommended an unsuitable investment that is not consistent with the needs of the customer or the risk attitude of the investor. The adviser has failed to properly explain the nature of the investment or justify why the investment is suitable.

3. CASE STUDY: MAHITA

The fact-find

Mahita is aged 35, single and a higher rate taxpayer. She pays into an occupational pension and has accumulated approximately £35,000 in savings that she keeps in deposit accounts outside an ISA. She also has approximately £20,000 in gilt holdings, and these pay interest income of approximately £700 every six months. The gilts are held outside of an ISA. Finally, she has a repayment mortgage of £150,000.

In a fact-find meeting with her financial adviser, she states that her primary objective is to have sufficient income when she retires. She also wants investments that are tax-efficient.

After using a risk profiling program, she agrees with her adviser that she is willing to take a medium amount of risk with her investments. An analysis of Mahita's income and expenditure reveals that she has surplus income every month of approximately £1,500.

Recommendations

The adviser recommends that Mahita uses some of her cash deposits to pay off some of her mortgage but keeps sufficient deposits for emergency funds. The adviser also suggests that she sells some of her gilts and invests in some regulated collective investment schemes that match her risk profile.

In addition, her maximum ISA allowance for the current tax year could be used to shield part of her gilts or collective investment scheme investments, or some combination of the two. The adviser then suggests that the surplus monthly income be used to make monthly payments into a collective investment scheme. The choice of investment schemes would reflect her attitude to risk and the principle of diversification.

The adviser sends Mahita a suitability report setting out the facts ascertained during the fact-find and the reasons for the recommendations. The limitations and risks of the recommended investments were clearly set out.

Comments on the fact-find and recommendations

Overall, the fact-find is thorough and the recommendations are suitable.

- The areas in which advice was given were agreed with Mahita, although the adviser could have warned her about the limitations of just advising on the one area.

- Information was collected on customer needs and objectives, attitude to risk, affordability and tax status. It may have been helpful to explore Mahita's attitude to risk across all her objectives and ensure that there is a common understanding of what this means in practice.

Also, it is good practice to explore all aspects of risk, including product risks and underlying fund risks, where applicable, as well as the circumstances in which these risks might occur.

- It will be important to consider whether the advice provided will remain suitable if Mahita's circumstances change – for example, changes in income, employment, residence and health.
- A suitability report was provided, setting out the limitations and risks of the recommendations.

4. CASE STUDY: STEVE AND DIANE

Steve and Diane are meeting with their investment adviser to review their investments, which currently are:

- UK equities and OEICs: £56,000.
- UK corporate bonds: £61,000.
- Fixed-interest savings accounts in a UK bank: £72,000.
- Property (part-owned with friends): £75,000.

None of the investments are currently held in an ISA.

They also give the following facts during the meeting:

1. Steve is a higher rate taxpayer and Diane is a basic rate taxpayer.
2. They have no children.
3. Both Diane and Steve would like to see more capital growth.
4. Neither Steve nor Diane is a member of a pension scheme.

Questions

1. Which of the four facts given during the meeting is not a hard fact?

(a) *Fact one.*

(b) *Fact two.*

(c) *Fact three.*

(d) *Fact four.*

2. **By investing a large part of their portfolio in fixed-interest savings accounts, they are most exposed to which kind of risk?**

(a) *Credit risk.*

(b) *Market risk.*

(c) *Operational risk.*

(d) *Inflation risk.*

3. **Over the long term, which of the following asset classes is most likely to achieve growth if they choose a pension scheme?**

(a) *Equities.*

(b) *Cash.*

(c) *Gilts.*

(d) *Corporate bonds.*

4. **Which of the investments held by Steve and Diane exposes them to credit risk?**

(a) *Property.*

(b) *Equities.*

(c) *Fixed-interest savings accounts.*

(d) *UK corporate bonds.*

5. **Given Steve and Diane's preferences revealed in fact three, which one of the following recommendations is most likely to be given by the adviser?**

(a) *Increase fixed-interest savings accounts.*

(b) *Sell property and increase holdings of corporate bonds.*

(c) *Reduce holdings of corporate bonds and purchase gilts.*

(d) *Reduce holdings of fixed-interest savings and increase holdings of equities.*

6. **If the adviser recommends to Steve that he invests in a personal pension, what kind of document must the adviser provide to Steve if he agrees?**

(a) *An appropriateness report.*

(b) *A suitability report.*

(c) *A key facts report.*

(d) *A needs and objectives report.*

Answers

1. (c) – this is a soft fact, as it cannot be verified using documentary evidence.

2. (d) – fixed-interest savings are most likely to see their value eroded by inflation over a long investment horizon.

3. (a) – over a long investment horizon, equities are most likely to see the highest amount of capital growth.

4. (d) – credit risk is associated with debt instruments; it is the risk that the borrower defaults and as a consequence the investor loses money. Out of the two debt instruments listed, fixed deposit accounts and UK corporate bonds, it is UK corporate bonds that face the highest risk of default. Fixed deposit accounts at a UK bank have a lower risk of default, and if the bank does default, the deposits are protected by the deposit protection scheme.

5. (d) – again, because equities will show the highest capital growth over the long term.

6. (b) – when recommending a designated investment to a retail client, the firm must provide the client with a suitability report.

5. CASE STUDY: ANYA

Anya is 40 years old and has inherited a sum of £300,000, which she is looking to invest. She is a member of her firm's defined benefit pension scheme and has no mortgage. She has had a meeting with a financial adviser, and the following facts about Anya have been identified:

1. Anya wants to have investments that are tax-efficient.

2. Anya would like her investments not to have their value eroded by inflation.

3. Anya is a higher rate taxpayer.

Questions

1. Which of the facts about Anya is a hard fact?

(a) *Fact one.*

(b) *Fact two.*

(c) *Fact three.*

(d) *None of them are hard facts.*

2. **Which of the following investments best meet Anya's first requirement?**

(a) *Personal pension scheme.*

(b) *OEICs.*

(c) *Real estate investment trusts (REITs).*

(d) *Direct investment in property.*

3. **If Anya decides to invest in a VCT, how long must she hold the shares in the VCT before their disposal is exempt from capital gains tax (CGT)?**

(a) *No minimum period of investment is needed.*

(b) *One year.*

(c) *Three years.*

(d) *Five years.*

4. **Which one of the following investments is least likely to meet Anya's second requirement over a 20-year investment horizon?**

(a) *UK equities.*

(b) *Property.*

(c) *Fixed-rate deposit invested through an ISA.*

(d) *Index-linked gilts.*

5. **The financial adviser suggests the following investments to Anya as part of a diversified portfolio. Which one of these investments is exempt from income tax?**

(a) *UK shares invested through an ISA.*

(b) *Gilts.*

(c) *Corporate bonds.*

(d) *Investment trusts.*

6. Calculate the maximum amount of income tax relief Anya can receive if she invests £100,000 in some unlisted stocks that qualify under the enterprise investment scheme (EIS).

Answers

1. (c) – a hard fact is something that can be verified by documentation.
2. (a) – of these options, only a personal pension scheme has tax advantages of income tax relief.
3. (a) – there is no minimum period for VCT investments. (The taxation treatment of VCTs is covered in chapter 6, section 1.)
4. (c) – cash investments are most likely to see erosion in value due to inflation over the medium/ long term.
5. (a) – shares sheltered in an ISA are exempt from income tax on dividends. (The taxation treatment of investments is covered in chapter 6, section 1.)
6. £30,000 – income tax relief on an EIS investment is 30% of the investment, i.e. £100,000 × 0.3 = £30,000. If her income tax liability (before relief) is less than £60,000, then she will get less than £10,000 (100% relief) – hence the £15,000 is the maximum relief. (The taxation treatments of EISs is covered in chapter 6, section 1.)

CHAPTER 5 SECTION 7

THE OBJECTIVES OF PENSION FUNDS, LIFE ASSURANCE AND GENERAL INSURANCE COMPANIES AND THE FACTORS THAT IMPACT UPON THEIR INVESTMENT DECISIONS

SECTION AIMS

By the end of this section, learners should be able to:

- Explain the features and objectives of the following funds in the UK:
  - Pension funds (defined benefit and defined contribution)
  - Life assurance
  - General insurance.
- Distinguish among the typical asset allocations for DB and DC pension funds, life assurance and general insurance funds.
- Explain the return objectives of the major fund types.
- Classify funds by their income/ capital growth requirements.
- Explain the effect of each of the following on a fund's asset allocation:
  - Time horizons
  - Liability structure
  - Liquidity requirements.
- Explain the taxation of the various types of funds in the UK.
- Explain the effect that tax legislation may have on the stock selection and asset allocation of a fund.
- Identify the other types of legal requirements that affect pension funds, insurance funds and retail clients.

The extent of institutional involvement in modern financial markets cannot be exaggerated. In the UK, a large proportion of gilts and UK equity are held and managed by investment institutions. These institutions enable small investors to purchase a stake in large, well-diversified portfolios of assets, where they would otherwise only be able to purchase a small number of securities. Indirect investment via an investment institution is now the most popular way for retail investors to invest.

The most important investment institutions in the UK are pension funds, insurance companies and unit trusts. In December 2013, these institutions managed combined assets estimated to be worth £3.95tn (based on a survey by the Investment Association). For institutional clients, around 46% was invested in equities, 34% in bonds and 6% in cash.

1. PENSION FUNDS

There are two main types of pension fund: defined benefit and defined contribution. In defined benefit, the sponsor agrees to pay members of the scheme a pension equal to a pre-determined percentage of their final salary, subject to the member's years of service. In defined contribution, contributions are used to buy investments, and it is the return on these investments that determines pension benefits. Occupational pension schemes, where the sponsor is the employer, may be either defined benefit or defined contribution, while personal pensions are defined contribution. For both occupational schemes (excluding 'pay as you go' schemes) and personal pensions, there is a regular inflow of funds to the scheme, and these funds are accumulated and invested.

The other source of pension provision is from the state, which provides a basic flat rate pension and an additional tier, the state second pension (S2P), which is earnings-related. It is possible to opt out of S2P. The existing two-tier system will be replaced by a single-tier system from 6 April 2016. To qualify for the new state pension, an individual will need at least 10 qualifying years on their National Insurance contribution (NIC) record. They will need at least 35 qualifying years to get the full new state pension. They will receive a proportionate amount of the full new state pension if they have between 10 and 34 qualifying years.

Unlike other types of institutional investment, pension funds benefit from certain tax exemptions. Contributions to a pension scheme are not taxable, and the accumulated interest and capital gains in the fund are also not liable to taxation. However, the pension payments received by a pensioner are liable to income tax. The other main feature of pension funds is the long-term nature of their liabilities. Given this, pension fund managers are required to concentrate their investments in long-term assets (see Table 5.1, which shows the allocation of funds to different asset classes by pension funds in aggregate).

Actuaries take into account, for example, death rates in order to determine the average length of time that an employee will draw a pension and calculate pension fund liabilities for occupational schemes. Given the estimate of the future liability stream, the occupational scheme's trustees – who are appointed to ensure that the pension fund is managed competently – will then determine the overall investment strategy for fund assets that are held to meet these liabilities. The trustees will often determine, for instance, the proportion of assets to be held in different asset classes, such as equity, fixed-income securities and property. This asset mix may be determined, at least in part, by the maturity of the pension fund.

A fund with a high proportion of contributing employees close to retirement should be more mature than a fund with a larger proportion of young contributors. As the maturity of the fund increases, trustees may wish to invest more fund assets in fixed-income securities and less in equity, thereby reducing the uncertainty about the fund's future cash flows. Conflicts may arise between the managers of a firm and the pension fund trustees. Management may be keen to set investment objectives that maximise the return on fund assets in the short term in order to reduce the sponsor's contribution rate. By contrast, trustees may prefer a less risky investment policy, trying to ensure that their value will always be sufficient to meet the fund's future liabilities. Professional fund managers, often commercial bank subsidiaries and life assurance companies, manage pension funds.

The investment policy of both retail investors and investing institutions will be partially determined by their tax status. Pension funds are exempt from both income tax and CGT, which should mean that they can invest without having to concentrate, for example, on low coupon gilts like higher rate taxpayers. However, pension funds may still wish to avoid low coupon fixed-income securities because their popularity with higher rate taxpayers reduces the yield on these issues. Despite not having to pay CGT, pension fund managers may still prefer to receive dividend income rather than capital gains. To adjust a portfolio by realising capital gains incurs transaction costs: firstly on the sale of securities to realise the capital gain, and secondly through the purchase of new securities. However, if the fund can be rebalanced by using dividend or coupon income, transaction costs will only be incurred on the purchase of securities. Therefore, pension fund managers may prefer dividend or coupon payments to capital gains.

The selection of specific assets for a pension fund is usually determined by the pension fund manager according to the general guidelines laid down by the trustees. Since pension funds have a regular flow of income from contributors, fund managers may be able to take advantage of pound cost averaging. If assets are purchased and sold during both market peaks and troughs, the effect of pound cost averaging will be to ensure that the fund manager pays the 'average' price for the assets. Alternatively, fund managers may wish to time their purchases, thus accumulating contributions so that they can buy when security prices are low.

A number of developments have affected the pensions sector over the last 15 years. First, there has been a decline in defined benefit schemes and an increase in defined contribution schemes. This is particularly true for private sector schemes, where less than half of schemes are now defined benefit schemes (compared to 78% in 1999). There are a number of reasons for the closure of defined benefit schemes:

- Increasing longevity, which increases costs for the scheme.
- Disclosure of the schemes' funding position in accounts (see chapter 10).
- Increasing pension deficits – this is partly caused by increasing longevity, but is also a consequence of falling returns on assets held by the schemes.

This has led many defined benefit schemes, particularly those in deficit, to switch away from equities towards bonds. A number of schemes have adopted liability-driven investment (LDI) strategies that involve not just a switch to bonds, but also the use of swaps and other derivatives to more accurately match assets to liabilities. See chapter 15 for more information on LDI strategies. For those defined benefit schemes that have closed to new members, the average age of their members has begun to rise, making a bond-based strategy more attractive. Of course, there are limits to a shift to bonds. It is recognised that using a LDI strategy simply locks in the deficit. Some schemes have adopted partial LDI strategies against some of their liabilities and are using traditional equity investments in an attempt to reduce the deficits. There is also a shortage of long-dated bonds and index-linked bonds.

2. INSURANCE COMPANIES

Insurance companies that provide personal pensions are a significant proportion of pension fund provision. However, owing to the different tax treatment of pension funds compared to the other funds under the management of insurance companies, the insurance company pension funds are quoted and managed separately. In this section, we will look at non-pension insurance company business, which consists of two parts: life assurance and general insurance.

Life assurance companies

Life assurance generally involves long-term liabilities, which are based on the insurance contracts sold by the company. A term assurance policy covers the life of an individual over a specific period (usually ten years or more). In the event that the insured person survives the period, no payment is made. A whole of life policy will insure the life of an individual and pay a capital sum on the policyholder's death, whenever the death should occur.

The contract that grew most in popularity in the UK over the 1980s and 1990s was the endowment policy. An endowment policy combines a savings element with a life assurance element. In return for regular premiums, an endowment policy will pay a fixed sum of money in the event of the policyholder's death, or at least the same fixed sum if the holder survives for a pre-specified period. Endowments are often taken out as insurance cover for mortgages where the sum assured is equal to the outstanding value of the mortgage. If the holder dies during the life of the mortgage, the mortgage provider receives the sum assured, thus paying off the mortgage. Alternatively, if the holder survives the period of the mortgage, the value of the endowment is designed to be equal to the value of the mortgage when the mortgage is due to be redeemed.

Endowments attracted much publicity in the years after 2000, particularly in relation to their mis-selling. The regulator fined many organisations for failing to make investors fully aware of the risks involved (as the savings element is invested in many asset classes, including equities) and not ensuring that the investments were appropriate for the customers' attitude to risk. Many mortgage holders were unexpectedly left short of the amount required to repay their mortgage following the downturn in the global equity markets from 2000 to 2002.

Since the liabilities of life assurance business are long-term in nature, the portfolios of assets held and managed by insurance company fund managers also tend to be long-term. Details of the performance of unit-linked life funds can be found in the *Financial Times* managed funds service.

The tax position of life fund business is different from that of pension fund business. The investment returns of life companies are subject to both CGT and income tax, and, as a consequence, life assurance fund managers will adjust their investment strategy to attempt to minimise the tax which they pay on their funds. Life assurance premiums are paid by policyholders out of post-tax income. Some life assurance policies, such as endowment policies, can be qualifying, meaning that the proceeds of the policy are not taxable. This contrasts with the proceeds from pension funds, which are paid in gross and are taxable.

General insurance companies

General insurance business provides insurance cover against specific contingencies, for example, fire, theft, storm damage, etc. In return for the payment of an insurance premium, an individual or company can insure property with general insurance policies, usually over a fixed period of one year. Liabilities from this type of insurance business are short term in nature, since most claims are made immediately after the relevant event. In order to meet these claims, general insurance companies pool the premiums into reserves, usually in the form of securities which are highly liquid.

3. ASSET ALLOCATION

Fund objectives and constraints

The decision as to what proportion of a portfolio to allocate to the various asset classes is determined by reviewing the objectives and constraints of the fund.

For example, a defined benefit pension fund aims to cover projected liabilities – some of which are immediate and short term (for employees already retired), and some of which are long term (for employees many years from retirement age). The two key kinds of objective are to maximise returns; or to match projected liabilities.

In achieving these objectives, only a certain degree of risk will be acceptable to the stakeholders. There is a definite trade-off between the returns achievable and the risk taken. More risk-averse funds will allow a lower degree of risk in the fund, and thus the potential for high returns is diminished.

The return objective (and risk tolerance) is in turn dependent on a number of portfolio constraints that can fall into the following categories:

- Liquidity needs: cash or near cash assets will be required to cover day-to-day operating expenses and payments out of the fund, and to respond to unanticipated changes in those needs. Fixed income instruments (particularly short-term government bonds) will give easier access to cash should it be required.
- Time horizon: the longer the time horizon of the fund, the more risks the fund can afford to tolerate. A young pension fund, for example, with a low proportion of retired to active members can afford to allocate more of its portfolio to long-term, higher risk assets, such as equity and property. A more mature pension fund with a shorter average duration of liabilities would allocate a larger portion of its fund to fixed income – with a duration to match that of its liabilities.
- Tax: the tax status of the fund will affect the return objective and make some asset classes less desirable than others. For example, charitable funds and pension funds, which pay no income tax or CGT, should consider carefully investments where tax is deducted at source as it may not be possible to reclaim this tax deduction. Even if it is, there is a delay in recovering the tax, which represents a time delay and opportunity cost. Gross funds will also avoid 'tax-free' investments, since these come at a premium that provides no added advantage to a tax-free fund.
- Legal and regulatory: these constraints may exist and need to be borne in mind when constructing the fund. For example, authorised unit trusts in the UK have restrictions as to which asset classes they can invest in.
- Other constraints may exist that do not fall into the above categories: for example, a trust deed may exist that constrains the manager to certain asset classes, or prevents investment in certain types of company stock, such as life science companies. Ethical constraints have become more widespread in the last ten years.

Bearing this outline in mind, the following section gives an overview of asset allocation among the major institutions – pensions and insurance companies.

4. ASSET CLASS DISTRIBUTIONS

Table 5.1 summarises the distribution of assets by the three major classes of institutional investor: pension, life and general insurance funds.

Pension funds

At the end of 2013, UK self-administered pension funds had total net assets of £1,706bn. This was many times greater than the holdings of German and French pension funds respectively. The principal reason for these differences in holdings across Europe is the differing levels of social security provision in each country; for example, in Luxembourg, state benefits are so high that private pension provision is rare.

Since equities offer a suitable match for long horizon pension fund liabilities – which are closely related to wages – it is no surprise to find that around 44% of net assets in Table 5.1 comprise equity investments including direct UK and foreign equity holdings, and more indirect equity holdings held in the form of mutual fund investments.

Table 5.1: Portfolio holdings of UK insurance funds (life and general) and pension funds (end 2013)

	PENSION FUNDS (%)	INSURANCE – LIFE (%)	INSURANCE – GENERAL (%)
Net short-term assets	3.2	54.8	10.4
UK GOVERNMENT BONDS (GILTS)			
Total gilts	13.3	12.3	8.1
(of which, index-linked)	(70.0)	(40.0)	(18.0)
OTHER FIXED INCOME	9.4	20	19.5
EQUITY			
UK equities	6.4	11.8	4.9
Overseas equities	10.0	13.5	1.7
Total equities	16.4	25.3	6.6
MUTUAL FUND INVESTMENTS	27.9	24.9	2.9
OTHER ASSETS	29.8	11.7	52.5
TOTAL ASSETS	100	100	100

Source: Office for National Statistics.

Fixed income securities play a smaller role in the overall picture, with about 23% of pension assets in fixed income securities (approximately 13.3% in UK gilts). In most other European countries, this percentage is much higher: in the recent past in Denmark, approximately 70% of private pension assets have been held in domestic bonds, rising to 75% for Germany and 76% for Portugal. The holdings of gilts are currently particularly low as a consequence of the Bank of England's policy of quantitative easing which has seen the Bank of England buy large quantities of gilts from institutional investors.

Short term asset holdings were low in 2013, reflecting a reduction in uncertainty about the outlook for long term investments following the increase in uncertainty during the 2008 financial crisis. Other assets include derivative positions and property and other asset holdings have been increasing in recent years as a proportion of total assets.

Life assurance

Table 5.1 also shows that the second largest group of institutional investors are the long-term insurance funds, whose assets totalled over £1,449bn by the end of 2013. This sector includes annuity business, various forms of long-term savings policies and life assurance itself.

Like pension funds, life funds also have very long term liabilities; therefore approximately 50% of life fund investments are equities (including mutual fund investments). A significant portion (just over 32%) is invested in fixed income securities (UK government bonds and corporate bonds), particularly those with over five years to maturity. This reflects the nature of the business of selling annuities – fixed income securities with a higher degree of certainty of cash flows provide a degree of cash flow matching for these institutions' annuity liabilities. Short term assets were also low for the same reasons noted above for pension funds.

General insurance

The net assets of general insurance companies are small relative to that of pension and life funds assets. At the end of 2013, general insurance net assets totalled around £161bn. General insurance refers to the pooling of household, motoring, personal accident and other short term risks, where policies are usually renewed on an annual basis. As one might expect, general insurance companies hold substantial proportions of short term assets, to match the short term nature of their liabilities. The typical insurance company business cycle is no more than three to five years.

Time horizons

Pension funds can have very long term liabilities, which may not fall due for 45 years and may last for 20 or more years. However, many analysts prefer to think of this long term horizon as comprising a series of shorter, possibly five-year, horizons. This facilitates a more sensible evaluation of investment objectives based on reasonably foreseeable changes in conditions and circumstances, though as financial and economic conditions become more volatile, there is an increasing tendency to focus on shorter periods.

The liquidity requirements for defined benefit plans may be quite different from defined contribution schemes. The former depend very much on the current age distribution of future beneficiaries. Clearly, immature plans in new companies have few current retired members and hence low liquidity needs. As a pension fund matures, liquidity needs tend to rise. Liquidity needs for a defined contribution (or money purchase) scheme will depend upon the specific circumstances of the plan, including employee turnover rates, withdrawal provisions and the average age of the contributing employees. A relatively new high technology company might require high liquidity for its scheme if there is extensive job turnover, whereas a small, family-run company with little job turnover and no retirement intentions will require low liquidity for its scheme. Clearly, projected death and retirement rates also determine liquidity requirements for defined contribution plans.

There has been a decline in fixed benefits and a rise in with-profits policies offered by long term insurance companies. Consequently, the liabilities of such companies have elements similar to both defined benefit and defined contribution pension schemes. Furthermore, the liquidity needs of life funds are similar to, but slightly greater than, those of pension funds, reflecting the shorter term liability structure of the former.

Compared to long term insurance funds, cash flows for general insurance funds are much more uncertain; hence liquidity has been a higher priority for such funds. In addition, the time horizon for general insurance companies is much shorter than that for life companies. To meet its liquidity needs, a general insurance company will maintain a portfolio of short term securities as an immediate liquidity reserve.

Taxation

Pension funds are exempt from taxation on income and capital gains, with two exceptions. Since 1997, the tax credits paid on dividends earned on UK shares held by the fund are no longer recoverable. In addition, there may be withholding tax on overseas investments, which may not be recoverable. This would seem to suggest that pension funds should be indifferent between high and low coupon fixed income securities (all things being equal). The lower tax on capital gains relative to dividends would also suggest a preference for returns in the form of capital gains. However, there are other factors that influence pension funds investment behaviour including a preference for cash flows (through dividends) which allows the fund to change its investment stance without having to sell existing assets.

Both general and life insurance businesses are taxed on their profits, though the tax on the latter varies according as to whether it is (tax-exempt) pension, life assurance with-profits business or annuity business. The standard rate of corporation tax is charged on life business, unless it relates to investments defined for policyholders, in which case it is reduced to the basic rate of income tax. Clearly, investment via a gross pension scheme has tax advantages over life assurance-linked savings policies.

General insurance and life assurance companies operate within a detailed legal framework intended to prevent such companies from being unable to meet future liabilities and to keep the possibility of fraud to a minimum. Firstly, there is a separation between general insurance and longer term life assurance business. Secondly, general insurers are required to keep solvency margins expressed as a percentage of net assets to net premiums written. However, UK rules do not specify which sort of assets insurers must hold, in contrast to US regulators, who favour bonds. There are few restrictions on the investments available as assets for life funds.

CHAPTER 05 KEY FACTS

5.1

1. The two main types of investors are retail investors and institutional investors.

2. The FCA categorises retail investors according to their wealth and experience in order to restrict promotions of and investments in more risky types of investments.

3. A high net worth investor is defined as a person with an annual income of £100,000 or more, or net investable assets of £250,000 or more.

4. A certified sophisticated investor is a person who has a certificate in the required form confirming that they have been assessed by a firm as being sufficiently knowledgeable to understand the risk of a particular investment.

5. The FCA's treating customers fairly (TCF) initiative aims to deliver six improved outcomes for retail clients:

    i. Consumers can be confident that they are dealing with firms where the fair treatment of customers is central to the corporate culture.

    ii. Products and services marketed and sold in the retail market are designed to meet the needs of identified consumer groups and are targeted accordingly.

    iii. Consumers are provided with clear information and are kept appropriately informed before, during and after the point of sale.

    iv. Where consumers receive advice, the advice is suitable and takes account of their circumstances.

    v. Consumers are provided with products that perform as firms have led them to expect, and the associated service is both of an acceptable standard and as they have been led to expect.

    vi. Consumers do not face unreasonable post-sale barriers imposed by firms to change product, switch provider, submit a claim or make a complaint.

6. The three main factors affecting an investor's needs/objectives are:

    - Time horizon.

- Return requirement.
- Risk tolerance.

7. Other factors affecting a client's needs include liquidity, tax considerations, regulatory requirements, religious or ethical restrictions or other unique circumstances.

5.2

1. Establishing a client's objectives is a vital first stage in the financial planning process.
2. Financial objectives should be quantified in terms of both how much is required and when.
3. Some objectives may need to be prioritised and amended in the light of affordability.

5.3

1. Collecting data regarding a client's current circumstances is also a key stage in financial planning.
2. It may be necessary to clarify detail with third parties, in which case a 'letter of authority' will be needed.

5.4

1. Clients often have limited understanding of investment risk and thus limit it to capital risk. They may need an explanation of inflation risk, interest rate risk and shortfall risk.
2. Diversification between different asset classes is a way of limiting risk, because different asset classes have different exposure to the four types of investment risk.
3. A client may have more than one 'attitude to risk' if they have different investment objectives with different timescales.

5.5

1. The financial planning process contains six main steps, including a review after implementation.
2. Asset allocation is always the main driver of performance, and must be appropriate to the client's objectives and attitude to risk.
3. If collective products are part of the recommendation, then past performance, charges and (if relevant) the financial strength of the provider should be taken into account.

5.6

1. The fact-find should capture all pertinent details, including: current and future circumstances, objectives, current and expected income levels, expenditure, current financial status, entitlement of benefits, attitude to risk.

2. Advisers should ascertain whether a client has sufficient emergency funds.

3. It is good practice to explore all aspects of risk, including product risk and underlying risk, as well as the circumstances where these risks might occur.

4. It is also good practice to consider whether the advice provided remains suitable if the client's circumstances change – e.g. a client may expect their income to fall if their company begins to perform badly.

5.7

1. There are two main types of pension fund: defined benefit and defined contribution.

2. Pension funds are exempt from both CGT and income tax (except they cannot claim back the 10% tax deducted at source on dividend payments), and therefore their investment policy is generally not determined by tax considerations (as is the case for other types of investor).

3. The liabilities of pension funds are usually long term in nature, and the asset mix of a fund will depend in part upon the maturity of the fund.

4. Life assurance companies also have long term liabilities. Traditionally, one of the main liabilities came from the sale of whole of life policies, although today much of a fund's liability will come from endowment policies.

5. General insurance companies tend to have much shorter liabilities arising from the sale of contingency specific insurance policies. The short term liabilities of general insurance funds mean that these funds are more heavily focused upon shorter term assets.

6. Life assurance and general insurance funds are not tax-exempt.

7. Funds' asset allocations are primarily determined by analysing the fund objectives (return and risk) and constraints (liquidity, time horizon, tax, legal, regulatory and any other specifics, such as ethical constraints).

8. The largest institutional funds in the UK are pension funds, followed by insurance funds, unit trusts and then investment trust companies. Pension and life funds tend to be dominated by long term assets.

CHAPTER 05 SELF-ASSESSMENT QUESTIONS

1. **Harry and Bridget are aged 38 and 35, respectively. Harry will soon be able to join his new employer's pension scheme; Bridget currently has no pension arrangement. They would like to retire when Harry reaches age 60 and retain their current lifestyle. Which of the following is likely to be the most important starting point for advice?**

(a) *An analysis of their household income and expenditure.*

(b) *Details of their wills.*

(c) *Details of all of their existing life assurance policies.*

(d) *A copy of their last income tax return.*

2. **Which of the following investors is likely to have the MOST flexibility in achieving their retirement objectives, assuming they all wish to retire with the same living standard?**

(a) *An investor aged 32 wishing to retire at 55.*

(b) *An investor aged 42 wishing to retire at 60.*

(c) *An investor aged 35 wishing to retire at 50.*

(d) *An investor aged 23 wishing to retire at 65.*

3. **Which of the following statements regarding a client fact-find is true?**

(a) *A client must complete a fact-find prior to their first meeting with an adviser.*

(b) *A fact-find must be documented on paper and signed by both the client and the adviser.*

(c) *A copy of the client fact-find must be attached to any recommendations.*

(d) *There are no regulatory requirements regarding the nature and content of a fact-find.*

4. **In the course of establishing a client's current circumstances, advisers sometimes make use of letters of authority to third parties. Which of the following enquiries should not require the adviser to use a letter of authority?**

(a) *To determine which funds a single premium life assurance bond is invested in.*

(b) *To determine how much capital is outstanding on a repayment mortgage.*

(c) *To determine whether the client is a basic or higher rate taxpayer.*

(d) *To determine the underlying funds of a client's ISA investments.*

5. **Which of the following asset classes is likely to have the lowest level of capital risk?**

(a) *Overseas equities.*

(b) *UK equities.*

(c) *Gilts.*

(d) *Cash deposits.*

6. **Which of the following is least likely to affect a client's attitude to risk?**

(a) *The timescale of the investment.*

(b) *Whether their investment objective is income or capital growth.*

(c) *Whether the client is a basic or higher rate taxpayer.*

(d) *The asset allocation of the client's existing investments.*

7. **Which of the following statements regarding asset allocation is true?**

(a) *Asset allocation is influenced by a client's attitude to risk and their investment objectives.*

(b) *Asset allocation must remain fixed for the duration of the portfolio and cannot be changed.*

(c) *Asset allocation is less important than fund or investment selection.*

(d) *Asset allocation must be revised each year as part of the annual review.*

8. **Collective investment products may form part of a recommended portfolio. Which of the following factors is least critical to the fund selection process?**

(a) *The level of annual management charges within the product.*

(b) *The past performance of the fund compared with its peer group.*

(c) *The quality of customer service given by the product provider.*

(d) *The size of the fund.*

9. Which of the following statements regarding institutions' asset allocation is typically correct?

(a) *Life assurance funds have a higher allocation to equities and a higher allocation to fixed income securities compared to general insurance funds.*

(b) *Life assurance funds have a higher allocation to equities and a lower allocation to fixed income securities compared to general insurance funds.*

(c) *Life assurance funds have a lower allocation to equities and a higher allocation to fixed income securities compared to general insurance funds.*

(d) *Life assurance funds have a lower allocation to equities and a lower allocation to fixed income securities compared to general insurance funds.*

10. Which of the following statements relating to defined benefit pension funds is correct?

(a) *A mature fund will have a higher liquidity requirement and thus have a higher allocation to short dated securities.*

(b) *A mature fund will have a lower liquidity requirement and thus have a higher allocation to short dated securities.*

(c) *A mature fund will have a higher liquidity requirement and thus have a lower allocation to short dated securities.*

(d) *A mature fund will have a lower liquidity requirement and thus have a lower allocation to short dated securities.*

ANSWERS

1. *(a) An analysis of affordability based on a cash flow statement of income and expenditure is the most likely starting point out of the four alternatives.*
2. *(d) Generally the more time there is to invest, the more flexibility in achieving investment objectives.*
3. *(d) There are no regulatory requirements in relation to a fact-find.*
4. *(c) The advisor should be able to identify a client's tax status by asking the client.*
5. *(d) Deposits are generally not exposed to capital risk – the risk of loss of value of the amount invested.*
6. *(c) The tax rate faced by the investor on income is unlikely to affect their attitude to risk.*
7. *(a) Asset allocation will be affected by the client's attitude to risk and their objectives.*
8. *(d) Fund size will be less important than charges, past performance and customer service in determining fund selection.*
9. *(b) Life assurance companies have longer term liabilities than general insurance companies so have a preference for assets that deliver higher returns in the long run i.e. equities. General insurance ompanies need to manage cash flows over a shorter horizon (to meet expected claims) and so invest more in fixed income and cash.*
10. *(a) A mature fund will need more access to cash to pay a greater proportion of maturing claims so will prefer to invest in short dated securities.*

LINK TO CFA LEVEL 1

The material in this chapter is not covered in CFA Level 1.

CHAPTER 6

TAXATION IN THE UK

The ways in which the UK tax system applies to individuals, companies, trusts and investments themselves are covered in this chapter.

The UK tax system is very complicated and this chapter addresses the most common elements and the way in which the elements impact on the majority of investors.

Income tax, capital gains tax and inheritance tax all have unique characteristics related to their application, allowances, exemptions, rates and bands. This chapter builds an understanding of all of these taxes, together with an ability to perform common tax calculations.

Further taxes such as value added tax and stamp duty, as well as National Insurance contributions, are also described.

Investment advice needs to take account of all tax implications for a client. Various indirect investments offer potential tax benefits. These include pension investments, individual savings accounts, onshore and offshore collective investment schemes and life assurance policies, real estate investment trusts, venture capital trusts and enterprise investment schemes. The application of each must be understood.

In addition to specific tax advantaged investments, investment advisers should consider a variety of additional tax planning approaches such as full use of available allowances, the optimum timing of asset sales and the lifetime disposal of assets. The ability to make the best investment decision for a client's individual tax circumstances may be tested in the examination.

This topic will be examined using questions that test both an understanding of the nature of taxation and also numerical taxation calculations applied to the most common elements of personal taxation.

CHAPTER 6 SECTION 1

THE UK TAX SYSTEM AND THE TAXATION OF INVESTMENTS

SECTION AIMS

By the end of this section, learners should be able to:

- Describe the principles of income tax applicable to earnings, savings and investment income in the UK.
- Describe, in relation to income tax, the system of allowances, reliefs and priorities for taxing income.
- Explain the taxation of the income of trusts and beneficiaries.
- Describe the system of National Insurance contributions (NICs).
- Describe the principles of capital gains tax (CGT) in the UK.
- Describe the principles of inheritance tax (IHT).
- Explain the limitations of lifetime gifts and transfers at death in mitigating IHT.
- Explain the implications of residence and domicile in relation to liability to income tax, CGT and IHT.
- Describe the system of UK tax compliance, including self-assessment, pay as you earn (PAYE), tax returns, tax payments, tax evasion and avoidance issues.
- Describe the principles of stamp duty land tax (SDLT) as applied to property transactions (buying/selling and leasing).
- Describe the principles of stamp duty reserve tax (SDRT).
- Explain how companies are taxed in the UK.
- Describe, in outline, the principles of value added tax (VAT).
- Analyse the taxation of direct investments, including cash and cash equivalents, fixed interest securities, equities and property.
- Analyse the key features and taxation of indirect investments, including pension arrangements, different types of individual savings accounts (ISAs) and child trust funds, onshore and offshore life assurance policies, real estate investment trusts, venture capital trusts and enterprise investment schemes.

1. INCOME TAX

Income tax is normally paid at either the basic or higher rate according to a person's total yearly income. The tax year runs from 6 April to 5 April the next year, and all figures used in this section relate to the 2015/16 tax year. Every taxpayer has a personal allowance of £10,600, although this is gradually withdrawn at the rate of £1 for every £2 earned where a taxpayer's income exceeds £100,000, Therefore someone with income of £121,200 or more will have no personal allowance. In addition, non-domiciled taxpayers using the remittance basis of taxation are not able to claim a personal tax allowance – see part 5 in this section for a discussion of domicile.

For those able to claim the personal allowance, income up to £10,600 is tax-free. Those born before 6 April 1938 may qualify for a higher personal allowance. For 2015/16, a person can transfer a fixed amount (known as the marriage allowance) of £1,060 (10% of their personal allowance) to a spouse or civil partner. A transfer will be beneficial where one spouse/civil partner has little or no income, with the result that their personal allowance is wholly or partly unused. However, a transfer is only permitted where the other spouse/civil partner does not pay tax higher than at the basic rate. The potential tax saving for 2015/16 is therefore £212 (£1,060 at 20%). This is given to the recipient as a deduction from their tax liability.

Income in excess of the personal allowance is 'taxable income'. The first £31,785 of taxable income each year is generally taxed at 20%, i.e. the basic rate. Taxable income beyond this and up to £150,000 is taxed at the higher rate of 40%, or 32.5% for dividend income. The threshold for the higher rate tax can be increased beyond £31,785 by certain types of pension contributions and charitable donations (explained later in this chapter). For taxable income above £150,000, there is an additional tax rate of 45%.

In addition, there is a 0% starting rate band of £5,000 for savings income only, which is not available if taxable non-savings income is above this limit. If this is the case, savings income is taxed first at 20%, then at 40% if it falls into the threshold for higher rate tax. For additional rate taxpayers, savings income is taxed at 45%.

A new personal savings allowance was announced in the March 2015 Budget that will apply from 6 April 2016. The amount of allowance will depend on the rate of income tax paid by a taxpayer:

- Basic-rate taxpayers will have an allowance of £1,000, so there will be no tax on this amount of interest (a maximum tax saving of £200 compared to the current tax year).
- Higher-rate taxpayers will have an allowance of £500 (a maximum tax saving of £200).
- Additional-rate taxpayers will not receive any.

The income tax system takes an individual's total taxable income and breaks it down into three elements:

- Non-savings income is taxed first at either 20% or 40% if it is above the threshold for higher rate tax.
- Non-dividend savings income is taxed next, again at either 20% or 40%.
- Dividend income is taxed at either 10% or 32.5% if it is above the threshold for higher rate tax. For additional rate taxpayers, dividend income is taxed at 37.5%.

Table 6.1: Income tax rates for 2015/16

	2015/16
Starting rate for savings: 0%	£0–£5,000
Basic rate: 20%	£0–£31,785
Higher rate: 40%	£31,786–£150,000
Additional rate: 45%	Over £150,000

An individual's income from all sources is brought together to produce a personal tax computation, as shown in the following example:

	NON-SAVINGS INCOME (£)	SAVINGS INCOME (£)	DIVIDENDS INCOME (£)	TOTAL (£)
Income from employment	56,000			
Bank/building society interest		1,200		
Dividends (gross)			2,200	
Total income	56,000	1,200	2,200	59,400
Less interest paid	(2,000)			(2,000)
Net income	54,000	1,200	2,200	57,400
Less personal allowance	(10,600)			(10,600)
Taxable income	43,400	1,200	2,200	46,800

	£
Income tax on non-savings income	
£31,785 @ 20%	6,357
£11,615 @ 40%	4,646
Tax on savings income £1,200 @ 40%	480
Tax on dividend income £2,200 @ 32.5%	715
Tax liability	12,198

Note that deductible interest is deducted from total income to give net income.

An individual who pays interest in a tax year is entitled to relief in that year if the loan is for a qualifying purpose, which could be:

- buying plant or machinery for partnership use;
- buying plant or machinery for employment use;
- buying an interest in an unquoted employee-controlled company;
- investing in a partnership;
- investing in a co-operative; or
- buying ordinary shares in, or lending money to, a close company (a close company is one that is controlled by five or fewer shareholders or by its directors, regardless of their number).

The final tax liability for higher and additional rate taxpayers may be reduced by the effect of certain payments made, principally:

- Pension contributions: an individual who is under the age of 75 is entitled to tax relief on contributions to a registered pension scheme in a tax year. The maximum tax-relieved contributions that can be made are the higher of:
  - The individual's relevant earnings subject to an annual cap of £40,000 (2015/16 tax year).
  - A basic amount of £3,600.

  Tax relief is at the taxpayer's marginal tax rate, so an additional rate taxpayer can obtain 45% tax relief on their pension contributions.

- Donations to charity, such as gift aid charitable donations, earn tax relief at the taxpayer's marginal tax rate.

Taxation of the income of trusts and beneficiaries

Where the trustees can accumulate income and/or distribute it at their discretion, trusts are taxed as set out below.

The rate of income tax payable depends on the type of income and whether or not the income falls within the 'standard rate band', which applies to the first £1,000 of income.

Table 6.2: Tax rates on accumulation/discretionary trust income (the first £1,000 or 'standard rate band')

TYPE OF INCOME	TAX RATE 2015/16
Dividend-type income	10% (the 'dividend ordinary rate')
All other income (rent, business income, savings)	20% (the 'basic rate')

Table 6.3: Tax rates on accumulation/discretionary trust income (over £1,000)

TYPE OF INCOME	TAX RATE 2015/16
Dividend-type income	37.5% (the 'dividend trust rate')
All other income (rent, business income, savings)	45% (the 'trust rate')

How the standard rate band works

The standard rate band is applied in the following sequence to different types of income:

- First to non-dividend income (rent, business income, savings).
- Then to dividend income.

If the person who set up the trust (the settlor) has created more than one trust, the £1,000 standard rate band is divided equally among the trusts. However, if the settlor has five or more trusts, the standard rate band for each trust is £200 (£1,000 ÷ 5).

Where trust income is paid out to a beneficiary at the trustees' discretion, it is treated as having already been taxed at the trust rate of 45%. If the beneficiary's overall level of income means they are a non-taxpayer or a basic or higher rate rate taxpayer, they may be able to reclaim some or all of this tax back.

2. NATIONAL INSURANCE CONTRIBUTIONS

National Insurance is a scheme where people in work (either employed or self-employed) make payments towards benefits. The payments are called National Insurance contributions (NICs), and certain benefits are only paid out if NIC conditions are met.

Employees under the state pension age working in the UK have to pay class 1 NICs on part of their earnings. The amount paid depends on earnings. If earnings are below a certain amount (called the primary contribution threshold), then no NICs have to be paid. There are other classes of NICs:

- Class 1A NICs are paid by an employer if an employee receives certain taxable benefits with their job, such as the use of a company car.
- Class 1B NICs are paid by an employer if they have entered into a pay as you earn (PAYE) settlement agreement with HM Revenue & Customs (HMRC).
- Class 2 NICs are paid by the self-employed. If earnings are below a certain limit (called the small profits threshold), then the self-employed person does not have to pay contributions.
- Class 3 NICs are mainly voluntary contributions that someone can choose to pay if they do not have to pay any compulsory contributions – for example, if their earnings are too low. People can choose to pay class 3 contributions to help fill gaps in their NIC record.
- Class 4 NICs may have to be paid by someone who is self-employed and earns profits over a certain amount each year. These contributions are usually paid with income tax under the self-assessment system.

Some married women and widows have the right to pay reduced class 1 and class 2 contributions, but this right was only available for those people who applied before 21 May 1977. It normally means the person cannot get contributory benefits and may get less state pension.

The number of years that someone needs to have paid NICs in order to qualify for the maximum basic state pension is currently 30 years, but the single-tier state pension introduced from 6 April 2016 will increase this requirement to 35 years. From 12 October 2015, class 3A NICs will be introduced for a limited period until 5 April 2017. They will give people who have reached or will reach state pension age before 6 April 2016 an opportunity to boost their additional state pension entitlement – and hence their future pension entitlement.

3. CAPITAL GAINS TAX

Capital gains tax (CGT) is payable by UK residents on the disposal of a chargeable asset. Most assets are chargeable, including shares, foreign currency (not for personal use) and property. A chargeable disposal occurs when an asset is sold (in whole or part) or given away.

The rate of CGT for basic rate income taxpayers is 18%. More precisely, a CGT rate of 18% applies where a taxpayer's taxable income (including gains) does not exceed the upper limit of the income tax basic rate band (£31,785 for 2015/16). For higher and additional rate taxpayers, the rate of CGT is 28%. The only exception to this is a rate of 10% paid on the disposal of certain business assets under entrepreneurs' relief.

A portion of any gains made in one tax year is exempt from CGT – for the tax year 2015/16, this is £11,100. Also, only net chargeable gains are taxed (i.e. capital losses can be deducted from chargeable gains). Any losses that exceed gains in a particular year can be carried forward indefinitely to be set against gains made in the future.

Certain assets are exempt from CGT, including:

- An individual's main home.
- Private cars.
- Individual savings accounts (ISAs).
- National Savings and Investment (NS&I) savings certificates.
- Betting and lottery winnings.
- Premium bond prizes.
- British government stock and most corporate bonds.
- Shares under the enterprise investment scheme (EIS) or seed enterprise investment scheme (SEIS), provided income tax relief has not been withdrawn.
- Foreign currency for personal use (e.g. spent on holidays abroad), although currency bought and sold for gain is chargeable.
- The first £50,000 of shares provided under an employee shareholder agreement (an employee shareholder can be given between £2,000 and £50,000 of shares in their employer company).

To illustrate the calculation of a CGT liability, consider the case of Susan who is a basic rate taxpayer and, in the tax year 2015/16, makes capital gains of £15,000 and capital losses of £1,500. What CGT will she pay?

	£
Capital gains	15,000
Capital losses	(1,500)
Net capital gains	13,500
Annual exempt amount	(11,100)
Taxable gain	2,400

Susan is a basic rate taxpayer, so CGT is chargeable at the rate of 18%. The CGT payable by Susan will therefore be £432. CGT is due on 31 January following the tax year of the disposal, so in this case the tax of £432 will be due on 31 January 2017.

4. INHERITANCE TAX

Inheritance tax (IHT) is charged on an individual's estate at death on gifts made in the seven years prior to death, and also on chargeable lifetime transfers (CLTs) – most transfers to trusts are CLTs.

IHT applies if the taxable value of a person's estate when they die is above £325,000 (2015/16). IHT is payable on the excess above this nil rate band at a rate of 40%. Any unused nil rate band on a person's death can be transferred to their surviving spouse or civil partner for use on their death.

Where a claim to transfer an unused nil rate band is made, the nil rate band that is available when the surviving spouse or civil partner dies will be increased by the proportion of the nil rate band unused on the first death.

For example, if on the first death the chargeable estate is £150,000 and the nil rate band was £300,000, 50% of the nil rate band would have been unused. If the nil rate band on the second death is £325,000, then this will be increased by 50% to £487,500. It is the percentage of the unused band that is transferred, not the amount.

There are also a number of exemptions which allow a person to pass on amounts (during their lifetime or on their death) without any IHT being due, for example:

- If a person's estate passes to their spouse or civil partner and they are both domiciled in the UK, there is no IHT to pay even if the estate is above the £325,000 nil rate band. This exemption applies to lifetime gifts and to estates passing on death.
- Certain other gifts, such as wedding gifts and gifts in anticipation of a civil partnership up to £5,000 (depending on the relationship between the giver and the recipient), gifts to charity and the first £3,000 given away each year are also exempt.

- Anyone leaving more than 10% of their estate to charity benefits from a reduced IHT rate of 36%.

If a person makes a lifetime gift to another individual and it is not covered by one of the exemptions, it is a potentially exempt transfer (PET). A PET is only free of IHT if the donor lives for seven years after the gift is made.

Most transfers into trusts are immediately liable to IHT if the transfer exceeds the donor's nil rate band. These are known as chargeable lifetime transfers (CLTs). The only type of transfer into trust that counts as a PET is where the trust is for the disabled. CLTs in excess of the donor's available nil rate band are subject to an immediate IHT charge of 20%.

A CLT will only be subject to an immediate 20% IHT charge if the reduction in the value of the donor's estate (after allowable deductions such as the £3,000 annual exemption) exceeds the donor's available nil rate band. This will be the nil rate band applicable to the tax year in which the CLT is made less any other CLTs made within the previous seven years.

Effectively, therefore, property can be passed out of an estate into a trust every seven years to the value of the current nil rate band. Alternatively, property can be passed out of an estate into a trust every year to a value of one-seventh of the current nil rate band, or any other combination of gifts to a trust that uses up the current nil rate band over seven years.

A CLT will not be subject to any further IHT charge provided the donor survives for at least seven years after making the gift. If that does not happen, then the CLT will be added to the estate of the deceased and taxed at 40% if any part remains chargeable after deducting the nil rate band and any other available reliefs. A credit will be allowed for the 20% paid on the lifetime transfer and taper relief may also apply if the donor survived at least three years after making the gift – but if the eventual IHT charge turns out to be less than the 20% already paid, no rebate is given.

If a person makes a lifetime gift with strings attached (technically known as a gift with reservation of benefit), it will still count as part of their estate, no matter how long they live after making it. For example, if someone gives their house to their children but carries on living there without paying a full commercial rent, the value of the house will still be included in their estate and liable to IHT.

An additional nil rate band will be available when a main residence is passed on death to direct descendants from 2017/18. The main residence nil rate band will initially be set at £100,000, and will be transferable to a surviving spouse or civil partner in the same manner as the normal nil rate band. If the net value of the estate exceeds £2m, then the main residence nil rate band will be tapered away.

5. RESIDENCE AND DOMICILE

Since 6 April 2013, a statutory residence test has been used to determine an individual's residence status, which has to be determined each tax year. Essentially, the test divides taxpayers into three separate categories, each with their own rules:

- Automatically non-resident;
- Automatically resident; or
- Those who need to review connecting factors with, and the amount of time spent in, the UK.

Each step should be considered, and if it does not conclude a person's status, they then move on to the next step. As soon as a conclusion is reached then no further parts of the test need to be considered. The test is in three parts.

Part A – Automatically non-resident

A person is non-resident if any of the following conditions are met:

- they visit the UK for fewer than 16 days during the tax year;
- they are non-UK resident in all of the previous three tax years and visit the UK for fewer than 46 days during the tax year; or
- they work full-time overseas and visit the UK for fewer than 91 days during the tax year (with no more than 30 days spent working in the UK).

Part B – Automatically resident

A person is resident if Part A does not apply and any of the following conditions are met:

- they are present in the UK for 183 days or more during the tax year;
- they have their only home in the UK. The conditions for this test are quite complex, but it is necessary to have the UK home for a period of at least 91 days, and to live there for at least 30 days during the tax year; or
- they carry out full-time work in the UK.

Part C – Sufficient ties test

If neither Part A nor Part B applies, then a further series of tests are applied based on ties to the UK such as family connections, work and accommodation.

Domicile

A person is domiciled in the country in which they have their permanent home. Domicile is different from nationality or residence. A person can be resident in more than one country but can only be domiciled in one country at a time.

A person acquires a domicile of origin at birth. This is normally determined by the domicile of the father (or mother if the father died before the person's birth or the parents were not married). After the age of 16, a person can acquire a domicile of choice. This involves the person settling in another country with the intention of making it their permanent home.

From April 2017, individuals who were born in the UK to UK-domiciled parents will no longer be able to claim non-domicile status whilst they are resident in the UK.

Generally, a UK resident is liable to UK income tax on their UK and overseas income. A non-resident is liable to income tax only on income arising in the UK. A UK resident who is not UK-domiciled may use the remittance basis of taxation, although this is only relevant if they have foreign income and/or gains.

With the remittance basis of taxation, a person pays UK tax on UK-sourced income and capital gains as they arise or accrue. However, they only have to pay UK tax on overseas income and/or capital gains when they are brought (remitted) into the UK. Normally, the remittance basis must be claimed, but it applies automatically if the individual has unremitted overseas income and/or capital gains of less than £2,000 in a tax year. However, the personal allowance is not available if the remittance basis is claimed.

If an individual decides to claim the remittance basis and has been a 'long term' resident in the UK, they may have to pay the remittance basis charge (RBC). The RBC is an annual tax charge fixed at £30,000 if a person has been resident for at least seven of the last nine tax years. If a person has been resident for at least 12 of the last 14 tax years, then a higher RBC of £60,000 applies.

An even higher RBC of £90,000 applies where a person has been resident for at least 17 of the last 20 tax years. It is a tax on the unremitted overseas income and/or gains which are left outside the UK, and is payable in addition to any UK tax that the individual has to pay on UK income and/or gains, or on foreign income and/or gains remitted to the UK. The RBC is payable if, in a tax year, the individual has £2,000 or more of unremitted overseas income and/or gains, and:

- they make a claim to use the remittance basis;
- they are aged 18 or over; or
- they are a 'long term' resident of the UK.

In general, non-UK residents are not entitled to either the income tax personal allowance or the CGT annual exempt amount. However, citizens of the European Economic Area and Commonwealth countries, and residents in the Isle of Man and the Channel Islands, are entitled to these allowances.

Generally, if a person is domiciled or deemed to be domiciled in the UK, IHT applies to their assets wherever they are situated. If a person is domiciled abroad, IHT applies only to their UK assets. From April 2017, a non-domiciled individual will be deemed domiciled for all tax purposes after being UK resident for at least 15 out of the previous 20 years. The £90,000 RBC will then be redundant because the remittance basis is only available where an individual is nondomiciled.

6. THE SYSTEM OF UK TAX COMPLIANCE

A large amount of income is taxed at source, either through PAYE or through basic rate deductions. If additional tax is payable, a system of self-assessment is used. This requires taxpayers to keep sufficient records in order to prepare a tax return if required by HMRC. Business records must be kept for five years after the 31 January following the tax year. A tax return must be submitted by 31 October following the end of the tax year if it is filed on paper, and a return filed electronically must be submitted by 31 January following the end of the tax year.

For taxpayers who are self-employed or who pay less than 80% of last year's income tax at source, a system of payments on account is used. Here, the taxpayer will pay two equal payments on account of their tax on 31 January in the tax year and 31 July following the end of the tax year. These are payments to cover tax over the current year and are designed to improve HMRC's cash flow. There is a final balancing payment on the following 31 January based on the submitted tax return.

Tax evasion should not be confused with tax avoidance, which is the legal structuring of tax affairs to ensure the lowest possible tax bill. Tax evasion involves deliberate actions on the part of a taxpayer in order to evade paying the proper and full amount of tax due. Tax evasion can lead to a criminal investigation and prosecution. However, criminal investigations are generally only conducted for large-scale, blatant tax frauds.

Where HMRC suspects individuals of tax evasion, it will normally use the civil investigation of fraud procedures to obtain a civil monetary settlement. HMRC has increasingly encouraged taxpayers to make voluntary disclosure via various campaigns focused on particular target groups. Another approach HMRC has used is task forces for an intensive burst of activity targeted at specific business sectors and locations where there is a high risk of tax evasion.

The total amount payable to HMRC in respect of the tax offences will include the tax due, plus statutory interest (for late paid tax) and a penalty based on a percentage of the tax due. Individuals and businesses involved in tax avoidance schemes may have to pay HMRC the disputed amount of tax upfront while the dispute is being resolved – known as accelerated payments.

7. LAND TAXES

Stamp duty land tax (SDLT) is a self-assessed tax on land transactions involving any estate, interest, right or power in or over land. In Scotland, land and buildings transaction tax (LBTT) applies instead of SDLT.

As part of the conveyancing process, agents (usually) complete a SDLT tax return, giving:

- the effective date of the transaction;
- the purchase price of the property; and
- a calculation of the SDLT payable.

Table 6.4: Rates of SDLT

RESIDENTIAL		NON-RESIDENTIAL	
Slice of purchase price	Rate	Purchase price	Rate
£0 to £125,000	0%	£0 to £150,000	0%
£125,001 to £250,000	2%	£150,001 to £250,000	1%
£250,001 to £925,000	5%	£250,001 to £500,000	3%
£925,001 to £1,500,000	10%	Over £500,000	4%
Over £1,500,000	12%		

In December 2014, the basis for taxing residential land transactions changed. For non-residential land transactions, tax is paid at a single rate on the entire purchase price. However, for residential transactions, tax is paid at the rate of tax on that part of the purchase price within each tax band. This basis removes the distortions in house prices previously associated with bunching of sales around the SDLT thresholds. For example, the SDLT calculation for a non-residential property bought for £400,000 would be £400,000 at 3% = £12,000. However, for a similar residential property, the calculation would be: (£125,000 at 0%) + (£125,000 at 2%) + (£150,000 at 5%) = £10,000.

For leasehold property, SDLT is charged at the rate of 1% on the present value of rent over the term of a lease where this value exceeds £125,000 for residential property and £150,000 for nonresidential property. SDLT is only paid on the excess over the threshold, and is in addition to SDLT on any premium received.

An anti-avoidance rate of 15% is charged on the entire purchase price where companies and collective investment schemes buy residential properties with a value over £500,000.

Land and buildings transaction tax

LBTT has been used for land transactions in Scotland since 1 April 2015. The tax is applicable to residential and non-residential land transactions in a similar manner to the bands used for SDLT on residential property. Tax is therefore only paid at the rate of tax on that part of the purchase price within each tax band.

Table 6.5: Rates of LBTT

RESIDENTIAL		NON-RESIDENTIAL	
Slice of purchase price	Rate	Slice of purchase price	Rate
£0 to £145,000	0%	£0 to £150,000	0%
£145,001 to £250,000	2%	£150,001 to £350,000	3%
£250,001 to £325,000	5%	Over £350,000	4.5%
£325,001 to £750,000	10%		
Over £750,000	12%		

8. STAMP DUTY RESERVE TAX AND STAMP DUTY

Stamp duty reserve tax (SDRT) is paid on paperless transactions when an investor buys:

- Shares in a UK company (except for AIM companies and those listed on a recognised growth market, such as ICAP Securities and Derivatives Exchange (ISDX)).
- Shares in a foreign company with a share register in the UK.
- An option to buy shares.
- Rights arising from shares already owned.
- An interest in shares, such as an interest in the money made from selling them.

SDRT may also be payable when units in unit trusts or shares in open-ended investment companies (OEICs) are purchased. However, there is no SDRT payable when an investor buys units from the fund manager, or where units are surrendered. As mentioned earlier, SDRT is not payable on the purchase of shares listed on AIM or ISDX and the high growth segment of the London Stock Exchange main market.

Transfers using CREST

Most paperless share transactions that SDRT is paid on are carried out electronically through CREST, the electronic settlement and registration system. CREST automatically deducts the

SDRT and sends it to HMRC. An investor's stockbroker then settles with CREST and bills the investor for the SDRT and their own fees.

The amount of SDRT paid by an investor is worked out at a flat rate of 0.5% (rounded up or down to the nearest penny) based on what the investor paid for the shares, not what the shares are worth. So if it is a cash transaction, the amount of SDRT is based on the amount of cash paid. For example, if an investor buys shares for £1,000, they will pay £5 in SDRT no matter the value of the shares themselves.

When buying shares where the price paid is greater than £1,000, and the purchase is recorded on a stock transfer form, the form will need to be stamped by HMRC and stamp duty will need to be paid. For purchases less than £1,000, no stamp duty is payable. Note that stamp duty is only payable where the purchase is recorded on a stock transfer form. For paperless (CREST) transactions, SDRT is paid as detailed above.

9. CORPORATION TAX

A UK-resident company is liable to corporation tax on its worldwide profits and chargeable gains arising in an accounting period. Other companies are taxed on profits generated in the UK. An accounting period cannot be longer than twelve months.

For the financial year 2015 (which covers the period 1 April 2015 to 31 March 2016), there is a single rate of corporation tax of 20% whatever the level of a company's profits.

A company's trading losses can normally be set against:

- Income and gains of the same accounting period.
- Income and gains of the previous year.
- Trading profits from the same trade in future years.

Losses incurred in the final twelve months of trading can be carried back for three years, being set against more recent periods before earlier periods.

A company's corporation tax liability is self-assessed, with the majority of companies paying their corporation tax nine months and one day after the end of their accounting period. However, large companies are required to pay their corporation tax in four quarterly instalment payments. These payments are based on the company's estimate of its current year tax liability. A large company is one whose profits for the accounting period in question are more than £1.5m.

10. VALUE ADDED TAX

Value added tax (VAT) is chargeable on the taxable supply of goods and services in the UK and the import of goods and some services by a taxable person in the course of business carried on by that person. A trader must register for VAT with HMRC if their businesses' VAT taxable turnover is more than £82,000. However, a business can register voluntarily if its turnover is below the registration threshold.

VAT is charged on taxable supplies at one of three rates in the UK: 0%, 5% or 20%. A zero-rated supply (such as children's clothes and printed books) is different from exempt items, because businesses supplying zero-rated items can reclaim VAT on any of their purchases; a business supplying exempt items cannot reclaim VAT. The 5% rate applies to energy products/services, and the 20% rate (called the standard rate) applies to most other goods and services.

Where a financial adviser arranges the sale of a retail investment with a customer, then the charges made to the customer are exempt from VAT, regardless of whether the sale of the product is finally concluded. However, where the service provided to the customer is purely advice or recommendation, any charges to the customer are subject to VAT at the standard rate. VAT liability for ongoing services will depend on the type of services that the adviser has agreed to perform.

11. TAXATION OF DIRECT INVESTMENTS

Savings income comprises:

- Interest (from banks, building societies, gilts and corporate bonds).
- The income part of a purchased life annuity.
- Chargeable gains on life assurance policies.

Some savings income is paid gross, such as:

- Interest on NS&I accounts.
- Interest paid to individual investors by listed UK companies in relation to corporate bonds (debentures and loan stocks) held.
- UK government bond interest.

Most savings income is paid to individuals net of basic rate tax:

- Bank and building society interest.
- Interest paid by unlisted companies in relation to corporate bonds.
- Savings income from non-discretionary trusts.
- The income portion of a purchased life annuity.

If the individual is not subject to income tax, then the tax deducted can normally be reclaimed or, in the case of bank and building society interest, an election could be made to have interest paid gross (provided the individual can prove non-taxpayer status). From 6 April 2016, all savings income will automatically be paid gross, eliminating the need to make repayment claims.

The first £5,000 of savings income benefits from a starting rate of 0%. However, as income tax is charged first on non-savings income, for most individuals their savings income will fall outside the starting rate limit. Savings income will therefore be charged at the basic, higher or additional rate.

Dividends are automatically taxed (called 'taxed at source') at the rate of 10%. The 10% deducted is called a tax credit. The taxation of dividends is as follows:

- Basic rate taxpayers: no further tax to pay.
- Non-taxpayers: cannot reclaim the tax credit.
- Higher rate taxpayers: pay a further 22.5% of the gross dividend (making a total of 32.5%).
- Additional rate taxpayers: pay a further 27.5% (making a total of 37.5%).

In the July 2015 Budget, the government announced a reform to dividend taxation from 2016/17. The 10% tax credit will be abolished and replaced with a £5,000 dividend tax allowance – the first £5,000 of dividend income will then be tax free.Once the allowance is exceeded, dividends will be taxed at 7.5% for basic rate taxpayers, 32.5% for higher rate taxpayers and 38.1% for additional rate taxpayers. This will increase the rate of tax on dividends above the new allowance by 7.5% compared to the rates for 2015/16.

The main target of this change is not ordinary shareholders, but private company directors who draw dividends rather than a salary in order to avoid paying NICs.

EXAMPLE

Dave is aged 45 and in the current tax year (2015/16) earns a salary of £11,000 from his part-time employment. He also receives bank interest (net of tax) of £3,200.

Calculate Dave's tax liability.

	NON-SAVINGS INCOME (£)	SAVINGS INCOME (£)	TOTAL (£)
Employment income	11,000		
Gross bank interest £3,200 x 100/80		4,000	
Gross income	11,000	4,000	15,000

	NON-SAVINGS INCOME (£)	SAVINGS INCOME (£)	TOTAL (£)
Less personal allowance	(10,600)		(10,600)
Taxable income	400	4,000	4,400
Income tax			
Non-savings income £400 @ 20%	80		
Savings income £4,000 @ 0%		0	
Tax liability	**80**	**0**	**80**

Rental income from property letting is liable to income tax, but any running costs (such as repairs and interest costs on a loan used to purchase the property) can be offset against rental income to reduce the tax liability. However, the government will restrict the amount of tax relief for loan interest to the basic rate of 20%, with this restriction being phased in over four years from 2017/18.

Interest income from gilts and corporate bonds is taxed as savings income.

Shares and property are subject to CGT if the asset is sold (or gifted). However, any gain from the sale of property that is classed as the individual's primary residence is exempt from CGT. Any gains made from the sale of gilts or corporate bonds are also exempt from CGT.

12. TAXATION OF INDIRECT INVESTMENTS

Pension arrangements

An individual who is under the age of 75 is entitled to tax relief on contributions to a registered pension scheme made during the tax year. The maximum tax-relieved contributions that can be made are the higher of:

- the individual's relevant earnings subject to an annual cap of £40,000 (2015/16 tax year); or
- a basic amount of £3,600.

Tax relief is at the taxpayer's marginal tax rate, so a higher rate taxpayer (with income between £31,786 and £150,000) can obtain 40% tax relief on their pension contributions. An additional rate taxpayer obtains relief at 45%. If contributions to a pension scheme exceed the annual cap of £40,000, then tax is payable at the taxpayer's marginal tax rate on the excess over £40,000.

At retirement, a tax-free cash lump sum equal to 25% of the accumulated fund is available, with the remaining fund used to produce an income taxable at the pensioner's marginal rate. Since 6 April 2015, the government has allowed those with defined contribution pension schemes greater flexibility when it comes to withdrawing their pension fund at age 55.

Pensioners can now drawdown their pension savings whenever and however they wish. Any amount taken in excess of the 25% tax-free lump sum is simply treated as income and subject to the normal rates of income tax for the year of drawdown. However, once a pension fund has been accessed flexibly, the future level of annual allowance is reduced to £10,000. This is known as the money purchase annual allowance. The £10,000 allowance generally applies regardless of the method used to access the pension fund, but it is not triggered if just a tax-free 25% lump sum is taken without there being any income drawdown.

If an individual dies before they reach age 75, they can leave their remaining defined contribution pension to anyone they want tax free.

There is a lifetime allowance of £1.25m for the 2015/16 tax year. This will reduce to £1m from 6 April 2016. If an individual's pension fund exceeds this limit at retirement, the excess will be subject to a lifetime allowance charge of 25% if the excess is taken as income, or 55% if the excess is taken as a lump sum.

From 2016/17, a tapered reduction to the amount of the annual allowance of £40,000 will be introduced for individuals with income of over £150,000. The rate of reduction will be £1 for every £2 of income exceeding £150,000, down to a minimum annual allowance of £10,000. In preparation for the introduction of the tapered reduction, there are some complex transitional rules which mean that the amount of annual allowance for 2015/16 could actually be between £40,000 and £80,000 depending on various factors.

Individual savings accounts

An individual savings account (ISA) is not an investment in itself, but rather a wrapper in which investments can be placed to shield them from taxation. To invest through an ISA, an individual must be resident in the UK when the investment is made.

There are two types of ISA:

- Cash ISAs: money is normally invested in a cash deposit with a bank or building society where there is no capital uncertainty.
- Stocks and shares ISAs: money can be invested in:
  - Shares and corporate bonds issued by companies listed on a recognised stock exchange, including AIM shares, and also securities issued by companies trading on certain small and medium-sized enterprise (SME) markets.

- Securities and shares issued by housing associations and other co-operative or community benefit societies.
- Shares and corporate bonds issued by companies listed on a recognised stock exchange.
- Gilts issued by the UK government or by governments of countries in the European Economic Area.
- Units or shares in funds authorised by the Financial Conduct Authority (FCA), e.g. unit trusts or OEICs.
- Units or shares in non-UCITS (undertakings for collective investment in transferable securities) retail schemes authorised by the FCA for sale to retail investors in the UK.
- Shares and securities in investment trusts.
- Units or shares in UCITS funds based elsewhere in the European Union.
- Any shares which have been transferred from an HMRC-approved save as you earn (SAYE) share option scheme or share incentive plan.
- Life insurance policies.
- Stakeholder medium term products.
- Core capital deferred shares issued by building societies (core capital deferred shares are a new form of equity which can be issued by mutual societies).

ISAs have an annual investment limit in 2015/16 of £15,240. This limit is flexible and can be split between the two types of ISA as desired – such as £14,000 in a cash ISA and £1,240 in a stocks and shares ISA.

Junior ISAs (JISAs) are available to children under the age of 18 who were either born after 2 January 2011 or who were not eligible for a child trust fund (CTF). The maximum investment in a JISA is £4,080 per tax year (2015/16) which may be split between a cash JISA and a stocks and shares JISA as desired. A child can have a maximum of two JISAs (one of each type) over their childhood.

A JISA can be opened by anyone with parental responsibility for the child or by children themselves from age 16. There is no access to the proceeds of a JISA until the child's 18th birthday. Any income generated in a JISA that a parent has funded is not taxable on that parent. Since 6 April 2015, it has been possible to transfer the savings in a CTF to a JISA.

Investments within an ISA are exempt from income tax and CGT. However, the 10% tax credit currently paid with dividends from UK shares is not recoverable.

Onshore and offshore collective investment schemes and investment companies

UK collective investment schemes are exempt from tax on gains made within the fund. This gives them an advantage over life funds. Any income (other than dividend income from UK or overseas companies, which is not taxable) is subject to corporation tax at 20%. Management expenses can be offset against income.

The tax treatment of dividend distributions from UK collective investment funds is the same as the tax treatment of direct holdings of equities. Where a fund holds more than 60% of its investments in interest-bearing securities, the income (including dividend income) is deemed to be interest and the distribution is made net of 20% tax. This is then treated by a taxpayer in the same way as interest received net of tax.

An investor is liable to CGT on disposals of collective investment schemes including switching between subfunds of an umbrella fund. Investment trusts are exempt from tax on gains, and non-dividend income is subject to corporation tax. An investment trust shareholder is subject to the same taxation treatment as a normal shareholder of company shares.

For offshore funds, there will (in general) be no tax payable by the fund, although in some jurisdictions a small local tax may be payable. The tax treatment of a UK investor in an offshore fund will largely depend on whether the fund has reporting or non-reporting status.

Reporting funds are those which have applied to HMRC for that status and meet certain criteria, including providing reports of their 'reportable income'. The actual distributions from such a fund are paid gross. A UK investor will have to declare both the actual distributions received plus their reportable income in excess of the sums distributed. They currently pay tax as follows:

- A non-taxpayer will have no liability to tax.
- A basic rate taxpayer will pay tax at a rate of 10%.
- A higher rate taxpayer will pay tax at a rate of 32.5%.
- An additional rate taxpayer will pay tax at a rate of 37.5%.

Any chargeable gain arising from a fund disposal or transfer will be subject to CGT.

Non-reporting funds, often termed 'roll-up' funds, accumulate income in the fund. A UK investor is liable to income tax on any distribution or encashment of such a fund.

Onshore and offshore life insurance funds

Any proceeds from a qualifying life assurance policy are usually free of income tax and CGT for the original beneficiary. However, where a policy is surrendered or sold within the shorter of ten years or 75% of the term of the policy, 20% tax is payable by higher rate taxpayers on the surplus of proceeds over premiums paid. The tax charge is 25% for additional rate taxpayers. There are a complex set of rules that determine whether a policy is a qualifying one. These include:

- Premiums must be payable for at least ten years.
- Premiums must be paid annually or more frequently.
- For policies issued on or after 6 April 2013, premiums are restricted to £3,600 per year, with this limit applying across all policies owned by an individual.

Thus a single premium policy cannot be a qualifying policy, and therefore is subject to income tax on encashment. Life assurance bonds are single premium policies, and one-off or regular payments from a UK life assurance bond for a basic rate taxpayer will normally incur no further income tax, because it is already deemed to have paid basic rate tax on both income and gains within the life fund. However, there are occasions when there is an additional personal liability to income tax.

An investor is allowed to take a payment from the bond of up to 5% of the original premium each policy year, until 100% is reached (i.e. after 20 years) without an immediate liability to income tax. If this allowance is not used in any one year, it can be carried forward. If an investor takes more than this allowance, then there may be a personal income tax liability if, when taking this payment, the gain makes them a higher (or even an additional rate) taxpayer when added to the investor's taxable income for the year.

If someone invested £100,000 and took no withdrawals in year one but at the end of year two made a withdrawal of £15,000, the gain would be the withdrawal amount less the allowance. In this instance, it would be £15,000 less £10,000, which is £5,000. This £5,000 is divided by the number of complete policy years the investor has held the bond – in this case two years – which is known as 'top slicing'. If this £2,500 (i.e. £5,000 ÷ 2) when added to the investor's taxable income makes them a higher rate taxpayer, they would be liable to income tax at 20% on the portion of the gain that is over the higher rate threshold. The tax charge is 25% for an additional rate taxpayer. This would then be multiplied by the same number of years used in the top slicing calculation. The additional income tax liability for a higher rate taxpayer in this example would be £2,500 @ 20% = £500 × 2 = £1,000.

Income tax may also be payable when the investor cashes in their bond. The profit on the bond (gain) is calculated and divided by the number of complete policy years the investor held the bond. If this amount, when added to the investor's taxable income, makes them a higher or additional rate taxpayer, they will have an additional liability to income tax. They will pay income tax at 20% on the portion of the gain that is over the higher rate threshold, and 25% if over the additional rate threshold. Once again, the tax liability is multiplied by the number of years used in the top slicing calculation.

The effect is that higher and additional rate taxpayers can draw an annual payment from the bond of up to 5% of the initial investment each year for 20 years, without an immediate tax liability. If they are still higher or additional rate taxpayers when the bond is cashed in, they will have to pay income tax of 20% or 25% on the profits made from the bond. This represents the difference between the higher or additional rate of tax of 40% or 45%, respectively, and the basic rate of 20%, which has already been paid by the life assurance company.

Offshore life assurance bonds do not pay corporation tax on income and gains within the fund, although withholding tax on dividends is not reclaimable. This 'gross roll-up' of income and gains generally has the effect of causing the fund to grow more quickly than an onshore fund. Provided annual withdrawals do not exceed 5% of the initial investment, no liability to tax will arise until the bond is encashed in full. Withdrawals in excess of 5% per year are liable to UK income tax at the taxpayer's highest rate, as is the overall gain on final encashment. On final encashment, any 'gain' in the value of the investment bond (taking into account any previous withdrawals) is added on to the investor's taxable income and is subject to tax in the normal way.

Real estate investment trusts

Any rental income and capital gains are exempt from tax at the real estate investment trust (REIT) level but are taxed at the investor level when they are paid as dividends. To ensure income and gains are taxed at the investor level, REITs are required to distribute the majority of their tax-exempt rental income (but not gains) to shareholders. Basic rate tax at 20% is generally withheld from the dividend, with the dividend then taxed as income at the investor's marginal tax rate.

Venture capital trusts

An investor in a venture capital trust (VCT) obtains the following tax benefits on a maximum qualifying investment of £200,000 per year:

- A tax reduction of 30% of the amount invested. This relief is withdrawn if the shares are sold within five years or if the entity ceases to qualify as a VCT.
- Dividends received are tax-free (whatever the holding period).
- Capital gains on the sale of shares in the VCT are exempt from CGT (whatever the holding period).

Also, any capital gains made by the VCT itself on its investments are exempt from tax.

Enterprise investment schemes

- Income tax relief: An individual with an interest of 30% or less in a company can reduce their income tax liability by 30% of the amount invested, provided an EIS qualifying investment is held for three years from the date of issue, or three years from commencement of trade (if later). The maximum in respect of which a subscriber may obtain income tax relief in any tax year is £1m. Individuals may elect to treat their subscription for EIS shares, up to their maximum annual investment limit, as if made in the previous tax year, thereby carrying income tax relief back one year.

EXAMPLE

Initial investment	£50,000
Less income tax relief @ 30%	(£15,000)
Net cost of investment	£35,000

- CGT exemption: no CGT is payable on disposal of shares after three years (or three years after commencement of trade if later) provided the EIS initial income tax relief was given and has not been withdrawn on those shares.
- CGT deferral: An investor can defer a CGT liability by reinvesting gains in EIS shares. Deferral only applies if the investment is made no more than one year before or three years after the disposal of the asset giving rise to the gain. So, in the above example, if further relief at the higher CGT rate of 28% was obtained in respect of CGT deferral, the net cost of the investment would effectively fall to £21,000 (£35,000 less (£50,000 at 28%)).
- Loss relief: if EIS shares are disposed of at any time at a loss (after taking into account income tax relief), the loss can be set against the investor's income in the tax year of disposal or the previous tax year. The net effect is to limit the investment exposure to 42p in the £1 for a 40% taxpayer, or to 38p in the £1 for a 45% taxpayer, if the shares become totally worthless (ignoring CGT deferral). Alternatively, a loss can be offset against chargeable gains – saving CGT at the rate of 18% or 28%.
- Seed enterprise investment scheme (SEIS): this runs alongside the EIS, but is targeted at start up companies. The SEIS provides 50% income tax relief for investment of up to £100,000 per tax year, and there is also a CGT exemption for 50% of any reinvested gains. In addition, the investment is exempt from CGT on disposal if it has been held for three years.

CHAPTER 6 SECTION 2

INVESTMENT ADVICE AND TAX PLANNING

SECTION AIMS

By the end of this section, learners should be able to:

- Evaluate the tax considerations shaping clients' needs and circumstances.
- Analyse the key principles of income tax planning.
- Analyse how the use of annual CGT exemptions, the realisation of losses, the timing of disposals, and the sale and repurchase of similar assets can mitigate CGT.
- Calculate the most common elements of income tax, NICs, CGT and IHT, including the impact of lifetime transfers and transfers at death.
- Select elementary tax planning recommendations in the context of investments and pensions advice.

Most clients seek to manage their affairs in such a way that they mitigate the amount of tax they pay. The main personal taxes are IHT, income tax and CGT.

1. INHERITANCE TAX PLANNING

IHT is a tax which is normally paid on death by individuals where the value of their estate exceeds their nil rate band; any excess is taxed at 40%. For the tax year 2015/16, the nil rate band is £325,000.

EXAMPLE

John died during the 2015/16 tax year with an estate valued at £800,000, which he leaves to his children. His estate will be liable for IHT on £475,000 (the excess above £325,000) at 40% – in other words, an IHT liability of £190,000. If John was a widower, his estate would have the potential to inherit his late spouse's unused nil rate band. If his spouse's estate had not made any use of its nil rate band, then John's estate would have two nil rate bands totalling £650,000. This would have reduced his IHT liability to £60,000.

A liability to IHT can also arise as a result of gifts to trusts (CLTs) if the value gifted is in excess of the settlor's available nil rate band at the time of the transfer. The rate of IHT on such lifetime gifts is 20%. Outright lifetime gifts to individuals are PETs and are not subject to any immediate IHT. Furthermore, they fall outside the donor's IHT estate if the donor survives for seven complete years from the date of the gift.

Most IHT planning focuses on reducing the value of an individual's estate through lifetime gifts. The client has to balance the wish to reduce their estate in order to limit potential IHT liability, with the need to retain sufficient wealth to support their required standard of living. The gift with reservation rules mean that it is difficult to gift wealth away and still retain any benefit; for example giving away a house, but continuing to live in it without paying full market rent.

2. INCOME TAX PLANNING

As mentioned earlier in this chapter, the marginal rates of income tax on savings income depend upon both the nature of the savings income and the tax bracket of the investor.

The following table is for the tax year 2015/16.

LEVEL OF TAXABLE INCOME (NET OF THE PERSONAL ALLOWANCE)	NON-DIVIDEND SAVINGS INCOME	DIVIDEND SAVINGS INCOME
Basic rate taxpayers £1 to £31,785	20%	10%
Higher rate taxpayers £31,786 to £150,000	40%	32.5%
Additional rate taxpayers £150,001 and above	45%	37.5%

There is also a 0% starting rate for savings income only. The starting rate limit for savings income is £5,000.

Taxable income is the total of an individual's income which is subject to income tax net of their personal allowance. Strategies for mitigating income tax make use of the fact that not all 'income' is subject to income tax and that taxpayers are entitled to a personal allowance (although this is gradually withdrawn once income exceeds £100,000). The basic personal allowance for 2015/16 is £10,600.

Non-taxable 'income'

ISAs produce non-taxable income; otherwise, the income from most investments is taxable. Other tax-free investments include NS&I savings certificates and NS&I children's bonds, but these do not produce regular returns.

There are investments which are deemed to be 'non-income producing' as far as the tax system is concerned, but which can pay regular returns to the investor akin to income. Single premium life assurance bonds have an effective annual allowance based on 5% of the original investment. For example, Sally, a higher rate taxpayer, invested £50,000 in a single premium bond on 2 January 2008. She immediately set up a regular monthly withdrawal of £200. Her 5% annual allowance is £2,500, so none of these regular withdrawals need to be declared on her income tax return. This is particularly useful as Sally is a higher rate taxpayer.

However, the 5% annual allowance is not tax-free income; rather, it is tax deferred. Assume that Sally encashes her bond on 10 August 2015 for £48,000. The calculation of the gain on encashment will include all of her 5% withdrawals to date (say, £18,400), so the gain will be £48,000 plus £18,400 = £66,400 less the original premium of £50,000 = £16,400. UK-based life bonds have already had their income and gains taxed at 20%, so they are deemed to be 'basic rate tax paid'. A basic rate taxpayer has no further tax to pay on this gain, but a higher rate taxpayer is liable to a further 20% income tax. This will therefore result in a 2015/16 income tax bill for Sally of £3,280.

Making use of the income tax personal allowance

Even a one-month-old baby has an income tax personal allowance of £10,600. Only income subject to income tax in excess of this amount is taxed. It therefore makes sense for a married couple (or members of a civil partnership) to make full use of each of their personal allowances and to avoid investments being held in the name of the individual who has the highest marginal rate of income tax.

For example, if one spouse is a higher rate taxpayer and the other spouse is having a career break, it makes sense to transfer ownership of investment capital, which generates taxable income into the name of the non-working spouse in order to make use of their personal allowance and their lower marginal rate of income tax. Another more cautious approach would be to put ownership into joint names. However, such planning may not be necessary when the tax-free personal savings allowance is introduced from 6 April 2016.

Where a person has total income between £100,000 and £121,200, then their marginal income tax rate on this band of income is 60% (40% higher rate income tax plus a further 20% due to the loss of personal allowance). Again, investment income could be transferred to a spouse or civil partner, but it also makes sense to make pension contributions given the 60% tax relief that is available.

There is, however, a rule which restricts parents from making gifts in order to use the personal allowances of their own children while the children are under the age of 18 and unmarried. If the income generated from capital gifted by a parent exceeds £100 a year, then all of the income will be taxed as if it is still the parent's own income. This rule only applies to income arising from parental gifts of capital. It does not apply to capital gifted by grandparents, aunts and uncles, etc. The rule also only applies to income, but not to investment returns, which are taxed as capital gains.

Since 6 April 2015, a person is able to transfer up to £1,060 of their personal allowance to their spouse or civil partner. This is beneficial where someone is a non-taxpayer and their personal allowance is unused, although a transfer is only permitted where the recipient is a basic rate taxpayer.

Other income tax mitigation schemes

- Contributions to a registered pension scheme qualify for tax relief. This is particularly advantageous for higher or additional rate taxpayers, who will obtain tax relief at 40% or 45%, respectively, on any contributions made during the tax year. Of course, the investment cannot be accessed until retirement (although there is now much more flexibility as regards drawdown from 6 April 2015), and contributions are effectively restricted to an annual allowance of £40,000. There is also a lifetime allowance.

- Investment under the EIS attracts 30% income tax relief, although the EIS shares have to be held for three years. SEIS investment attracts income tax relief of 50%, although such an investment carries more risk.

- Investment in a VCT attracts income tax relief of 30%.

- Making use of the ISA allowance of £15,240 for 2015/16, thus providing a shelter against income tax.

3. CAPITAL GAINS TAX PLANNING

Each taxpayer has an annual CGT exempt amount; for the tax year 2015/16, this is £11,100. Only gains, net of losses, in excess of £11,100 are subject to CGT at a rate of 18% for basic rate taxpayers and 28% for higher and additional rate taxpayers. Any unused annual exempt amount cannot be carried forward to future tax years.

In practice, very few private individuals pay CGT. Common strategies to mitigate CGT include:

- Spreading ownership of assets between family members to make use of the maximum number of annual exempt amounts. Transfers between spouses and civil partners are free from CGT. There is also scope for CGT reduction where one spouse would pay CGT at the rate of 28%, while the other would only pay at the 18% rate.

- Phasing encashments over several tax years (if possible) in order to benefit from more than one annual exempt amount. For example, if two separate disposals were made in, say, late March 2016 (tax year 2015/16) and late April 2016 (tax year 2016/17), this would utilise two annual exempt amounts. This would better mitigate CGT than selling all the investments in March 2016 and being entitled to only one annual exempt amount.

- Deliberately realising paper losses in order to reduce gains that would otherwise exceed the annual exempt amount and become taxable.

'Bed and breakfasting' by selling shares and purchasing them back the next day, with only a small risk of the market going against the investor. However, the government has acted against bed and breakfasting by introducing a 30-day rule. Over 30 days must elapse between the sale and purchase in order for the arrangement to be effective for tax purposes.

One way of overcoming the restriction is for the investor to take advantage of the fact that investments can be transferred between spouses (and civil partners) without incurring CGT. The investor sells the shares in the market (creating the gain), while the spouse simultaneously repurchases in the market to avoid price movement – and sometime later transfers the shares back to the investor.

- Deliberately realising gains within the annual exempt amount so that there is no actual taxable gain, then repurchasing a similar (but not identical) investment. This has the effect of increasing the base cost of the investment and thus reducing the risk of future gains exceeding future annual exempt amounts. Any unused annual exempt amount cannot be carried forward.

- Using ISAs to shield investments from CGT.

4. TAX PLANNING: CASE STUDIES

We will now look at three case studies that illustrate computations for the main taxes combined with elementary tax planning recommendations.

There are a further two case studies at the end of this chapter, each with six associated questions. These case studies are of a similar format to those in the Investment Management Certificate exam and allow you to test your ability to apply the basic principles of tax planning.

Table 6.6: Tax rates and allowances for 2014/15 and 2015/16

2014/15 TAX RATES AND ALLOWANCES	2015/16 TAX RATES AND ALLOWANCES
Personal tax allowance: £10,000	Personal tax allowance: £10,600
INCOME TAX RATES	**INCOME TAX RATES**
Starting rate for savings (10%): £0–£2,880	Starting rate for savings (0%): £0–£5,000
Basic rate (20%): £0–£31,865	Basic rate (20%): £0–£31,785
Higher rate (40%): £31,866–£150,000	Higher rate (40%): £31,786–£150,000
Additional rate (45%): £150,001 and above	Additional rate (45%): £150,001 and above
DIVIDEND INCOME TAX RATES	**DIVIDEND INCOME TAX RATES**
Non/basic rate taxpayers: 10%	Non/basic rate taxpayers: 10%
Higher rate taxpayers: 32.5%	Higher rate taxpayers: 32.5%
Additional rate taxpayers: 37.5%	Additional rate taxpayers: 37.5%

2014/15 TAX RATES AND ALLOWANCES	2015/16 TAX RATES AND ALLOWANCES
CAPITAL GAINS TAX	**CAPITAL GAINS TAX**
Exempt amount: £11,000	Exempt amount: £11,100
Basic rate taxpayer: 18%	Basic rate taxpayer: 18%
Higher/additional rate taxpayer: 28%	Higher/additional rate taxpayer: 28%
INHERITANCE TAX	**INHERITANCE TAX**
Nil-rate band: £325,000	Nil-rate band: £325,000
Rate: 40%	Rate: 40%
CORPORATION TAX	**CORPORATION TAX**
Main rate: 21% Small profits rate: 20%	Single rate: 20%
PENSIONS	**PENSIONS**
Annual allowance: £40,000	Annual allowance: £40,000

2014/15 TAX RATES AND ALLOWANCES	2015/16 TAX RATES AND ALLOWANCES
ISA ANNUAL LIMITS	**ISA ANNUAL LIMITS**
Investment limit: £15,000	Investment limit: £15,240
ENTERPRISE INVESTMENT SCHEME	**ENTERPRISE INVESTMENT SCHEME**
Tax relief rate: 30%	Tax relief rate: 30%
VENTURE CAPITAL TRUSTS	**VENTURE CAPITAL TRUSTS**
Tax relief rate: 30%	Tax relief rate: 30%

CASE STUDY 1: INCOME TAX MITIGATION

Jeremy was born in 1961 and he is married to Simone. For 2015/16, Jeremy has gross employment earnings of £60,000, on which PAYE of £13,750 has been paid. He has gross savings income from bank and building society accounts of £1,000 (paid net of 20% tax) and gross dividend income (paid with a 10% tax credit) of £760. Simone is currently unemployed and does not have any income.

Show Jeremy's income tax liability for 2015/16.

	NON-SAVINGS INCOME (£)	SAVINGS INCOME (£)	DIVIDEND INCOME (£)	TOTAL (£)
Income from employment	60,000			
Bank/building society interest		1,000		
Dividends			760	
Total income	60,000	1,000	760	
Net income	60,000	1,000	760	61,760
Less personal allowance	(10,600)			(10,600)
Taxable income	49,400	1,000	760	51,160
Income tax on non-savings income £31,785 @ 20%	6,357			
Income tax on non-savings income £17,615 @ 40%	7,046			

	NON-SAVINGS INCOME (£)	SAVINGS INCOME (£)	DIVIDEND INCOME (£)	TOTAL (£)
Tax on savings income £1,000 @ 40%		400		
Tax on dividend income £760 @ 32.5%			247	
Tax liability	13,403	400	247	14,050

Notes:

1. Income tax is charged first on non-savings income. So the 0% rate of tax on savings income does not apply in this case.
2. The figures for non-savings income, savings income and dividend income shown above are the gross amounts. So if the net figures for savings income and dividend income are available, these need to be grossed up by multiplying by 100/80 for savings income and 100/90 for dividend income.
3. Jeremy is a higher rate taxpayer because his total income (after deduction of the personal allowance) is greater than the threshold of £31,785.

How much tax is payable by Jeremy? Jeremy has already paid tax (at source) on all of his total income. Therefore this needs to be subtracted from the tax liability to determine any additional tax to be paid.

	£
Tax liability	14,050
Less tax suffered:	
PAYE on employment income	(13,750)
Tax paid on bank and building society interest (£1,000 at 20%)	(200)
Tax credit on dividend income (£760 at 10%)	(76)
Tax payable	24

What tax planning advice could have been given to Jeremy at the start of the tax year 2015/16 to enable him to reduce his tax payable?

- Simone is not using her personal allowance, so transferring ownership of the savings accounts and shares to her will reduce the tax paid by Jeremy. As Simone is a non-taxpayer, she could claim back the 20% tax paid on bank and building society interest, or she could certify in advance that she is a non-taxpayer and have the interest paid gross. In terms of dividend income, the 10% tax credit is not reclaimable, but no further tax would be payable.
  The tax saving would be £571 (£400 + £247 – £76)

- Should Simone subsequently commence work and become a basic rate taxpayer, then the tax saving will be reduced to £371 (£571 – £200) because there is no additional tax liability on dividend income for a basic rate taxpayer.

- If Jeremy has not used his ISA allowance for the tax year 2015/16, then he could place his savings accounts and shares in an ISA. As long as the overall investment limit for the year of £15,240 is not breached, the interest/dividend income from these investments would then be shielded from income tax. The total potential tax saving is again £571.

- Jeremy could contribute to a registered pension scheme. This would attract income tax relief of 40% on the contributions made as he is a higher rate taxpayer.

Say that Jeremy makes a (net) personal pension contribution of £10,000 during 2015/16. Then tax relief would be given at source, because the contribution is deemed to be made net of basic rate tax. As Jeremy is a higher rate taxpayer, further tax relief would be given when Jeremy submits his self-assessment tax return. The additional relief will be given by increasing the basic rate threshold for 2015/16 by the gross amount of contribution for which he is entitled to relief. This is shown in the revised computation below.

	£	£	£	£
Taxable income	49,400	1,000	760	51,160
Income tax on non-savings income £31,785 @ 20%	6,357			
£12,500 (£10,000 × 100/80) @ 20%	2,500			
£5,115 @ 40%	2,046			
Tax on savings income £1,000 @ 40%		400		
Tax on dividend income £760 @ 32.5%			247	
Tax liability	10,903	400	247	11,550

By making the pension contribution, Jeremy has reduced his tax liability by £2,500. Of course, this contribution is not immediately accessible like other savings/investments, because it is used to fund pension benefits upon retirement (although there is now more flexibility regarding pension drawdown).

Jeremy could also obtain tax relief by investing under the EIS, the SEIS or in a VCT. The EIS and VCT investments would attract income tax relief of 30% and the SEIS at 50%. Of course, these are risky investments, especially if Jeremy does not already have an investment portfolio.

CASE STUDY 2: CAPITAL GAINS TAX MITIGATION

Jenny is a higher rate taxpayer who has sold the following assets during 2015/16. Jenny's husband, Peter, is also a higher rate taxpayer but did not dispose of any assets during this year.

	PROCEEDS (£)	ORIGINAL COST (£)
Painting	35,000	25,000
Shares in ABC plc	20,000	25,000
Shares in XYZ plc	30,000	20,000
Gilts	20,000	18,000

The amount of CGT payable by Jenny for 2015/16 is:

	£	£
PAINTING		
Proceeds	35,000	
Less original cost	(25,000)	
Chargeable gain		10,000
SHARES IN ABC PLC		
Proceeds	20,000	
Less original cost	(25,000)	
Capital loss		(5,000)

	£	£
SHARES IN XYZ PLC		
Proceeds	30,000	
Less original cost	(20,000)	
Chargeable gain		10,000
Net chargeable gains		15,000
Less annual exempt amount		(11,100)
Taxable gains		3,900
CGT @ 28% on £34,900		1,092

Notes:

1. Capital losses are subtracted from chargeable gains to determine net chargeable gains.
2. Gains arising from the sale of gilts are exempt from CGT.

How could Jenny have reduced her CGT liability for 2015/16?

- Jenny might have had other assets standing at a loss which she could have sold during 2015/16 in order to realise further capital losses. These could have reduced the net chargeable gains figure of £15,000.
- Spouses and civil partners are taxed separately and each has an annual exempt amount. Jenny could therefore have transferred some of the assets to Peter prior to the sale taking place. For example, the painting could have been transferred. This would have resulted in Jenny and Peter each having net chargeable gains of less than the annual exempt amount, and therefore no CGT liability.
- The sale of some of the assets could have been delayed until after 5 April 2016 (i.e. into the tax year 2016/17). This would have allowed Jenny to utilise two annual exempt amounts.

CASE STUDY 3: INHERITANCE TAX MITIGATION

Daniel died on 21 August 2015 having not made any lifetime gifts. The value of his assets at the date of death came to £750,000 and he had liabilities totalling £80,000. Daniel made exempt legacies of £70,000. The nil rate band at the date of Daniel's death is £325,000. Calculate the IHT liability in respect of Daniel's estate.

	£
Assets	750,000
Liabilities	(80,000)
Exempt legacies	(70,000)
Chargeable estate	600,000
Inheritance tax due = (£600,000 – £325,000) @ 40%	110,000

How could this IHT liability have been reduced?

Most IHT mitigation comes from lifetime transfers.

- Daniel could have made gifts of his assets to his family before he died. As long as Daniel had survived for seven years after the gifts had been made, they would have been exempt from IHT. Of course, gifts might have been liable to CGT at the time the gift was made (unless it was cash or otherwise exempt). If Daniel had survived for fewer than seven years, the gift would have become liable to IHT. However, there is a sliding scale of IHT after the deceased survives more than three years.
- Daniel could have made gifts into trust prior to his death. Such transfers are liable to IHT at 20% (i.e. half the IHT death rate) at the date of transfer. The gift would have been exempt from any further IHT if Daniel had survived for seven years after making the gift. However, if Daniel had died within seven years, then additional tax would have been payable – again subject to taper relief.
- Daniel could have left his estate to his spouse/civil partner. All gifts between husband and wife or between partners in a civil partnership are exempt from IHT whether made during the donor's life or at death.
- Daniel could have left some of his estate to a charity, a political party or an important national institution (such as a museum or art gallery). All such gifts are exempt from IHT. Also, a reduced IHT rate of 36% would apply if Daniel left more than 10% of his chargeable estate to charity.
- Daniel could have made small value gifts to individuals for a number of years before his death (but not on death). Such gifts are exempt from IHT up to a limit of £3,000 a year.

Finally, to illustrate the transfer of the nil rate band between spouses/civil partners, let us consider the case where Daniel is survived by his wife, Jane. Assume that in his will Daniel left £150,000 to his son Geoff and the remainder of his estate to his wife. If Jane dies a year later, in August 2016, leaving an estate of £525,000 to Geoff, what is the amount of Jane's estate chargeable to IHT after deducting the nil rate band?

The nil rate band is still £325,000 for 2016/17:

- Daniel's unused nil rate band = £325,000 – £150,000 = £175,000.
- The unused nil rate band in percentage terms = 175,000/325,000 = 53.85%.

The amount of Jane's estate chargeable to IHT after deducting the nil rate band is:

	£
Estate left to Geoff	525,000
Less Jane's nil rate band	(325,000)
Less Daniel's unused nil rate band (53.85% of £325,000)	(175,000)
Amount chargeable	25,000

CASE STUDY 4: JIM

Jim died in July 2014 leaving an estate valued at £1m. Jim was survived by his wife, Evelyn, and in his will Jim left the whole of his estate to her. Evelyn died in July 2015, leaving an estate of £850,000 to her daughter, Tricia.

The nil rate band is £325,000 for both 2014/15 and 2015/16.

Questions

1. **What is the amount of IHT payable in respect of Jim's death?**
2. **What amount of nil rate band can be passed from Jim's estate to Evelyn's estate?**
3. **What is Evelyn's chargeable estate after deducting the nil rate band?**
4. **What is the maximum amount of gifts that Jim could have made to individuals in any year before his death that would have been definitely exempt from IHT?**
5. **If Tricia had married before Jim's death, what is the maximum amount of exempt IHT wedding gift that Jim could have given to her?**
6. **If Jim had decided to gift his house to his daughter before he died but continued to live in it (paying a market rent to his daughter), how many years would he then have to live before the gift was no longer liable to IHT?**

Answers

1. *£0 as gifts between spouses are exempt from IHT.*

2. *£325,000. Because Jim's nil rate band has not been used, it can be transferred in full to Evelyn.*

3.

Estate left to Tricia	*£850,000*
Less Evelyn's nil rate band	*(£325,000)*
Less Jim's transferred nil rate band	*(£325,000)*
Evelyn's chargeable estate	*£200,000*

4. *£3,000.*

5. *£5,000.*

6. *Seven years (Jim is paying a market rent so this is not a gift with reservation).*

CASE STUDY 5: DAVID

David was born in 1963. He has the following sources of income for 2015/16:

- Gross income from employment of £55,000.
- Savings interest of £480 from a bank account (paid net of basic rate tax). The total value of the account at the start of the tax year was £20,000.
- Net dividend income of £350 from a holding of ABC plc shares.

Questions

1. **How much income tax will be paid in respect of David's employment income?**

2. **How much additional tax will David have to pay on his dividend income?**

3. **David decides to make a (net) contribution of £10,000 to a personal pension scheme. If tax relief is given at the basic rate of tax at source, how much will actually be paid into David's pension fund?**

4. **If David decides to invest £10,000 in a VCT, how much tax relief will be deducted from his income tax liability?**

5. **David's wife did not use her personal allowance for 2015/16. How much tax could have been saved if David had transferred ownership of the ABC plc shares to her at the start of the tax year?**

6. **Assuming David has not used his ISA allowance for 2015/16, how much tax could he have saved by sheltering his savings from his bank account within an ISA?**

Answers

1. *Income tax paid on employment income:*

Employment income	*£55,000*
Less personal allowance	*£10,600*
Taxable income	*£44,400*
Tax paid: £31,865 @20%	*£6,357*
(45,000 – 31,865 @ 40%)	*£5,046*
Tax paid on employment income	*£11,403*

2. *Tax paid on dividend income:*

Gross dividend	*£350 × 100/90 = £389*
Therefore tax already paid	*£389 – £350 = £39*
Therefore additional tax	*(£389 @ 32.5%) – £39 = £87*

3. *£10,000 × 100/80 = £12,500.*

4. *Tax relief: 30% of £10,000 = £3,000. This relief will be lost if the shares are not kept for five years.*

5. *Tax saved: £389 @ 22.5% = £87 (i.e. the tax payable as per question (2)).*

6. *Tax savings from sheltering savings in an ISA:*

ISA allowance	*£15,240*
Gross interest	*£600 (480 × 100/80)*
Therefore tax saved	*(£600 x 15,240/20,000 @ 40% = £183)*

Only £15,240 can be sheltered using this year's cash ISA.

CHAPTER 06 KEY FACTS

6.1

1. The basic rate of tax on earned income is 20%. The higher rate of tax is 40%. There is also an additional rate of tax of 45% payable on income over £150,000.

2. A tax credit equal to 10% is paid with dividends from share investments, and this satisfies the 10% tax liability on dividends for lower and basic rate taxpayers. For higher rate taxpayers, the rate of tax on dividend income is 32.5%. For additional rate taxpayers, dividend income is taxed at 37.5%. Credit is given for the 10% tax attached to the dividend.

3. Investors who are non-taxpayers (and pension funds) are not able to claim back the 10% tax credit on dividend income.

4. The personal allowance is deducted from income to arrive at the amount which is taxable. Pension contributions and gift aid payments reduce the tax liability for higher and additional rate taxpayers.

5. Employees under pension age working in the UK have to pay class 1 NICs if their income is above the primary threshold.

6. CGT is payable by UK investors at a rate of 18% for basic rate taxpayers and a rate of 28% for higher and additional rate taxpayers. A portion of any gains made during each tax year is not subject to CGT (the annual exempt amount).

7. Only net chargeable gains are taxable (i.e. chargeable gains less capital losses).

8. IHT only applies if the taxable value of a person's estate when they die is over £325,000 (the nil rate band).

9. IHT on death is levied at a rate of 40% on the excess above the current nil rate band.

10. It is possible for spouses and civil partners to transfer their nil rate band so that any part of the nil rate band that was not used when the first spouse or civil partner died can be used against the estate of the surviving spouse or civil partner.

11. A PET is a lifetime gift that is free of IHT if the person who makes the gift lives for seven years after the gift is made.

12. A person's residence and domicile are different concepts and may influence their tax status. A person may be UK resident but not UK domiciled, or vice versa.

13. Stamp duty land tax (SDLT) is a self-assessed tax on land transactions involving any estate, interest, right or power in or over land in the UK. In Scotland, land and buildings transaction tax (LBTT) applies instead of SDLT.

14. There is a 0% starting rate band of £5,000, but this is for savings income only and is not available if taxable non-savings income is above this limit. If the starting rate is not available, then savings income is taxed at the investor's marginal tax rates.

15. Tax relief on pension contributions is at the taxpayer's marginal tax rate.

16. A tax-free lump sum of up to 25% can be taken from a pension fund upon retirement.

17. Investments held within an ISA are exempt from income tax and CGT.

18. UK collective investment schemes are exempt from tax on gains made within the fund. The tax treatment of dividend distributions from UK collective investment funds is the same as the tax treatment of direct holdings of equities. Note, if the funds are bond funds then distributions are taxed as savings income not dividends. Disposals of units/shares in collective investment are subject to CGT.

19. Any proceeds from a qualifying life assurance policy are usually free of income and CGT for the original beneficiary.

20. One-off or regular payments from a (single premium) UK life assurance bond for a basic rate taxpayer will normally incur no further income tax.

21. An investor is allowed to take a payment from a life assurance bond of up to 5% of the original premium each policy year, until 100% is reached (20 years) without an immediate liability to income tax. Any gains on maturity/encashment (including any previous withdrawals) are taxed as income on maturity.

22. For REITs, any rental income and chargeable gains are exempt from tax at the REIT level but are taxed at the investor's marginal rate when they are paid as dividends.

23. Investors in VCTs obtain a tax reduction of 30% of the amount invested if they hold the investment for at least five years. VCT investments are exempt from CGT.

24. Provided an EIS qualifying investment is held for no less than three years, an individual can reduce their income tax liability by an amount equal to 30% of the amount invested. No CGT is payable on the disposal of an EIS investment, provided the investor has held the shares for three years. The SEIS provides 50% income tax relief for investment of up

to £100,000 per tax year, and there is also a CGT exemption for 50% of any reinvested gains. There is also no CGT on the disposal of an SEIS investment.

6.2

1. IHT planning often focuses on lifetime gifts, but most gifts into trusts are chargeable. The gift with reservation rules mean that it is difficult to gift an asset and then to continue enjoying an ongoing benefit.

2. Income tax can often be mitigated by using investments where the investment returns are not treated as taxable income. Spreading ownership of investments between family members can also save income tax.

3. CGT can be reduced by managing the timing of disposals to make the most of annual exempt amounts and capital losses.

CHAPTER 06 SELF-ASSESSMENT QUESTIONS

1. How often are large companies required to pay corporation tax?

(a) *Every quarter.*

(b) *Every six months.*

(c) *Nine months after the end of the financial year.*

(d) *Twelve months after the end of the financial year.*

2. An investor purchases shares in Xanadu plc for £40,000 and shares in Connect plc for £30,000. These are sold within the same tax year for £55,000 (Xanadu plc) and £29,000 (Connect plc). If the annual exempt amount is £11,100 and the investor is a higher rate taxpayer, what is the capital gains tax payable?

(a) *£0.*

(b) *£522.*

(c) *£812.*

(d) *£2,900.*

3. A higher rate taxpayer receives a dividend of £800. If this is paid with a tax credit of 10%, what is the investor's income after the payment of all the tax that is due on the dividend?

(a) *£480.*

(b) *£540.*

(c) *£600.*

(d) *£800.*

4. What is the amount of stamp duty land tax payable on a residential property situated in England purchased for £200,000?

(a) *£4,000.*

(b) *£2,000.*

(c) *£1,000.*

(d) *£1,500.*

5. A gift (in excess of the nil rate band) to an individual will not be liable to inheritance tax after the donor survives for what period of time after making the gift?

(a) *Three years.*

(b) *Five years.*

(c) *Six years.*

(d) *Seven years.*

6. A higher rate taxpayer receives a dividend of £350 in a tax year. If this is paid with a tax credit of 10%, what is the additional tax to be paid by the investor?

(a) *£0.*

(b) *£87.*

(c) *£126.*

(d) *£156.*

7. What percentage of a pension fund can be taken as a tax-free lump sum on retirement?

(a) *10%.*

(b) *20%.*

(c) *25%.*

(d) *30%.*

8. Out of the total annual ISA allowance, what is the maximum percentage that can be invested in cash deposits?

(a) *25%.*

(b) *50%.*

(c) *75%.*

(d) *100%.*

9. What percentage of the initial investment of a life assurance bond can be withdrawn in a tax year without an immediate income tax liability?

(a) *5%.*

(b) *10%.*

(c) *15%.*

(d) *20%.*

10. An investment in a venture capital trust (VCT) will qualify for a tax reduction of what percentage of the amount invested?

(a) *10%.*

(b) *15%.*

(c) *20%.*

(d) *30%.*

11. George makes a gift of his second home in Cornwall to his son Nigel. George did not stay in the home following the gift. How long after making the gift does George need to live before the gifted home is completely exempt from inheritance tax?

(a) *Three years.*

(b) *Five years.*

(c) *Six years.*

(d) *Seven years.*

12. A chargeable lifetime transfer gift to a discretionary trust that is in excess of the settlor's nil rate band at the time of the transfer is subject to inheritance tax at which of the following rates?

(a) *0%.*

(b) *10%.*

(c) *20%.*

(d) *40%.*

13. **Which one of the following does not attract income tax relief?**

(a) *An investment in a life assurance bond.*

(b) *A contribution to a registered pension scheme.*

(c) *An investment in a venture capital trust.*

(d) *An investment in an enterprise investment scheme.*

14. **Joe is planning to sell some shares that will result in a chargeable gain of £30,000. Assuming the CGT-exempt amount for that tax year is £11,100 and Joe's wife is not planning to use her annual exempt amount, what is Joe's taxable gain if he transfers 50% of the shares to his wife prior to the disposal?**

(a) *£3,900.*

(b) *£9,450.*

(c) *£15,000.*

(d) *£18,900.*

ANSWERS

1. (a) Large companies are required to pay their corporation tax by instalments every quarter.

2. (c)

Xanadu plc shares purchase price	(£40,000)
Xanadu plc shares sales price	£55,000
Connect plc shares purchase price	(£30,000)
Connect plc shares sales price	£29,000
Chargeable gains	£14,000
Less annual exempt amount	(£11,100)
Amount chargeable to CGT	£2,900

CGT charged at 28%: £2,900 × 0.28 = £812

3. (c) Gross dividend $= \text{net dividend} \times \frac{100}{9}$

$$= £800 \times \frac{100}{9}$$

$$= £889$$

Investor's after tax income = £889 less 32.5%

= £600

4. (d) SDLT is £1,500 ((£125,000 at 0%) + (£75,000 at 2%))

5. (d) (5) The gift referred to in the question would be classed as a potentially exempt transfer. If the donor survives for seven years after making the gift then the gift would no longer be liable to IHT.

6. (b) Gross dividend $= \text{net dividend} \times \frac{100}{9}$

$$= £350 \times \frac{100}{9}$$

$$= £389$$

Tax payable at the higher rate = £389 × 32.5% = £126

Tax already paid at 10% = £389 × 0.1 = (£39)

Additional tax payable = £87

7. (c) The maximum percentage of a pension fund that can be taken as a tax-free lump sum on retirement is 25%.
8. (d) ISAs are flexible and allow a taxpayer to place any proportion (up to 100%) of their annual allowance into a cash ISA.
9. (a) The maximum percentage of the initial investment of a life assurance bond that can be withdrawn in a tax year without an immediate income tax liability is 5%.
10. (d) An investment in a VCT will qualify for an income tax reduction of 30%. The tax relief will be lost if the investment is not held for five years.
11. (d) This gift is a potentially exempt transfer and for it to qualify for exemption from IHT George has to survive for seven years after making the gift.
12. (c) A chargeable lifetime transfer that is in excess of the settlor's nil rate band is subject to IHT at 20%.
13. (a) No income tax relief is available for life assurance bonds. Any withdrawal from a life assurance bond of up to 5% of the initial amount invested is tax-free at the time of withdrawal, but this is effectively tax-deferred as the investor may still have to pay income tax on any gain when the bond is cashed in.
14. (a) No CGT arises from Joe's transfer of 50% of the shares to his wife.

    Taxable gain = £30,000 × 50% – £11,100

    = £3,900

LINK TO CFA LEVEL 1

As the material in this chapter is UK-focused, there is no direct link to the CFA Level 1 curriculum.

1. Which of the following activities is normally the responsibility of the compliance officer of an investment firm?

   (i) Ensuring advertisements comply with FCA rules.

   (ii) Ensuring new clients are correctly categorised.

   (iii) Ensuring client money is held separately from the firm's own money.

(a) *(i) only.*

(b) *(i) and (ii) only.*

(c) *(ii) and (iii) only.*

(d) *(i), (ii) and (iii).*

2. A basic rate taxpayer receives a dividend payment of £100. If this comes with an implied tax credit of 10%, what is the additional amount of tax to be paid by the investor?

   Important! You should enter only the answer in numbers (without spaces, letters or symbols) strictly using the following format: 0

3. Which of the following types of trading system is facilitated by SEAQ?

(a) *Order-driven.*

(b) *Quote-driven.*

(c) *Dutch auction.*

(d) *Over the counter.*

4. One of the conditions for a merger to qualify for referral to the Competition and Markets Authority is where the merged company controls more than what % of the market:

   Important! You should enter only the answer in numbers (without spaces, letters or symbols) strictly using the following format: 00

5. **Which of the following statements are correct in relation to applications to the FCA for approved person status?**

   (i) The individual wanting approved status must apply to the FCA for this.

   (ii) The FCA will NOT grant conditional approval.

   (iii) Approved person status is only required for persons undertaking controlled activities.

(a) *(i) and (ii) only.*

(b) *(i) and (iii) only.*

(c) *(ii) and (iii) only.*

(d) *(i), (ii) and (iii).*

6. **Which of the following investments are classed as packaged products?**

   (i) Life assurance policies.

   (ii) Personal pensions.

   (iii) Share options.

(a) *(i) only.*

(b) *(i) and (ii) only.*

(c) *(ii) and (iii) only.*

(d) *(i), (ii) and (iii).*

7. **If a UK listed company wishes to release a 'profit warning' announcement, it is required to release this through which one of the following?**

(a) *A meeting with analysts.*

(b) *A meeting with financial journalists.*

(c) *A circular to existing shareholders.*

(d) *A regulatory information service.*

8. **To obtain a premium listing on the London Stock Exchange, a company should normally have published and audited accounts covering the previous:**

(a) *One year of trading.*

(b) *Two years of trading*

(c) *Three years of trading.*

(d) *Five years of trading.*

9. **Direct management of the UK government's debt is undertaken by the:**

(a) *Bank of England.*

(b) *Treasury.*

(c) *Debt Management Office.*

(d) *Central Gilts Office.*

10. **An investor who acquires more than 3% of Baggins PLC shares must:**

(a) *Notify Baggins PLC.*

(b) *Notify the London Stock Exchange.*

(c) *Notify the Takeover Panel.*

(d) *Notify the Public Records Office.*

11. **Which one of the following is classed as an ancillary service under MiFID?**

(a) *Managing portfolios of investments.*

(b) *Investment advice.*

(c) *Safekeeping of financial instruments for clients.*

(d) *The operation of multilateral trading facilities.*

12. A firm, acting as a discretionary manager for a retail client, which undertakes transactions too frequently is breaking the conduct of business rule on:

(a) *Front-running.*

(b) *Churning.*

(c) *Best execution.*

(d) *Timely execution.*

13. If an investment firm is to treat a retail client as a professional client, it must:

(i) Obtain a written statement from the client stating that it wishes to be treated as a professional client.

(ii) Provide a written warning of the regulatory protections the client will lose.

(iii) Obtain a written statement from the client that it is aware of the consequences of losing regulatory protection.

(a) *(i) only.*

(b) *(i) and (ii) only.*

(c) *(ii) and (iii) only.*

(d) *(i), (ii) and (iii).*

14. Under which of the following circumstances is an unsolicited real time promotion to a retail client permitted?

(i) Where the client relationship allows for such promotions.

(ii) For the sale of generally marketable packaged products.

(iii) Where the customer is provided with a written statement of the terms of business before any agreement is entered into.

(a) *(i) only*

(b) *(ii) only.*

(c) *(i) and (ii) only.*

(d) *(i), (ii) and (iii).*

15. **The UK money laundering legislation covers the proceeds from which of the following?**

(i) Drug trafficking.

(ii) Terrorism.

(iii) General crime.

(a) *(i) only.*

(b) *(ii) only.*

(c) *(i) and (iii).*

(d) *(i), (ii) and (iii).*

16. **Which one of the following statements about an EU directive is not correct?**

(a) *An EU state can choose whether to implement the directive.*

(b) *The directive must be implemented by a particular date.*

(c) *The directive can be implemented by primary legislation.*

(d) *The aim of the directive is harmonisation of laws across EU member states.*

17. **A firm may provide which of the following services to a retail client without having to undertake an appropriateness check?**

(i) Arranging the purchase of UK listed shares.

(ii) Arranging the purchase of US listed shares.

(iii) Discretionary portfolio management.

(a) *(i) only.*

(b) *(i) and (ii).*

(c) *(ii) and (iii) only.*

(d) *(i), (ii) and (iii).*

18. In relation to corporation tax assessment, a company can normally set off trading losses against which of the following?

(i) Income and gains of the same accounting period.

(ii) Income and gains of the previous year.

(iii) Trading profits from the same trade in future years.

(a) *(i) only.*

(b) *(ii) only.*

(c) *(i) and (ii) only.*

(d) *(i), (ii) and (iii).*

19. A customer with a claim against an insolvent authorised firm must seek redress through:

(a) *The Financial Ombudsman Service.*

(b) *The Financial Services Compensation Scheme.*

(c) *The Financial Conduct Authority.*

(d) *The Department for Business, Innovation and Skills.*

20. An investor purchases some shares in Peach PLC for £30,000 and Rembrandt PLC for £20,000. These shares are then sold by the investor in the same financial year for £40,000 and £18,000. If the annual exempt amount for capital gain is £11,100 and the investor is a basic rate taxpayer, what is the amount of capital gains tax payable?

Important! You should enter only the answer in numbers (without spaces, letters or symbols) strictly using the following format: 0

21. **Which of the following goods and services is an investment firm able to purchase using dealing commission from a broker?**

(i) Historical price data feeds.

(ii) Subscription to publications.

(iii) Original research.

(a) *(i) only.*

(b) *(ii) only.*

(c) *(iii) only.*

(d) *(ii) and (iii) only.*

22. **Where an investment manager provides a discretionary management service to clients, this will normally involve which of the following?**

(i) Initiating transactions.

(ii) Executing transactions.

(iii) Monitoring transactions through to settlement.

(a) *(i) only.*

(b) *(i) and (ii) only.*

(c) *(ii) and (iii) only.*

(d) *(i), (ii) and (iii).*

23. **A firm which intends to publish a recommendation to customers but deals for itself ahead of publication is likely to be breaking which one of the following Conduct of Business Sourcebook rules?**

(a) *Churning.*

(b) *Timely execution.*

(c) *Best execution.*

(d) *Front running.*

24. For market abuse to occur:

(i) It must relate to a qualifying investment.
(ii) The investment must be traded on a prescribed market.
(iii) The transaction size must exceed £10,000.

(a) *(i) only.*

(b) *(i) and (ii) only.*

(c) *(ii) and (iii) only.*

(d) *(i), (ii) and (iii).*

25. A legal document where one person gives another person the power to take decisions over their financial affairs is known as a power of:

(a) *Attorney.*

(b) *Probate.*

(c) *Transfer.*

(d) *Authority.*

26. The general law on trusts places which of the following requirements on trustees?

(i) To take such care as any ordinary prudent person would take.
(ii) To give due consideration to all beneficiaries.
(iii) To follow investment advice obtained from competent investment advisers.

(a) *(i) only.*

(b) *(i) and (ii) only.*

(c) *(ii) and (iii) only.*

(d) *(i), (ii) and (iii).*

27. **Which of the following pieces of legislation endows the Financial Conduct Authority with its statutory powers?**

(a) *The Financial Services Act 1986.*

(b) *The Criminal Justice Act 1993.*

(c) *The Financial Services and Markets Act 2000 (as amended by the Financial Services Act 2012).*

(d) *The Investment Services Directive.*

28. **A firm must retain records of complaints relating to its MiFID business for a period of at least:**

(a) *One year.*

(b) *Three years.*

(c) *Five years.*

(d) *Indefinitely.*

29. **Which one of the following investment funds is not overseen by a trustee?**

(a) *A fund invested for a charitable organisation.*

(b) *An investment trust.*

(c) *An authorised unit trust.*

(d) *An occupational pension scheme.*

30. **The current settlement cycle for London Stock Exchange equities is T+...**

Important! You should enter only the answer in numbers (without spaces, letters or symbols) strictly using the following format: 0

31. **The name of the person who transfers property to be managed under a trust for the benefit of separate beneficiaries is legally known as the:**

(a) *Settlor.*

(b) *Benefactor.*

(c) *Possessor.*

(d) *Attorney.*

32. **Which of the following is not required to obtain Part 4A authorisation to undertake investment business in the UK?**

(a) *An accountant providing investment advice.*

(b) *A firm authorised in Germany to undertake investment business.*

(c) *The manager of a unit trust.*

(d) *The trustee of a unit trust.*

33. **A tax credit is applied to equity dividends in the UK. What rate is this tax credit?**

(a) *10%.*

(b) *15%.*

(c) *20%.*

(d) *40%.*

34. **Which body is responsible for accepting an exchange as a recognised investment exchange in the UK?**

(a) *The Treasury.*

(b) *The Department for Business, Innovation and Skills.*

(c) *The Financial Conduct Authority.*

(d) *The Bank of England.*

35. **Large UK stocks on the London Stock Exchange are traded via:**

(a) *ARROW.*

(b) *SETS.*

(c) *GEMM.*

(d) *SEAQ.*

36. **Where an investment firm issues a financial promotion to retail clients, it must ensure that the promotion:**

(i) Identifies the firm as the issuer.

(ii) Is fair and not misleading.

(iii) Identifies the FCA as the regulator of the firm.

(a) *(i) only.*

(b) *(i) and (ii) only.*

(c) *(ii) and (iii) only.*

(d) *(i), (ii) and (iii).*

37. **Which one of the following Acts of Parliament makes insider dealing an offence?**

(a) *Drug Trafficking Act 1994.*

(b) *Criminal Justice Act 1993.*

(c) *Financial Services Act 1986.*

(d) *Companies Act 1985.*

38. **The custody rules, with respect to clients' assets, are mainly designed to:**

(a) *Restrict co-mingling of client and firm assets.*

(b) *Ensure that the firm never lends out clients' assets.*

(c) *Ensure that the firm always has physical custody of its clients' assets.*

(d) *Prevent theft of a clients' assets.*

39. **Which of the following investments are the subject of insider dealing regulations?**

(i) Gilt-edged securities.

(ii) FTSE-100 Index futures.

(iii) Property.

(a) *(i) only.*

(b) *(i) and (ii) only.*

(c) *(i) and (iii) only.*

(d) *(i), (ii) and (iii).*

40. A firm principally involved in dealing in ICE Futures Europe derivatives would be regulated by which one of the following organisations?

(a) *The Financial Conduct Authority.*

(b) *ICE Futures Europe.*

(c) *The Bank of England.*

(d) *The London Stock Exchange.*

41. Unit trusts are regulated by:

(a) *HM Treasury.*

(b) *The AUT.*

(c) *The Financial Conduct Authority.*

(d) *The Department for Business, Innovation and Skills.*

42. Which body is responsible for recognising an overseas investment exchange?

(a) *The Bank of England.*

(b) *HM Treasury.*

(c) *The Financial Conduct Authority.*

(d) *The Department for Business, Innovation and Skills.*

43. Which of the following statements are correct in relation to the Principles for Businesses?

(i) A breach of a principle by an investment firm gives rise to a right for an action for damages by a private person.

(ii) A breach of a principle does not automatically lead to a disciplinary measure by the FCA.

(iii) The principles apply to all authorised firms.

(a) *(i) and (ii) only.*

(b) *(i) and (iii) only.*

(c) *(ii) and (iii) only.*

(d) *(i), (ii) and (iii).*

44. Which one of the following statements is not correct?

(a) *A professional client has less regulatory protection than a retail client.*

(b) *A per se professional client can request to be treated as a retail client.*

(c) *A retail client can request to be treated as an eligible counterparty.*

(d) *A retail client can request to be treated as a professional client.*

45. A retail client has a right to cancel a purchase of a collective investment scheme within how many days?

Important! You should enter only the answer in numbers (without spaces, letters or symbols) strictly using the following format: 00

46. The risk of a fall in the nominal value of an investment is best described as:

(a) *Shortfall risk.*

(b) *Capital risk.*

(c) *Inflation risk.*

(d) *Systemic risk.*

47. Which of the following asset classes is likely to have the highest level of capital risk over the medium/long term?

(a) *Equities.*

(b) *Gilts.*

(c) *Corporate bonds.*

(d) *Cash.*

48. Which of the following bears the risk of a fund being insufficient to pay a reasonable pension on retirement for an occupational defined contribution scheme?

(a) *The employer.*

(b) *The employee.*

(c) *The trustees.*

(d) *The Pension Protection Fund.*

49. An individual submits a request to an organisation seeking information about him/her self under the Data Protection Act 1998. What is the maximum number of days the organisation normally has to respond to such a request?

    Important! You should enter only the answer in numbers (without spaces, letters or symbols) strictly using the following format: 00

50. The FCA uses which of the following approaches to its regulation of authorised firms:

(a) *Theme-based approach.*

(b) *Sector-based approach.*

(c) *Least cost-based approach.*

(d) *Risk-based approach.*

Case 1 – the next six questions relate to this case

Jeremy is a 40% taxpayer and his wife Sandra is a basic rate taxpayer. They are considering realising some of their investments to finance a UK holiday property purchase. The investments include:

- £50,000 nominal of Treasury 8% 2016, currently worth £62,000 against a purchase price of £51,000 paid two years ago by Jeremy.
- 30,000 ABC shares Sandra bought for £50,000 in 2008, which are now worth £79,000.
- A property they bought for buy to let purposes three years ago for £200,000, which is now worth £255,000.
- 15,000 XYZ shares Jeremy bought four years ago at a cost of £20,000, which are now worth £6,000.

The annual exemption for 2015/16 is £11,100. Jeremy and Sandra have not realised any capital gains or losses since May 2008. Ignore costs of sale in your answers.

51. Which one of their investments is exempt from capital gains tax?

(a) *Treasury 8% 2016.*

(b) *ABC shares.*

(c) *The buy to let property.*

(d) *XYZ shares.*

52. What is the maximum chargeable capital gain that Jeremy can realise in 2015/16 without facing a capital gains tax charge?

(a) *£1,818.*

(b) *£5,300.*

(c) *£11,100.*

(d) *£21,200.*

53. If Sandra sells her ABC shares and makes no other disposals in 2015/16, what would be her UK capital gains tax liability in £s?

Important! You should enter only the answer in numbers (without spaces, letters or symbols) strictly using the following format: 0000

54. If Jeremy sells his XYZ shares in 2015/16 and makes no other disposals, for how long can he carry forward the loss?

(a) *One year.*

(b) *Seven years.*

(c) *Ten years.*

(d) *Indefinitely.*

55. If Jeremy and Sandra sell the buy to let property and Jeremy also sells his XYZ shares in 2015/16, how much capital gains tax would he pay in £s?

Important! You should enter only the answer in numbers (without spaces, letters or symbols) strictly using the following format: 000 or 0000

56. If the buy to let property is sold in 2015/16, what would be the capital gains tax bill for Sandra arising from this disposal?

(a) *£2,952.*

(b) *£4,872.*

(c) *£4,950.*

(d) *£7,700.*

57. Which of the following goods can be purchased using dealing commission?

(a) *Information regarding a broker's handling of a specific transaction.*

(b) *Accommodation.*

(c) *Computer hardware for the front office.*

(d) *Custody services.*

58. Which of the following is not a consideration within a 'best execution' policy

(a) *Price.*

(b) *Likelihood of execution and settlement.*

(c) *Order size.*

(d) *Ex-dividend date.*

59. Client money rules dictate that firms must place any funds received in approved accounts in a prompt fashion. Which of the following is not an approved institution?

(a) *A central bank.*

(b) *A qualifying commercial paper fund.*

(c) *A qualifying money market fund.*

(d) *A BCD credit institution.*

60. Which of the following questions is looking for a 'soft' fact?

(a) *What is your date of birth?*

(b) *How much do you have outstanding on your credit card?*

(c) *How do you feel about investing in commodities?*

(d) *What is your monthly mortgage repayment?*

61. **A financial advisor needs to collect information on a client from a third party. What does the advisor require from the client?**

(a) *Letter of authority.*

(b) *Letter of acceptance.*

(c) *Letter of acknowledgment.*

(d) *Letter of agreement.*

62. **Which of the following scenarios poses the most inflation risk for a saver who has cash deposits?**

(a) *Base rate = 5%, RPI = 3%.*

(b) *Base rate = 3%, RPI = 2%.*

(c) *Base rate = 6%, RPI = 7%.*

(d) *Base rate = 9%, RPI = 8%.*

63. **Which of the following best describes the risks associated with equities?**

(a) *High capital risk, high shortfall risk.*

(b) *High capital risk, low shortfall risk.*

(c) *Low capital risk, high shortfall risk.*

(d) *Low capital risk, low shortfall risk.*

64. **Suzanne is aged 47 and is seeking retirement planning advice. Which of the following should be the last step in the financial planning process?**

(a) *Verifying her projected state pension.*

(b) *Recommending a specific pension fund for future saving.*

(c) *Clarifying her intended retirement age.*

(d) *Clarifying her target retirement income.*

65. What must a firm provide if it offers a recommendation to a retail client and as a result they purchase units of a regulated collective investment scheme?

(a) *Availability report.*

(b) *Suitability report.*

(c) *Opportunity report.*

(d) *Affordability report.*

66. Which of the following is not a significant factor in fund selection?

(a) *Charges.*

(b) *Past performance.*

(c) *Financial stability of the provider.*

(d) *Fund size.*

67. What maturity of investments do general insurers typically hold?

(a) *Short term.*

(b) *Medium term.*

(c) *Long term.*

(d) *Equally weighted.*

68. What is the amount of stamp duty payable on a residential property bought for £600,000 in £s?

Important! You should enter only the answer in numbers (without spaces, letters or symbols) strictly using the following format: 00000

69. A higher rate taxpayer receives a dividend payment of £1,000. If this is paid with an implied tax credit of 10%, what is the investor's income after payment of all tax due (to the nearest £)?

Important! You should enter only the answer in numbers (without spaces, letters or symbols) strictly using the following format: 000

70. Which type of government security typically best matches the liabilities of life insurers?

(a) *T-Bills.*

(b) *Short dated.*

(c) *Medium dated.*

(d) *Long dated.*

71. Which of the following asset classes typically has the highest allocation within UK pension funds?

(a) *Commodities.*

(b) *Index-linked gilts.*

(c) *Equities.*

(d) *Real estate.*

72. Which of the following is not a category of the CFA Code of Ethics and Standards of Professional Conduct?

(a) *Unprofessionalism.*

(b) *Conflicts of Interest.*

(c) *Duties of Clients.*

(d) *Integrity of Capital Markets.*

73. Vince is a dealer for an investment brokerage company. He is aware that a negative recommendation is going to be made by the firm on a share that both he, in his personal account, and his clients hold. According to the CFA Code of Ethics and Standards of Professional Conduct, he should:

(a) *Sell his own shares before transacting his clients' holdings.*

(b) *Not be holding the same shares as his clients.*

(c) *Put the sell order in at the same time for both his personal account and his clients.*

(d) *Sell his clients' holdings first before selling his own afterwards.*

74. **Under the CFA Code of Ethics and Standards of Professional Conduct, the statement of a fact that is known to be false or misleading is called:**

(a) *Misrepresentation.*

(b) *Misconduct.*

(c) *Misinformation.*

(d) *Misbehaviour.*

75. **Tim is giving a presentation to prospective clients relating to an equity fund. He decides to show a chart containing a period of time where a model portfolio was used. Tim should:**

(a) *Display the chart but make no reference to it orally in his presentation.*

(b) *Assume that this would have been the actual performance of the fund.*

(c) *Make it clear that this was a model portfolio and that the actual investment experience may differ.*

(d) *Not use the chart in his presentation.*

76. **Greg is an investment adviser. He personally holds 5,000 shares of Cheap plc. Greg thinks the company has outstanding prospects with the shares undervalued and decides to recommend it to his clients. He should:**

(a) *Not recommend it to his clients.*

(b) *Recommend it but make no mention of his own holding.*

(c) *Get a colleague to make the recommendation.*

(d) *Make the recommendation and disclose his ownership.*

77. **An investor buys £16,000 of shares. How much stamp duty reserve tax is payable (to the nearest £)?**

Important! You should enter only the answer in numbers (without spaces, letters or symbols) strictly using the following format: 00

78. Roger is a dealer for a private client wealth management firm. He is asked to purchase a number of shares across a variety of accounts. The orders are only partially filled, though. According to the CFA Code of Ethics and Standards of Professional Conduct, he should:

(a) *Give priority to those paying most commission.*

(b) *Allocate the shares to the best performing accounts first.*

(c) *Allocate the shares pro rata according to the order size.*

(d) *Allocate the shares randomly.*

79. Upon retirement, what percentage of an accumulated pension fund can be withdrawn as a tax-free lump sum (assuming it is within the lifetime allowance)?

Important! You should enter only the answer in numbers (without spaces, letters or symbols) strictly using the following format: 00

Case 2 – the next six questions relate to this case

Rick is a 42-year-old member of his employer's final salary pension scheme. This was closed to new members in 2005, three years after Rick joined. In 2016, the scheme is set to close to existing members, too. Rick's employer is offering a group personal pension scheme as a replacement, with contributions averaging about three-quarters of the level of those paid to the current final salary scheme.

80. Which of the following is not a likely reason why Rick's original pension scheme closed?

(a) *Disclosure of the scheme's funding position in the accounts.*

(b) *Increased longevity of members.*

(c) *Falling returns on assets held within the scheme.*

(d) *Higher capital gains tax rates.*

81. Which of the following strategies is Rick's final salary scheme likely to move towards during the next decade?

(a) *Equity-based.*

(b) *Bond-based.*

(c) *Commodity-based.*

(d) *Cash-based.*

82. Which of the following is not a portfolio constraint that Rick's new pension scheme may face?

(a) *Time horizon.*

(b) *Liquidity.*

(c) *Interest rates.*

(d) *Legal regulations.*

83. Rick's defined benefit scheme is considering moving to a liability-driven investment strategy to more accurately match assets with liabilities. Which of the following is likely to be an integral part of the strategy?

(a) *Swaps.*

(b) *Physical gold.*

(c) *Real estate investment trusts.*

(d) *Blue-chip equities.*

84. What type of scheme is Rick's new (2016) pension?

(a) *Defined benefit.*

(b) *Defined contribution.*

(c) *Defined reward.*

(d) *Defined value.*

85. Given that higher rate taxpayers prefer capital gains to income, which type of fixed income securities may pension funds prefer to avoid?

(a) *Low coupon.*

(b) *Medium coupon.*

(c) *High coupon.*

(d) *Indifferent to the coupon.*

ANSWERS

1. (d)
2. 0
3. (b)
4. 25
5. (c)
6. (b)
7. (d)
8. (c)
9. (c)
10. (a)
11. (c)
12. (b)
13. (d)
14. (c)
15. (d)
16. (a)
17. (d)
18. (d)
19. (b)
20.

Peach PLC shares purchase price	(£30,000)
Peach PLC shares sales price	£40,000
Rembrandt PLC shares purchase price	(£20,000)
Rembrandt PLC shares sales price	£18,000
Annual capital gain	£8,000
Less annual exempt amount	(£8,000) [up to the limit of capital gain]
Amount chargeable to CGT	£0
Answer	**0.00**

21. (c)
22. (d)
23. (d)
24. (b)
25. (a)
26. (b)
27. (c)
28. (c)
29. (d)
30. 2
31. (a)
32. (b)
33. (a)
34. (c)
35. (b)
36. (d)
37. (b)
38. (a)
39. (b)
40. (a)
41. (c)
42. (c)
43. (c)
44. (c)
45. 14
46. (b)
47. (a)
48. (b)
49. 40
50. (d)
51. (a)
52. (c)

53. ABC shares purchase price (£50,000)
ABC shares sales price £79,000
Capital gain £29,000
Less annual exempt amount (£11,100)
Amount chargeable to CGT £17,900
Sandra is a basic rate taxpayer so CGT = £17,900 x 0.18
= **£3,222**

54. (d)

55. Jeremy:

Property purchase price	(£200,000)/2 = (£100,000)
Property sales price	£255,000/2 = £127,500
XYZ shares purchase price	(£20,000)
XYZ shares sales price	£6,000
Net capital gain	£13,500
Less annual exempt amount	(£11,100)
Amount chargeable to CGT	£2,400

Jeremy is a higher rate taxpayer so CGT = £2,400 x 0.28
= **£672**

56. Sandra:

Property purchase price	(£200,000)/2 = (£100,000)
Property sales price	£255,000/2 = £127,500
Net capital gain	£27,500
Less annual exempt amount	(£11,100)
Amount chargeable to CGT	£16,400

Sandra is a basic rate taxpayer so CGT = £16,400 x 0.18
= **£2,952**

57. (a)
58. (d)
59. (b)
60. (c)
61. (a)
62. (c)

63. (b)

64. (b)

65. (b)

66. (d)

67. (a)

68. Stamp duty on purchases from £250,000 to £925,000 is charged at 5%

Stamp duty payable = £600,000 x 0.05

= £30,000

69. Gross dividend = net dividend $\times \frac{1}{0.9}$

$= £1{,}000 \times \frac{1}{0.9}$

$= £1111.11$

Investor's after tax income = (1 – 0.325) x £1111.11

= £750

70. (d)

71. (c)

72. (a)

73. (d)

74. (a)

75. (c)

76. (d)

77. SDRT charged = 0.005 x £16,000 [SDRT charged at 0.5%]

= £80

78. (c)

79. 25

80. (d)	*81. (b)*	*82. (c)*
83. (a)	*84. (b)*	*85. (a)*

INDEX

CFA Society United Kingdom